D0253102

COMMUNITY-BASED RESEARCH
AND HIGHER EDUCATION

COMMUNITY-BASED RESEARCH AND HIGHER EDUCATION

Principles and Practices

Kerry Strand, Sam Marullo, Nick Cutforth,
Randy Stoecker, Patrick Donohue

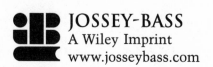

JOSSEY-BASS
A Wiley Imprint
www.josseybass.com

Copyright © 2003 by John Wiley & Sons, Inc. All rights reserved.

Published by Jossey-Bass
A Wiley Imprint
989 Market Street, San Francisco, CA 94103-1741   www.josseybass.com

No part of this publication may be reproduced, stored in a retrieval system, or transmitted in any form or by any means, electronic, mechanical, photocopying, recording, scanning, or otherwise, except as permitted under Section 107 or 108 of the 1976 United States Copyright Act, without either the prior written permission of the Publisher, or authorization through payment of the appropriate per-copy fee to the Copyright Clearance Center, Inc., 222 Rosewood Drive, Danvers, MA 01923, 978-750-8400, fax 978-750-4470, or on the web at www.copyright.com. Requests to the Publisher for permission should be addressed to the Permissions Department, John Wiley & Sons, Inc., 111 River Street, Hoboken, NJ 07030, 201-748-6011, fax 201-748-6008, e-mail: permcoordinator@wiley.com.

Jossey-Bass books and products are available through most bookstores. To contact Jossey-Bass directly call our Customer Care Department within the U.S. at 800-956-7739, outside the U.S. at 317-572-3986 or fax 317-572-4002.

Jossey-Bass also publishes its books in a variety of electronic formats. Some content that appears in print may not be available in electronic books.

Library of Congress Cataloging-in-Publication Data

Community-based research and higher education: Principles and practices / Kerry Strand ... [et al.].— 1st ed.
    p. cm. — (Jossey-Bass higher and adult education series)
    Includes bibliographical references and index.
    ISBN 0-7879-6205-8 (alk. paper)
    1. Community and college. 2. Student service. 3. Education—Research. I. Strand, Kerry. II. Series.
    LC237.C613 2003
    378.1'03—dc21   2003001613

Printed in the United States of America
FIRST EDITION
HB Printing   10 9 8 7 6 5 4 3 2 1

The Jossey-Bass
Higher and Adult Education Series

CONTENTS

FIGURES AND EXHIBITS

FIGURES

EXHIBITS

*I thank Arden for her love, support,
and encouragement over the years, and Asia and
Maya for the joy that they bring to my life.*—Nick

*I thank Tammy and Haley for their
understanding throughout this process.
This book meant time away from them—
always a difficult tradeoff.*—Randy

*I thank Sue for being my soulmate, my partner,
and my support in this work and in my life.
I also thank my parents, Bill and Marge,
for modeling for me a life of service.*—Sam

*I thank my remarkable parents, Jim and Marlene,
my wife, Donna, and my children—Patrick,
James, and Catherine—for their steady supply
of love, wisdom, support . . . and fun.*—Patrick

*To my main lifelines and favorite people,
Kirkley and Nathan.*—Kerry

FOREWORD

IF YOU THINK higher education in the United States should prepare students for active roles of reflective and committed citizenship in a multicultural and interracial democratic society, you will find this book important reading. If you realize that higher education is failing this role, you will treasure this book as a compass that points to the true north of academic reform and transformation.

The authors combine their years of experience with community-based research, in a broad range of higher education institutional settings, with systematic reflection. As a consequence, they make the case for community-based pedagogy and research, describe their methods, and outline operational options in detail. Their eye for specifics does not obscure a vision of human relationships and social justice enmeshed in education and research and expressed in trust of self, others, and the learning process. Their reflective practice makes it easier for faculty, staff, and administrators in higher education to understand community-based research in the evolution of recent educational reforms, such as service learning, and in the movement to a scholarship of engagement.

As I read these pages, conversations and events spanning three decades came to mind. I found in them echoes of campus turmoil, when students demand relevance in their education and social responsibility of their schools, and of numerous recent conferences, where college presidents called for the increased civic engagement of higher education.

The young star scholar of the department, where I was a graduate student, stormed out of his office complaining that the student protesters were making it impossible for him to work. The students had assembled to ask the board of trustees to put the university on record as opposed to the escalating war in Vietnam in 1972. As the departing academic pressed the elevator button, the department's administrative assistant tried to stop him with a pointed question. "You're not going anywhere. If you don't stay and make sense out of what's going on here, who's supposed to?"

The question did not deter him, he left.

Community-based research makes it more difficult for the faculty to excuse themselves from making sense of the public events and conditions around them. Others have already stepped forward. We stood, and perhaps cheered, as students shook off some of their apathy and took up the mantle of community service in the 1980s through the Community Outreach Opportunity League. This new activism ignored faculty because it pointedly avoided integration with the curriculum. We welcomed, and perhaps supported, college and university presidents in Campus Compact as they fashioned commitments to community service and the public responsibilities of higher education. They made few demands on us as well because our presidents did not dare spend their political capital on campus urging changes in teaching and research.

It is our turn now. Only faculty can explain by example how higher education can answer the calls for the renewal of civil society heard around the world. This wonderful book explains how it came to be our turn, what we can do about it, and that we have many collaborators and partners as we learn to make meaning of the scholarship of engagement. We find here a clear explanation of the unique role that faculty can play to make higher education an improved part of our civic infrastructure.

Lois Marie Gibbs, the housewife turned activist, who organized her neighbors at Love Canal and confronted company and public officials about the illnesses and hardship their actions had caused, started the national Citizens Clearinghouse on Hazardous Waste by the time I met her. I asked her how she handled campus partnerships in her work. She looked surprised and explained, "I don't find too many academics willing to jump over that wall to join us."

You will find in these pages plenty of evidence that many faculty and students have jumped and scaled the ivy-clad walls to join community partners in their efforts to increase and improve social services and to advocate for social justice. In the process, faculty-researchers have found the inadequacy of their disciplinary boundaries and research methodologies. We have had to devise and advocate new research approaches and new forms of accountability to people who address the social issues we study. We have had to reexamine the value-laden assumptions of objectivity and value-free scholarship. We have had to assert, as the authors do, that research *on and about* members of a community, especially a low-income community and without accountability to the members of that group, may "reproduce and legitimate" existing social arrangements of injustice and oppression.

Research efforts *for and with* community members, which "challenge and transform" existing social arrangements, simply bring to the forefront the issues of power and control inherent in all research. For example, my supervisor called me on the carpet and had the head of the Department of Family Medicine explain that "No self-respecting epidemiologist would do this work" [a community-based epidemiological study I was conducting with the residents along Yellow Creek in Eastern Kentucky]. I made a case of our responsibility to the people who lived in the path of exposure as well as to the academic practice of epidemiology. I conceded on one point, however; we began calling the work a community health-risk appraisal. Eventually, that work assisted the residents in winning a state court settlement that established a health care trust fund to provide services and examination for communities, like their own, that had some health risk because of exposure to chemical hazards.

Some of my students and I visited a juvenile detention center, during the course of a study described in this book, to interview some of the detained juveniles. We had walked through security doors buzzing open and locking shut and through curious stares. After conducting interviews and once outside the center, one of the students observed, "They're just like us. They're smart. They want the same things that we do. I had the breaks to get them differently. With just a few changes, they could have been visiting me."

Community-based research is about teaching and the cognitive and moral development of students. This student expressed the empathy that already distinguished her and this research reinforced. In addition to developing leadership traits such as empathy, when done well community-based research turns classrooms into learning communities. Imagine coming late to class and finding that the students had started without you because they had too much to cover. Or imagine a student asking, "Can't we read more than a book every two weeks?" It can and has happened because community-based research, as the authors show, offers students adult responsibilities with real stakes.

The authors give fair warning, however; a learning community can be far messier than a command-and-control classroom. There may be times when the faculty, with a few devoted students if she is lucky, will have to salvage a project that did not work out as planned or finish a project that lasted longer than the semester. Even these times, however, offer opportunities for effective teaching and research to "challenge and transform" existing social arrangements including our classrooms.

When presented with a proposal for a center for civic engagement that would sponsor participatory action research and campus community partnerships, a university administrator objected, "We're not a social service agency."

Indeed, as these pages make clear, higher education is about teaching, research, and service, but this book also explains how to combine them effectively with community-based research. The book helps explain that community-based research does not impose a burden on the roles of higher education but conveys a promise of their achievement. It explains that an expanded and improved role for higher education in the democratic civic infrastructure of participatory processes of problem solving offers students a path to engagement in their own learning and faculty a vital new avenue to renewed scholarship. And in a feature not to be discounted, advocates of community-based pedagogies and research will find charts, illustrations, and talking points to use in faculty workshops on their campuses or to use in convincing skeptical administrators, a dwindling group.

In the last analysis, this is a very dangerous book, not because it deters higher education from its mission but because it offers us a way to deliver on its promise to prepare students for active roles of reflective and committed citizenship in a multicultural and interracial democratic society. It is a dangerous book also because it challenges those of us in higher education to blend our disciplinary training with interdisciplinary inquiry that is both rigorous and relevant. It is dangerous because these problems require us to regain a sense of our creativity and to make a future for higher education that is better and more effective than its present practice.

These dangers and problems echo another fragment of conversation from the past. Paulo Freire, in an interview I conducted, urged that we make the future a problem. When we "problematize" the future, he suggested, we renew our human agency over the possible futures that we can create. In this sense, the authors have created a problem for us, fortunately. They have restored to our hands the capacity, responsibility, and possibility to shape a better future for higher education. They also distill and summarize a great deal of the scholarship of teaching, which gives us direction. They do so without offering recipes for success, which gives us the challenge to find our own agency. They provide an ideal while allowing for our limits in its pursuit. That combination offers hope for the future of higher education and for our own efficacy and effectiveness in its transformation.

RICHARD A. COUTO
Professor of Leadership and Change
Antioch University

PREFACE

WE HAVE ALL HEARD the litany of critical voices expressing frustration with higher education as it is perceived and practiced in the United States today.

Here is what some students have to say:

> "I get so bored sitting in a classroom, taking notes all the time. Why can't professors figure out a way to get us more interested in what they are trying to teach? And what does this stuff have to do with the real world? Why can't we study things that I can really use?"

> "Just volunteering doesn't seem to be enough. I've been tutoring this little boy three days a week. By Friday, I see a change, but by Monday we're back to square one. He's dealing with too many other problems—in his neighborhood, in his school. What can I do that will make a real difference for him, and for others like him?"

> "I really like my major, and I know what I'm learning will help me get started on a great career. But I also want to be able to use what I know to make the world somehow better for others. How can I do that with what I am learning here?"

Faculty members have concerns too:

> "I want to be an effective teacher, an active researcher, and also to contribute to the community on and off campus. At my institution, it is just about impossible to do all three well. Is there some way I can integrate all three of those—teaching, scholarship, and service—so as to help my career and give me a sense of accomplishment at the same time?"

> "I know active learning is best and that students should be developing a sense of commitment and caring about others—so lots of my students are involved in service-learning. I do my best to provide opportunities for reflection and to connect their service with the course material. But is their community service really giving

them the knowledge and skills they need to become effective, committed, active citizens? And how much are they doing to address real community problems?"

I don't want this!

"I went into higher education because I thought I could make some sort of difference. Instead, my research seems to have no value except to my own career and no relevance to anyone other than colleagues in my own discipline who have the same interests that I do. I want my work to be more useful and meaningful than that—to serve some sort of wider public good. But I still haven't figured out how I can make that happen."

Community-based organizations and service providers need help with their work, and they see local educational institutions as a possibility:

"We need help. We are under constant pressure to come up with new sources of money to support our work. That means having lots of hard data—about what grants are out there, what our community needs, how well our programs are working, and what the demand for our services will be down the road. You have lots of people who do research, don't you? Can't you give us a hand?"

"We're tired of being ignored by policymakers. We have people we are trying to serve, but policies keep changing and we have to keep rethinking what we're doing. They don't even ask us what we think of welfare-to-work! How can we get them to listen to us?"

"Where have you been? You've been aloof and distant and not too useful for us. Your university is the largest institution in our community, and a lot of resources go to you. Why don't we see any of it?"

"Student volunteers are great, because Lord knows we need help just getting things done—serving soup, mentoring kids, answering phones, running our after-school program. But this community has so many problems and needs that just aren't being addressed. How can you help us with those?"

Other community members seek a different kind of relationship with colleges and universities than they have had in the past:

"Researchers from the university come in here all the time with their clipboards and pencils, and I'm getting sick of being asked how poor I am. I'm fed up with being treated as a guinea pig. I'm answering more questions from folks like you, and I'm still not seeing any real change around here."

"You guys come in here for a day or two, and then we never hear from you again. Are you really interested in helping us solve some of our problems? Then why don't you spend more time here and really get to know us?"

"You don't have all the answers. Ask us sometimes about our community and our problems. We've been living here and we know a lot. Respect our knowledge. We can teach you a few things."

Funders want to see results for the money they give:

"We give a lot of money to academics for them to study community problems, but nothing much seems to come of it. How can we ensure that the research we fund makes a real difference in our communities?"

"Nonprofits and community-based organizations are always coming to us with proposals to support programs that address community problems and challenges. So often they have good ideas and great intentions but too little information: What's been tried before? What works, and why? What does the research in this area have to tell us? These groups need to do their homework!"

"We get lots of requests from professors at the local university who want to study ways to solve various problems in this city. In the meantime, the university has just built a beautiful new stadium and professors earn a whole lot more money than most of the working people in this town. Why should we give them our money when they are already so rich?"

— Researchers must do their homework.

Even college and university administrators voice concerns:

"Our institution is lagging in graduation rates, and we have to do something about it. We need to find a way to increase enrollment. That means being more innovative in the way we teach and coming up with ways to excite students about new educational options."

※ We must excite students!

"Politicians at every level are leaning on us. Every year the legislature cuts our budget and says our faculty isn't doing anything. They're asking me what our outreach programs are. Even the mayor is asking 'What have you done for us lately?'"

"There is a movement on campuses toward engagement with the community, and we're going to be left behind if we don't join in now. We say we're doing this, but where's the evidence? And what are our students getting from all this service to the community?"

Voices of frustration about business as usual in higher education have grown louder over the past two decades. Students want educational experiences that are engaging and relevant. Faculty members want to help provide those experiences while they apply their expertise in meaningful ways outside the confines of classroom, office, and laboratory. Communities have wide-ranging needs, some of which can be met by colleges and universities—provided those institutions demonstrate a genuine willingness to share resources and work toward developing respectful and reciprocal partnerships with those communities. Administrators are realizing that to thrive, their institutions must become more responsive to the growing needs of communities, the changing character of the student body, and the erosion in public trust that has challenged the ivory tower image of the academy from years past.

Responses to the crisis in higher education have been varied and, in a few cases, far-reaching. This book is about one such response. Community-based research (CBR) is research that is conducted *with* and *for*, not *on*, members of a community. In its multiple variations—participatory research, participatory action research, and empowerment research—CBR has a long and diverse history that spans the globe, and most of it does not involve higher education or academics at all. But the model of CBR that we detail here puts it at the center of partnerships between higher education institutions and the communities in which they are located. Unlike traditional academic research, CBR is collaborative and change oriented and finds its research questions in the needs of communities, which often require information that they have neither the time nor the resources to obtain. And in contrast to the participatory research conducted by individual faculty engaged in their own scholarship, our CBR model engages students alongside faculty and community members in the course of their academic work. CBR combines classroom learning and skills development with social action in ways that ultimately can empower community groups to address their own needs and shape their own futures. At the same time, CBR differs from most other experiential and service-learning pedagogies in its emphasis on the development of knowledge and skills that truly prepare students for active civic engagement.

We see CBR as a tool, a teaching technique, and an institutional change strategy for social justice, engaging universities' and communities' human

resources, expertise, and knowledge-generating capabilities to address social ills. The distinctive combination of collaborative inquiry, critical analysis, and social change that community-based research represents—as well
as its potential to unite the three traditional academic missions of teaching, research, and service in innovative ways—has led us to believe that
CBR is a next important stage of service-learning and engaged scholarship. We also see it as a compelling response to the voices of frustration in
contemporary higher education.

While CBR may well be a potentially transformative educational strategy, in fact remarkably little about it has been written for academics who
are drawn to this sort of work or for others—community members, administrators, funding agencies, students—who might want to know more
about it. This book is intended to be a guide to how and why to incorporate this promising new form of scholarship into academic settings.

We are five academics with varied and extensive experience in CBR as
teachers, researchers, administrators, scholars, and community activists.
We come from different disciplines and very different institutions: a liberal arts college for women, a community college, and mid- and large-size
public and private research universities. What we have in common is deep
involvement with CBR on our own campuses and in our communities, as
well as a shared commitment to the value of CBR as a response to many
challenges facing higher education today. This book is a product of that
deep involvement and shared commitment. It is also the product of a
rather extraordinary and richly rewarding collaboration among five very
different people who share a vision: that our work as teachers, scholars,
and citizens can make some difference in the worlds that we touch through
our work.

We have organized the book into discussions of the principles and the
practices of CBR and have also incorporated, wherever possible, voices
and experiences of people who are doing CBR on their campuses and in
their communities. We have been privileged to work together on this project as a result of a grant to the Bonner Foundation from the Corporation
for National Service, and it is largely our experiences through this grant,
and the experiences of our other colleagues on the grant, that we draw on
for this book.

Chapter One provides a brief history and overview of community-based
research and articulates its basic principles. Chapters Two and Three focus
on campus-community partnerships: Chapter Two looks at the principles
governing these partnerships, and Chapter Three provides extensive, concrete guidelines for establishing and sustaining those partnerships through
community-based research projects. The fourth and fifth chapters address

methodological considerations: Chapter Four looks at how CBR needs to be understood within the wider context of social change efforts of community organizations and agencies and what principles should guide decisions about research design and methods; Chapter Five details ways that the distinctive character of CBR shapes decisions at every stage of the research process. In Chapters Six and Seven, we turn to issues related to teaching CBR: its value as a pedagogic strategy (Chapter Six) and then, in Chapter Seven, a plethora of suggestions about how to incorporate CBR into courses and curricula, as well as how to manage the many details that come with doing CBR with graduate and undergraduate students. Chapters Eight and Nine address the complex questions of why and how we can transform our institutions to support new forms of community engagement, particularly the work of community-based research. Finally, in Chapter Ten we return to these voices—this time to imagine a vision of higher education that is based on research-oriented campus-community partnerships and to present a series of recommended action steps that we might take to help realize that vision.

Acknowledgments

We gratefully acknowledge the support of the Corporation for National Service, Learn and Serve grant 00LHENJ043, awarded to the Bonner Foundation, 1997–2000, of which we are subgrantees. We also acknowledge with deep appreciation and gratitude the support of the Corella and Bertram F. Bonner Foundation and, in particular, Robert Hackett for his tremendous support, vision, insight, and passion for mobilizing the scholarly resources of higher education for social justice.

Many people made this book possible. We thank the following people who have shared their expertise, experiences, resources, and examples of practice with us: John Saltmarsh, Natalie Avery, Terri Bailey, Anita Bonds, Dave Beckwith, Fleeta Bulle, José Calderon, Barry Checkoway, Jeff Collmann, Barbara Ferman, Dwight Giles, Zuline Gray-Wilkinson, Ira Harkavy, Jeffrey Howard, Marty Johnson, Chris Koliba, Katharine Kravetz, Matt Lawson, David Lisman, Gary Lichtenstein, Marlynn May, Paul McElligott, Roxana Moayedi, Tim Mungavan, Phil Nyden, Wayne Meisel, Beth Paul, Tom Plaut, Mary Rudolph, Jackie Valez, Ron Randall, Jerome Shindelman, Marycel Tuazon, LaTonya Webb, and Jason Willis.

None of our community-based research work would have been possible without the rich and rewarding collaborations over the years with our students and community partners. There are too many to name here, but we thank them all from the bottoms of our hearts.

We are indebted to Corella Bonner (1909–2002) for her vision that allowed the Bonner Foundation to become a national leader in the field of community-based research.

Thanks also to the faculty, staff, and students of the Bonner Community Research Program schools for their willingness to share information and insights; and to the always helpful and supportive folks at Jossey-Bass, especially Melissa Kirk, Cathy Mallon, and David Brightman, whose great enthusiasm for our project is ever appreciated.

ABOUT THE AUTHORS

KERRY STRAND is the Andrew G. Truxal Professor of Sociology at Hood College in Frederick, Maryland, where she has worked with undergraduate students and community partners on nearly two dozen community-based research projects over the past five years. She has published papers and presented numerous talks and workshops on service-learning, community-based research, and other topics related to undergraduate teaching and learning. Strand spent 2002 as a half-time visiting sociologist at the American Sociological Association (ASA) in Washington, D.C., and she continues her work as director of the ASA Honors Program and co-principal investigator of the Integrating Data Analysis project, working with sociology departments to infuse data analysis into their undergraduate curricula. Her areas of research include the medicalization of pregnancy and birth, gendered labor markets, and women's education, and most recently, the effects of reform-based mathematics pedagogy on college women's math-related attitudes and persistence. She holds a Ph.D. from the University of Maryland, College Park.

SAM MARULLO is associate professor of sociology at Georgetown University where, from 1997 to 2000, he served as the director of the Volunteer and Public Service Center, home of the university's service-learning credit program, student community service organizations, and the faculty support center for community-based research and service-learning. He also founded and codirected the Partners in Urban Research and Service-Learning Project, a collaborative university-community seminar that meets to study, research, and develop action initiatives to address community-defined problems. He serves as well as co-principal investigator on a grant from the Department of Housing and Urban Development to create a Georgetown-community outreach partnership center. In addition to his extensive administrative work, Marullo has developed and taught a large number of service-learning courses over the past decade and has sponsored over two hundred students in independent service-learning activities. His participatory research work in the community focuses on the causes of violence and community-based efforts to reduce and prevent violence. In spring 2000, he was named a finalist for the Campus Compact's Thomas Ehrlich Faculty Award for Service Learning. He has published over a dozen articles on service-learning and edited two special issues of *American Behavioral Scientist* (February 1999 and February 2000): "Universities in Troubled Times—Institutional Responses," and "Service-Learning Pedagogy as Universities' Response to Troubled Times." He holds a Ph.D. from Columbia University.

NICK CUTFORTH is an associate professor of curriculum and instruction in the College of Education at the University of Denver. His research in urban education, ethnographic methods, school-university collaboration, youth development and sport, and program evaluation have led to numerous presentations, grants, and publications. Most recently, he has coauthored, with D. Hellison and others, *Youth Development and Physical Activity: Linking Universities and Communities* (2000), and his article, "Connecting School Physical Education to the Community Through Service-Learning," appeared in the February 2000 issue of the *Journal of Physical Education, Recreation and Dance*. Cutforth is the recipient of awards from the University of Denver and from community organizations for his work on minority issues, and he is currently cochair of the DU/ Northwestside Schools Partnership, a collaborative venture between the University of Denver and three Denver public schools. He holds a Ph.D. from the University of Illinois, Chicago.

RANDY STOECKER is professor of sociology at the University of Toledo in Ohio. He has been doing community-based and participatory research since 1988, most recently with the Toledo Community Organizing Training and Technical Assistance program, the Cedar-Riverside neighborhood in Minneapolis, and the Bonner Foundation Community Research Project. He has published numerous articles on the method of participatory research, has coedited two special issues of the *American Sociologist* devoted to participatory research, and has edited two special issues of *Sociological Imagination* devoted to sociology and social action. He also moderates and edits "COMM-ORG: The On-Line Conference on Community Organizing and Development" (http://comm-org.utoledo.edu), a global academic-practitioner collaboration of over 850 people devoted to the practice of community organizing and its related fields. He holds a Ph.D. from the University of Minnesota.

PATRICK DONOHUE is an assistant professor of political science at Middlesex County College (MCC) in Edison, New Jersey. On campus, he is the director of MCC Community Scholars Corps, which organizes faculty and students to respond to the research and planning needs of local non-profit organizations. Off campus, he is active in his hometown of Trenton, where he is the interim director of the Trenton Center for Campus-Community Partnerships and has served as the president of Isles, a non-profit community development agency. Prior to joining MCC in 1994, Donohue was the assistant director of the New Jersey Youth Corps, a statewide program for high school dropouts, and he served previously as an investigator for the New Jersey Department of the Public Advocate. He holds a master's degree from Rutgers University's Eagleton Institute for Government and Politics.

COMMUNITY-BASED RESEARCH
AND HIGHER EDUCATION

ORIGINS AND PRINCIPLES OF COMMUNITY-BASED RESEARCH

Lastly, I would address one general admonition to all; that they consider what are the true ends of knowledge, and that they seek it not either for pleasure of the mind, or for contention, or for superiority to others, or for profit, or fame, or power, or any of these inferior things; but for the benefit and use of Life.

—Francis Bacon

OVER THE PAST TWO DECADES, many higher education institutions, from small, private, liberal arts colleges to massive state-supported research universities, have begun to rethink their institutional missions and implement a variety of community outreach efforts. Several forces have helped to create this state of affairs. Two of them—widespread criticism of higher education's disconnection from communities and growing concern about the professorate's exceedingly narrow definition of research—originated outside the institutions but quickly led to wide-ranging and often heated debate across campuses. The third force, recognition of the need to develop students' civic capacity and prepare them for active democratic citizenship, came largely from within the institutions themselves.

The Development of Campus-Community Partnerships

The contemporary criticism of higher education's inequitable and unresponsive relationship with the community echoes a historical chorus of voices weighing in about the nature and purpose of knowledge, from

Bacon's concern about the "true ends of knowledge" to John Dewey's warnings (1938) about the importance of linking knowledge with social inquiry rather than leaving it disconnected from action and isolated and mired in academic culture (Benson, Harkavy, and Puckett, 2000; Maurrasse, 2001). These ideas seem particularly relevant today, as the neighborhoods adjacent to many college and university campuses struggle with greater and greater challenges that university resources could help to address: urban decay, environmental threats, growing economic inequality, and the unmet needs of vulnerable children, families, and communities in areas such as education, health care, housing, criminal and juvenile justice, and employment. Some have even called for a widespread return of colleges and universities to the historical mission of land grant universities— regional institutions shaped by and responsive to local conditions, local problems, and local needs (Bledstein, 1976; Campbell, 1995; Kellogg Commission, 1999). What is the purpose of higher education, they ask, if not to reach out so as to provide something useful to society, starting with the communities that surround them?

At the same time, we have heard public demands for the work of professors to be more responsive to the public good. Ernest Boyer, in his widely cited book *Scholarship Reconsidered* (1990), criticized the narrow definition of scholarship as research in pursuit of new knowledge and took issue with how the "science of discovery" serves as the key, if not the only, kind of acceptable scholarship for faculty, especially those at research universities (Edwards and Marullo, 1999). He was concerned that other forms of scholarship—the scholarship of integration, of application, and of pedagogy—were undervalued and neglected with regard to both faculty roles and institutional credibility. In particular, he argued that the scholarship of application is best suited to address society's problems, and he challenged institutions to rethink their faculty reward systems and redirect their efforts by developing the resources needed to address the ills that confront society.

The third force for change was the growing realization on campuses that despite our best intentions, higher education is largely failing in its efforts to prepare students for lives of social responsibility and civic and political engagement. Slowly we learned that college and university graduates are no less likely than the rest of the population to be disengaged from political issues, disenchanted with the potential of government to effect positive change, and disinclined and ill equipped to participate actively in civic life. Invoking Dewey's treatise (1916) that education is where democratic participation is best learned, educators began to challenge colleges and universities to move beyond traditional courses and curricula to prepare students for democratic citizenship (Boyte and Kari, 1996; Ehrlich, 2000). Increasingly, the most widely promoted strategy for citizenship education has been some form of student involvement in communities, most typically in the form of volunteering and service-learning.

As a result of these three forces, the latter years of the twentieth century saw a dramatic increase in the involvement of higher education institutions in their surrounding communities. Today, a growing number of institutions are returning to the land grant ideal of American universities by forging connections with the communities that often lie just beyond their campuses. Many colleges and universities are partnering with schools, social service agencies, businesses, neighborhood organizations, and health care providers, often with government, corporate, or foundation support. These partnerships have resulted in a plethora of outreach initiatives in which thousands of students and faculty are participating in tutoring and sports programs; internships in areas such as education, social work, and psychology; research projects; and the provision of other services to their local communities (Maurrasse, 2001). The effectiveness of these partnerships has been enhanced by the establishment of the Campus Compact, an organization that focuses on increasing service opportunities for students and faculty, as well as a wide range of service-learning programs that have become more and more commonplace in community colleges, four-year colleges, and research universities (Eyler and Giles, 1999; Zlotkowski, 1999).

A particularly promising activity to come out of these academy-community partnerships is what has come to be called community-based research (CBR). CBR is a partnership of students, faculty, and community members who collaboratively engage in research with the purpose of solving a pressing community problem or effecting social change. *Community* in this context includes educational institutions (schools and day care centers), community-based organizations of various kinds (neighborhood associations, for example), agencies that provide services or otherwise work on behalf of area residents (such as a local health department or battered women's shelter), or groups of people who may not share a geographical association but do share an interest around cultural, social, political, health, or economic issues (for example, unions, Latinos, ex-offenders, breast cancer survivors, and identity groups such as the Gay, Lesbian, Bisexual, and Transgender Alliance). Sometimes the focus is on a local problem facing a neighborhood or an organization. The focus can also be regional, national, or global. In every case, the community consists of people who are oppressed, powerless, economically deprived, or disenfranchised—that is, who are disadvantaged by existing social, political, or economic arrangements.

In a broad but critical sense, then, CBR is about working for social and economic justice. By placing larger questions of social, political, and moral purpose at the center of higher education's historical missions of teaching, scholarship, and service, CBR addresses in a direct way higher education's public mandate to serve some larger public purpose as a citizen within a civil society.

Historical Influences on Community-Based Research

Community-based research has a long and diverse history. This diversity is reflected in the different terms used to describe this kind of research—*action research, participatory research, popular education,* and *participatory action research*—which illustrate historical distinctions concerning the political nature of the research enterprise and the degree of active participation of the community in the research (Sclove, Scammell, and Holland, 1998; Stoecker, 1999a). Moreover, practitioners of participatory research in different fields and different parts of the globe trace their history differently. Indeed, traces of CBR's historical roots can be found in several social science disciplines and professional fields both inside and outside academia. These multidisciplinary origins make it difficult to construct a precise history of CBR. However, these distinctions are less apparent today, and regardless of disciplinary origins or the terminology employed, many community-based researchers draw from several common historical and modern strands.

In the twentieth century, we have seen three basic influences that have converged into community-based research:

- A popular education model that emphasized the involvement of people in educating themselves for social change
- An action research model used by academics in conjunction with major social institutions
- A participatory research model that emphasized the involvement of people in doing their own research for social change

The Popular Education Model

The popular education influence on CBR has a number of important sources. In the early decades of the twentieth century, the settlement house movement swept the United States as young women from wealthy backgrounds moved into poor urban neighborhoods to provide services and, in some cases, to work for social change. Among the most famous of these was Hull-House, founded by Jane Addams and Ellen Gates Starr in 1889

(Polikoff, 1999). The important work of the Hull-House staff included a research project mapping the land use patterns in their Chicago neighborhood, involving neighborhood residents in a fascinating research and popular education process that became part of Hull-House's social service and social action agenda. The research itself provided a model that would later appear in depoliticized form and be credited to University of Chicago researchers Robert Park and Ernest W. Burgess (Deegan, 1988; Harkavy and Puckett, 1994). The model that Hull-House pioneered has become an important influence in the field of empowerment planning.

Another crucial popular education influence on CBR was the Highlander Folk School, now the Highlander Research and Education Center, founded by Myles Horton. Highlander was important for developing a model of popular education that emphasized people's ability to generate their own knowledge, independent of outside experts. Located in Tennessee, Highlander historically focused its efforts on the people of Appalachia and the rest of the South, among those groups in the United States most excluded from formal education and power.

Highlander's early development of a popular education and participatory research model included a project in support of a timber workers' strike in 1933. Highlander brought timber workers and their families together to research the logging industry in the area and develop a model of sustainable logging that would protect both the forests and workers' jobs in the long term (Adams, 1975; Bledsoe, 1969; Glen, 1988; Horton, 1989). In the 1950s, Highlander was involved in racially integrating labor organizations, as well as laying the groundwork for the 1954 *Brown v. Board of Education* school integration decision. After the major flood that devastated the Appalachian region in 1977, Highlander helped local residents, community organizers, and academic researchers investigate the conditions that produced the endemic poverty in the region, with the intent of bringing about changes through community action. In the process, citizens learned research skills and actively participated in civic politics to bring about changes in local tax codes that had been impoverishing the regional economy in favor of absentee landowners, mostly coal mining companies (Horton, 1993).

Highlander built a model of adult education focused on community-generated needs that set a standard for CBR as many researchers began to adopt some of its approaches. For example, Tax's Iowa Fox Indian Project (1958) involved anthropologists' combining research and action in their work with the tribe.

Paulo Freire was another central popular education influence on CBR, particularly through his book *Pedagogy of the Oppressed* (1970), which evolved from the author's experience in adult literacy work in Brazil. Freire believed in the power of education as a political tool for raising the consciousness of oppressed people at both the local and global levels. He tied education to an agenda of social change in which learning was to be coupled with the investigation of social conditions and then their transformation. Freire's writing served as a basis for a theoretical and practical model for participatory research and inspired scholars and activists to get together with community residents to research, educate, and plan for sustainable, community-controlled social change projects in which learning through investigation occupied the central role.

The Action Research Model

A second influence on community-based research, the action model, has its roots in the work of Kurt Lewin (1948). He coined the term *action research* to describe an approach that gained popularity in the 1950s as a tool to increase worker productivity and satisfaction through democratic relationships. Lewin's work is regarded as a conservative influence on CBR because it placed less emphasis on active community participation and did not challenge existing power relationships (Brown and Tandon, 1983). Nevertheless, it was useful for those who wanted to understand organizational change, innovation, and improvement by combining theory and practice. Decades later, a similar model emerged, in the work of William Foote Whyte (1991). Whyte's model, which he referred to as *participatory action research,* followed Lewin's in focusing on workplace management. Similarly, it was seen as ignoring class conflict, reigniting an earlier debate between action researchers and those who emphasized the importance of doing research in the service of lower classes struggling against oppression (Brown and Tandon, 1983).

The Participatory Research Model

The third influence on CBR comes from the more conflict-oriented participatory research model. Here, the widespread social and political critiques characteristic of the 1960s and 1970s also looked to the dominant approaches of social research, particularly its assumptions regarding the purposes of research, the possibility of objectivity, relationships between the researchers and the researched, the ethics of data collection, the ownership of research results, reporting findings, and epistemology (Sclove, Scammell, and Holland, 1998).

Forces emerging from community development efforts being undertaken in Third World countries increased the momentum of this critique. For example, during the early 1970s, young social scientists of the First World working as aid specialists in Tanzania became frustrated with the rigidity of the Western social science methods in the African setting (Park, 1992). These methods were based on rigid empiricism and positivism, with its obsession with instrument construction and rigor, defined by statistical precision and replicability. The scientists found that teams of students and village workers who were studying problems such as unemployment among youth and the socioeconomic causes of malnutrition were far more effective in eliciting needed information from the people than they, the scientists, had been. They attributed this success to the data collection methods that relied on the more communal sharing of knowledge specific to the local culture (Hall, 1992). The social scientists also came to realize that their own conventional research methods, which privilege the experts who control the production and distribution of knowledge, served only to reproduce a model that was tied to the Western domination of the newly emerging African nations. Based on these insights, development workers began to rely more and more on local knowledge for the technical solution of problems facing the people, who were encouraged to contribute their own experience, wisdom, and skills to the research.

Similar practices were adopted to address social change in parts of Latin America and Asia, which were also experiencing pains of struggle for liberation from foreign or dictatorial domination. Examples include Orlando Fals-Borda's work with peasants struggling for land in Colombia, people's struggles for protection against deforestation in India, and efforts to secure rights for farmer settlers in the southern Philippines (Park, 1992).

Critiques of positivistic research continued to surface and by the late 1970s, participatory research projects were being conducted in northern regions of the world, including Switzerland, Canada, the United Kingdom, the Netherlands, Italy, and the United States (Hall, 1992). By the early 1980s, several international groups were established and began writing on participatory research. These included the International Council for Adult Education's Participatory Research Group in Toronto and the Society for Participatory Research in Asia (Sclove, Scammell, and Holland, 1998). Participatory research projects were also undertaken in urban and rural North America in various disciplines, including public health, sociology, anthropology, community psychology, and community development.

In North America, participatory research has since been adopted in work with traditionally disadvantaged groups such as Latin American immigrants and First Nations councils (Hall, 1992), people with disabilities (Brydon-Miller, 1993), and Canadian aborigines (Jackson, 1993), as well as on women's issues (Cancian, 1993; Maguire, 1987), and community mental health issues (Schensul and Schensul, 1992).

Although books on participatory research appeared (see Maguire, 1987; Park, Brydon-Miller, Hall, and Jackson, 1993; Whyte, 1991), until recently much of the impetus for this work came from people in nonprofit research organizations rather than from academics in higher education settings. As we will see later in this chapter, the reasons for the limited faculty involvement in participatory research have to do in part with tensions between the traditional research emphases of colleges and universities and the needs of the communities beyond their campuses.

Principles of Community-Based Research

Our model of community-based research draws on these diverse historical influences and is guided by three central principles that represent the core tenets of CBR as it engages the resources of colleges and universities to help communities address pressing problems:

- CBR is a collaborative enterprise between academic researchers (professors and students) and community members.
- CBR validates multiple sources of knowledge and promotes the use of multiple methods of discovery and dissemination of the knowledge produced.
- CBR has as its goal social action and social change for the purpose of achieving social justice.

These principles are also perhaps best understood as features that differentiate CBR from business as usual in American higher education: that is, from conventional academic research including research *on* communities (see Exhibit 1.1) and from conventional approaches to teaching and learning at both the graduate and undergraduate levels.

Collaboration

From the perspective of the college or university, community-based research is the systematic creation of knowledge that is done with and for the community for the purpose of addressing a community-identified need. Ideally, CBR is fully collaborative, with those in the community working with academics—professors and students—at every stage of the research process: identifying the issue or problem, constructing research questions, developing research instruments, collecting and analyzing data, interpreting

Exhibit 1.1. A Comparison of Traditional Academic Research and Community-Based Research.

	Traditional Academic Research	Community-Based Research
Primary goal of the research	Advance knowledge within a discipline	Contribute to betterment of a particular community; social change, social justice
Source of the research question	Extant theoretical or empirical work in a discipline	Community-identified problem or need for information
Who designs and conducts the research?	Trained researcher, perhaps with the help of paid assistants	Trained researchers, students, community members in collaboration
Role of researcher	Outside expert	Collaborator, partner, and learner
Role of community	Object to be studied ("community as laboratory") or no role at all	Collaborator, partner, and learner
Role of students	None, or as research assistants	Collaborators, partners, learners
Relationship of the researcher(s) and the participants-respondents	Short-term, task-oriented, detached	Long-term, multifaceted, connected
Measure of value of the research	Acceptance by academic peers (publication, for example)	Usefulness for community partners and contribution to social change
Criteria for selecting data collection methods	Conformity to standards of rigor, objectivity, researcher-control; preference for quantitative and positivistic approaches	The potential for drawing out useful information, sensitivity to experiential knowledge, conformity to standards of rigor, and accessibility; open to a variety and combination of approaches
Beneficiaries of the research	Academic researcher	Academic researcher, students, community
Ownership of the data	Academic researcher	Community
Mode of presentation	Written report	Varies widely and may take multiple and creative forms (for example, video, theater, written narrative)
Means of dissemination	Presentation at academic conference, submission to journal	Any and all forums where results might have impact: media, public meetings, informal community settings, legislative bodies, and others

results, writing the final report, issuing recommendations, and implementing initiatives. To be effective, this collaboration requires mutually respectful relationships between university and community people and a fundamental sharing of authority. Everyone in the group is regarded as both a researcher and a learner. In this way, the research process itself becomes a means of change and growth for everyone involved in it.

This sort of collaboration clearly distinguishes the roles and relationships in CBR from those that characterize conventional academic research. Much research, of course, does not involve communities at all. But even with conventional approaches, where the community serves as the research "laboratory," there is a definite distinction between the researcher and the researched, or at least between the researcher and the clients for whom the research is being conducted. The traditional community researcher as outside expert typically has a limited and task-oriented relationship with the community rather than the more multifaceted and long-term relationship that characterizes CBR. This does not mean, however, that academic expertise is irrelevant in CBR. Indeed, professors and students can bring to the table a level of objectivity and broader knowledge and experience (including experience with other initiatives) that may be lacking within the community and are valuable precisely because they may encourage community members to consider new directions and new approaches.

The collaborative nature of CBR also makes it a distinctive and highly effective mode of teaching, learning, and empowerment for everyone involved. Students—who may undertake CBR for an independent study project, a graduate-level thesis, a term project with a class, or to fill a research requirement in a course, such as research methods or a capstone—are engaged in active learning and problem-centered pedagogy and benefit in several important ways from the sort of collaboration that characterizes this research approach. CBR offers the chance to learn through the best combination of experiential and intellectual learning strategies. As equal members of CBR teams, students learn how to listen to one another, engage in critical discussions about problems and issues, arrive at solutions mutually, and work together to implement them (Couto, 2001)—all skills that are important in the increasingly team-oriented work world.

The community's involvement in the research process also can have powerful outcomes for them. The capacity of community organizations, schools, and social agencies can be strengthened so that they are able to collect, analyze, and use data independently. Indeed, an important goal of CBR is to transfer information expertise into these organizations through training and resources provided initially by the college or university. If this goal is realized, the organizations become self-sufficient and no longer need to rely on outside experts, but can continue to draw on them when necessary (Stoecker, 1999a). The learning that results from involvement in information gathering and analysis can be an empowerment, or capacity-building, tool for the community (Sclove, Scammell, and Holland, 1998).

In practice, however, the full and equal participation of community members in every phase of the research may be somewhat problematic. Sometimes university researchers are unable or unwilling to relinquish their traditional roles as authoritative experts. Students may be insensitive to the importance or meaning of collaboration, or community members may have insufficient interest, time, or expertise to participate in every phase of the research. However difficult full and equal collaboration may be to achieve, though, it is a tenet and a goal of CBR. At the very least, the community must be fully involved in the first phase of the project—identifying the research need and questions—and in the final phase, where the results are disseminated and implemented. The degree and form of both community and student participation in other phases of the project also may depend on factors such as the nature of the project, characteristics of the community, the level of the students, and the availability of different kinds of expertise from both the university and community.

New Approaches to Knowledge

The second principle—that CBR validates multiple sources of knowledge and promotes the use of multiple methods of discovery and dissemination—refers to the distinctive ways that CBR defines knowledge and approaches the production of knowledge.

First, in the same way that CBR requires the equal participation of academic and community people in the research process, it also values equally the knowledge that each party brings to that process—both the experiential (or local) knowledge of community people and the specialized knowledge and skills of university faculty and students. CBR answers the question, "Whose knowledge counts?" in distinctive ways. It places the less powerful members of society at the center of the knowledge creation process. This means that people's daily lives, achievements, and struggles are no longer at the margins of research but are placed firmly at the center. CBR requires acknowledging the validity of the local knowledge generated in and through practice in community settings and weighing this alongside institutionalized, scientific, and scholarly professional knowledge familiar to faculty and students. Put simply, community-based researchers are interested in the epistemology of practice and, in particular, how each form of knowledge informs and guides the other.

A second distinctive feature of CBR's approach to knowledge is that it recognizes and may incorporate multiple research methods. It also encourages practitioners to develop and apply unconventional criteria for determining the appropriateness of those methods. CBR requires that we eschew rigid methodological rules or protocols. Rather, methods are chosen or developed because they have the potential for drawing out useful, relevant knowledge and because they invite the involvement of all parties, or stakeholders, in identifying, defining, and struggling to solve the problem. For example, because CBR places high value on local or experiential knowledge of community members, research approaches that are particularly sensitive to discerning the voice and perspective of participants, such as informal interviews or open-ended questions, might be chosen over more structured, researcher-controlled data collection methods. Generally, CBR also requires a willingness on the part of researchers to be flexible and adaptable: to be willing to rely on a variety and multiplicity of data collection methods and instruments, work to develop unconventional ones, ignore discipline-bound methodologies, and even change methodological direction in the middle of the study if it will enhance community participation and empowerment or enhance the usefulness of data collected.

A third feature is that CBR often requires innovative, user-friendly approaches to the dissemination of knowledge as well. Neighborhood residents and community organizations want tangible results that they can use. Indeed, the value of the entire research project rests on its potential to produce results that can be used by the community. This may mean that professors and students who are used to thinking in terms of research reports and scholarly standards of proof must think instead of the need for concrete results presented in a form that is comprehensible to neighborhoods, organizations, politicians, agency personnel, and others who might make use of the research findings. It requires that researchers demystify the language used in research reports, and it might also call for the use of innovative, creative methods of describing and reporting results that may not involve writing at all: video, art, community theater, or quilting, for example.

The distinctive approach to defining, discovering, and disseminating knowledge that is essential to CBR poses yet another challenge to conventional research paradigms in the sciences and social sciences. The collaborative nature of CBR calls into question conventional assumptions about who should be allowed to participate in the production of knowledge. That is, it challenges the exclusive authority of the trained researcher and argues for the value of nonspecialist participation in decisions relating to research processes and priorities. CBR's approach to knowledge—its insistence on democratizing and demystifying knowledge—goes further. CBR also challenges conventional assumptions about knowledge itself: what constitutes valid knowledge, how it is best produced or acquired, and who gets to control it. In this sense, CBR engages some of the provocative epistemological debates that have emerged in the sciences and social sciences in the form of feminist theory, critical science studies, and other important challenges to traditional thinking and dominant canons, including rigid disciplinary boundaries that can stand in the way of addressing research questions that are seldom confined to the content or methods of one discipline. To engage students with some of these epistemological questions, by modeling CBR as an alternative to conventional approaches, is yet another way that CBR differs from traditional teaching.

Social Action and Social Change

The third principle of CBR is its commitment to social action and social change in the interest of advancing social justice. Community organizations often need information as part of their efforts to make needed changes: improve their programs, promote their interest, attract new resources, understand their target populations, or in other ways contribute to a social action agenda aimed at improving the lives of people in the community, particularly those who are most limited in their access to resources and opportunities. The kind of information that CBR produces can explicate issues and challenges facing communities, create awareness of the need for action, focus attention on areas of particular concern, identify resources that can help address those concerns, design strategies for change, and assess the impact of those strategies. In other words, CBR offers a chance for community organizations and agencies to have a strong information base from which to plan and act. Hence, the central purpose for engaging in CBR is to produce information that might be useful in bringing about needed change.

The social change that is the goal of CBR may be of a substantial and long-lasting nature, but typically the social action it implies, or the improvement that it brings, is fairly modest. This may be by design—for example, an assessment of an after-school program has as its ultimate goal producing information that will improve that program, a useful but limited kind of change. It also may be a result of other factors, such as the failure of the project to produce truly useful results or, as is often the case, the inability to get decision makers to pay attention and act on the results that the project produces. Because the research project is often one relatively small item on a larger community social action agenda, its impact may be minimal or may not be discernible for some time. For example, a project whose purpose is to identify areas of community concern might be little more than a first stage in a long series of efforts to get those concerns analyzed and addressed.

Finally, the research process itself, quite apart from any results that it produces, may contribute to social change by empowering and helping to build capacity among community members. Some of this has to do with skills and knowledge that academics share with the community members. Another is simply the fact of community members coming together to identify collective needs and talk about potential solutions, which may help revitalize democracy in the community and otherwise set into motion structures and processes for social change quite beyond any particular research project. This aim of CBR has its roots in Freire's popular education model, where the process of coming together to educate, learn, and talk about social change serves as a means of consciousness raising and organization among community members, who are then empowered to work for change themselves.

The social action–social change goal of CBR distinguishes it in yet another clear way from both conventional academic research and, when it is used as a pedagogical strategy, conventional approaches to teaching as well. The dominant research paradigm dictates that the central purpose for doing research is to advance knowledge within disciplines. The careers of college and university faculty members—decisions about hiring, promotion, and tenure—rest primarily (or at least partially, at more teaching-oriented institutions) on their being successful researchers. Such success is measured mainly by the researchers' ability to attract grant money and the favorable judgment of their research by academic peers, as evidenced by presentation at disciplinary conferences and publication in peer-reviewed professional journals. The measure of the value of community-based research, in contrast, is its potential to bring about social change. And the research questions that drive CBR come not from the mandate to build theory in a discipline, but rather from a need for information that might help advance the social justice and social action agenda of a community organization or agency. CBR's social change objective, like its unorthodox approach to issues of knowledge and expertise, renders it at least somewhat suspect within traditional academic reward structures.

All of the basic principles of CBR distinguish it from conventional modes of teaching that is classroom based and lecture oriented. However, its social action orientation also makes CBR different from other forms of service-learning, much of which involves students in charity-oriented, direct-service-providing roles in the community. CBR's goal of social change means, among other things, that students must engage in some amount of critical analysis of causes of social problems and also must consider solutions and strategies for change. Its advocates argue that this makes CBR a particularly effective pedagogy for helping students acquire knowledge and skill for active citizenship and democratic participation.

Summary

Community-based research has emerged in response to the criticism that colleges and universities are insufficiently responsive to the needs of communities. CBR has a long and diverse history, and this history provides a basis for the three major principles that guide our model of CBR for higher education institutions: collaboration, validation of multiple sources of knowledge and methods of discovery and dissemination, and the goals of social change and social action to achieve social justice.

2

WHY DO COMMUNITY-BASED RESEARCH?

BENEFITS AND PRINCIPLES

OF SUCCESSFUL PARTNERSHIPS

PERHAPS THE MOST DISTINGUISHING feature of community-based research is that it is collaborative, and the foundation for that collaboration is the campus-community partnership. Faculty and students work with community-based organizations to define the research questions and develop appropriate strategies to address those questions. In this process, the scientific process is demystified and the results are produced to be useful to the community as they pursue their social change and community improvement agenda. However, as Nyden, Figert, Shibley, and Burrows (1997) note, "Successful collaborative projects typically have at their foundation a working relationship that has been built up over time" (p. 5). In this chapter, we focus on the partnership aspect of CBR: how it is that the community can benefit from the partnership and some of the principles that govern successful campus-community collaboration.

Before turning to our examination of the benefits of CBR to the community, we must first address the question, "Who is *the community?*" What we mean by community encompasses a variety of social organization forms that operate at a number of levels of size and complexity. At the basic level, the members of a community share a common interest or identity. Typically, these individuals create a form of social organization to further their common interest or advance their notion of common identity. The community entities with which we collaborate in CBR are those that share a common position in society that places them in a disadvantaged position in structural or cultural terms: they have access to fewer

resources and opportunities due to the way that the larger society's institutions, social structures, or policies operate or the way in which they are
perceived (and perceive themselves) in relation to the others in society.
Based on this position of disadvantage, members sharing this identity or
structural location come together to improve their opportunities and access to resources. The CBR process may collaborate with such communities
at any and all levels of this process: constructing the social organization,
defining its goals and strategies, implementing its social change initiatives,
assessing the effects of its change efforts, and reevaluating its initial goals
and strategies in the light of its experiences.

The social bases of these communities may take a variety of forms:

- Geographical location (for example, neighborhood groups,
  public housing residents)
- Position within an institution or social structure (for example,
  juvenile offenders, students in public schools, poor people,
  service sector laborers, senior citizens)
- Personal identity or status (for example, immigrants, women,
  people of color, gays and lesbians)
- Alliances with such constituencies (such as faith-based
  organizations and service agencies)

The actual community partners with which we conduct CBR are typically nonprofit organizations, public agencies, or small grassroots groups
organized for any number of purposes:

- Provide services to those in need
- Advocate for the disadvantaged or oppressed
- Empower people who are disenfranchised
- Alter structures that limit opportunities and generate poverty,
  violence, and suffering
- Ally themselves with such efforts

In some cases, these partner organizations are made up of, or controlled
by, members of those communities. In those situations, there is a clean fit
between the goal of working with the community and actual practice. In
many cases, however, those partners are a step removed from the community because community members do not control those organizations.
They are often, however, connected to it by staff or board members who
come from the community. Those "link people," or "bridge people," or

"translators," as they are variously called, are the connection between the organization and the community.

Other partners are two steps removed from the community because they have no direct connection to the people with the problem. Their staff or boards may share some structural characteristics—of class, race, gender, sexual orientation, disability, or other important characteristic—but they do not share the experience of the problem. Service providers, institutions, government, and other similar organizations trying to help a community when they have no community base, no community participation or control, and no bridge people are often suspect in a community. It is with these twice-removed groups that many academics partner, which introduces a series of concerns about how well the community itself is being empowered. In later chapters we discuss mechanisms for addressing these issues and strengthening community empowerment. We now turn to an examination of the ways that CBR may provide benefits to such community-based organizations.

Benefits to the Community

The leaders, staff, and organizers in community-based organizations (CBOs) confront enormous challenges and often feel overwhelmed, largely due to the nature of their work and the environment in which they operate. They labor on society's most complex problems—such as poverty, homelessness, child abuse, illiteracy, hunger, and lack of affordable housing—armed with woefully inadequate resources. They operate in a context that affords them fairly limited opportunity to effect structural changes and even fewer resources to devote to such changes. They are further hampered by frequent policy shifts and the resistance of entrenched elites allied behind the status quo. All too often, they find themselves so busy confronting the immediate threats to individual or family survival or well-being that they have little time and energy left to address the underlying causes of the problems that command their efforts.

Increasingly, these organizations have been asked not only to do more with less but to document with quantitative data that they have succeeded in their efforts. They are asked to undertake research on the extent of need and to select best practices for program implementation within a specific context. CBR partnerships can help alleviate some of these pressures, especially the need to demonstrate impact, and they can be an important resource for those who are working to improve the quality of life for disadvantaged people in our communities.

The South West Improvement Council

The South West Improvement Council (SWIC) is a nonprofit organization that provides housing and other services in a low-income, ethnically diverse neighborhood in southwest Denver. Jan Marie Belle, director of SWIC, needed solid data to support her community organization's case for grants, public funding, and political debates, but she lacked the resources to collect such information. Deb Moulton, a University of Denver doctoral student in quantitative research methods, worked with Belle to analyze the demographics relevant to affordable housing in southwest Denver.

Belle used the graphics that resulted from Moulton's study in a presentation to local foundations and politicians about housing issues in the city. The study's findings had important implications for charitable giving and public policy. "I got lots of thoughtful dialogue; council members commented how helpful it was to have graphics. One of the council members is a lawyer and president of the Colorado Mortgage Banker's Association. He exchanged cards with me, and we talked about forming a coalition to work on these issues in a way that nonprofits alone cannot. Folks like that really like data—factual information to make decisions. We had information he hadn't seen, and that was powerful for us."

In an e-mail note to Moulton, Belle said, "Thanks again, for the respect you are showing and the knowledge you are sharing. You are objective, fair, respectful, truly wanting to empower, not insecure, not trying to take what we have." Belle describes what she learned from her collaboration with Moulton: "Deb showed me how to analyze the data, to update things, and to use the computer program she uses. This was most empowering. I am gratified that she realizes that I can learn new things. It's so empowering to have this kind of data. It puts me on equal footing with those who have the money and political power. With my own data, I can negotiate service for the community. I don't have to rely on someone else's figures."

From the community's point of view, the primary incentive for entering into a CBR collaboration is to help it achieve its social change goals. Although CBO leaders, staff, and organizers may be willing, and even eager, to help educate students or advance the frontiers of knowledge, their objective for partnering with higher education students and faculty is to mobilize additional resources to fulfill their organizational mission. From the CBO perspective, such a partnership may be a significant asset for them. In the short run, the partnership may provide the CBO with access to new resources as well as the opportunity to leverage the resources that are already under its control. From a somewhat longer-term perspective, CBR partnerships have the potential to develop the capacities of community groups by increasing the skills of the staff, thereby enhancing the organization's ability to operate more effectively and better assess its operations and outcomes. Finally, and on a more abstract level, if we shift our focus away from the internal operations of community groups, we can see how these partnerships are able to make a meaningful contribution to democracy. In the following sections, we examine the potential for CBR to advance the social change objectives of community-based organizations by helping those organizations: leverage new resources and better mobilize the ones they have, develop their capacity, and participate more effectively in our democracy.

Accessing and Using Resources

CBR partnerships are valuable to community groups to the extent that they provide access to new, relatively stable, and diverse resources. In a typical CBR project, a group of students and their professor work on a question that the agency has identified. The significance to the CBO is that it receives a substantial infusion of real energy and expertise. At its best, such a partnership provides a temporary research and development staff for the CBO that it otherwise could not afford. It is temporary in the sense that any one professor and his or her class may share their talents during the course of a one-semester or two-semester CBR class. As the partnership deepens over time and broadens to cover a range of matters, the potential becomes even more powerful. In such a case, the partnership can provide an ongoing mechanism that will connect the community group with faculty members and students from a variety of disciplines, presumably over a long period of time during which a number of research initiatives can be undertaken.

Clearly, CBR is a vehicle to help nonprofits do more of what they are already trying to do daily. The additional resources brought to bear by faculty and students help the CBOs complete more activities that already appear on their short-term agenda. Consider how a simple CBR project can help an organization that runs a mentoring program for at-risk children, but does not have enough volunteers to serve all of them. In this situation, a group of students can produce a directory of all volunteer, service, and service-learning programs in the area. They can interview current volunteers and find out what brought them to the organization and what barriers they overcame to serve there. They can produce a directory of potential funding agencies and explain their distinctive application processes. Perhaps in a follow-up project the next semester, another group of students will draft a grant proposal on behalf of the organization, surveying the alternative program options, analyzing the strengths and weaknesses of the program, and documenting the program's existing practices. Each of these projects would help the program accomplish its short-term goal: matching more at-risk youths with positive role models.

CBR can also leverage funding sources well beyond their initial limits. Phil Nyden, director of the Center for Urban Research and Learning at Loyola University in Chicago, notes that "the roughly $10,000,000 in grants received by the Center for Urban Research and Learning at Loyola has leveraged at least another $10,000,000 in tuition, faculty time, student time, and other university resources. Easily one-third of this has directly gone to community partners, or has been of direct benefit to them" (Nyden, personal communication, 2002). Even when sharing a grant with a higher education institution that takes a large amount of it in overhead, the possibilities of using the remaining funds to leverage faculty time, student time, physical resources such as computer analysis and laboratory testing facilities, and other institutional resources for a CBR project can make an initial grant stretch considerably.

The University of Denver's six-year relationship with La Clinica Tepeyac also illustrates how a CBR partnership can be beneficial for a community-based organization. La Clinica is located in a Denver neighborhood that the university has been connected with through various community-based learning projects for several years. It is referred to as a first-tier partner of the university because whenever possible, La Clinica's research needs receive priority from the university when CBR projects are being planned, and the partners share a high degree of mutual trust. One of the research projects that illustrates how CBR can help CBOs better use existing resources and access new ones to meet goals was conducted by three University of Denver graduate students, who conducted a six-month evaluation of the Reach and Teach Program, an outreach program designed to familiarize local women in the community with La Clinica's breast and cervical screening services. The research team's report made several suggestions for improvement, which were incorporated into the following year's implementation of the program. The program director also used some of the report's positive findings to strengthen grant proposals, and some received funding.

CBR partnerships also provide community groups with a mechanism to leverage and maximize their own resources, which includes their own in-house expertise and staff time. For example, research on best practices— examining how other programs provide similar services, perhaps in comparable contexts—may provide useful suggestions for program changes that would lead to better service provision for clients. In terms of the research process itself, community groups have a significant amount of knowledge that could enhance the quality of any research effort, but it is often the case that they are unable to make this a high enough priority to which to divert staff time. Most of our community partners simply do not have the right combination of staff time and expertise to design and execute a research project that will provide useful results and withstand serious scrutiny. However, when they enter into a CBR partnership, they join a larger team effort. There are members on that team who complement what the community representatives bring to the table, and vice versa. Thus, it is not necessary, for example, that the community agency has a staff member who understands sampling. Instead, their staff can inform the campus experts about the nature of their population, warn of unique challenges that might confound standard sampling techniques, and advise on the content of the survey questionnaire that will be administered to the sample.

Enhancing Capacity

Working collaboratively on a CBR project enhances the capacity for all the parties involved in the project. Students learn how to conduct research, and both students and faculty learn about the community and the practical challenges confronting people in disadvantaged positions in society. All of the participants acquire skills, learning from others and learning how to interact with others from different positions and with different backgrounds. Community members also acquire technical skills in research, strategic planning, and evaluation. Furthermore, the CBOs within which the community members operate enhance their organization's systems for strategic planning and evaluation, leading to improvements in the organization's self-governance and internal democratization. A parallel development occurs within higher education institutions as well, as we discuss in Chapter Eight.

The participatory nature of many CBR projects also gives community members the opportunity to acquire new skills or develop others by working with academics and students. This may take place informally, as in the case of an agency director who participates in a training session on how to facilitate focus groups that was organized by a professor for her students. Or it may arise out of a more formal approach. At Georgetown University, for example, community partners can participate in community research seminars at no cost, learn how to conduct CBR and undertake a community-driven project, and receive academic credit. At a minimum, these opportunities make it easier for community members to become better consumers of research and savvier when it comes to analyzing the recommendations that may emerge from a research project. At a higher level, community members may find it easier to play a meaningful role in any participatory research effort that seeks their input in the design and implementation of a project. Finally, and perhaps ideally, community members who participate in CBR projects may learn how to conduct research on their own

However, it is not enough for a community group to gain access to new skills or even to develop their own skills. Rather, the most desirable goal is that CBOs establish the appropriate internal systems that use and control such information creation and dissemination processes. Here, too, a strong CBR partnership can make a significant contribution. For example, in Trenton, New Jersey, a shelter for runaway and abused children had completed hundreds of intake forms over a twenty-year period for each child who had walked through its doors in order to satisfy a federal reporting requirement. Yet the staff did not have the ability to enter these data onto a computer and examine them. A professor at a local college and his class entered and analyzed the data as part of a CBR project. This proved helpful but was not the most important outcome of this partnership. That came about when the professor later recruited a student from the computer science department to build on the work of the first class project. This second student designed a software program that the staff was able to use at their own site to generate monthly reports. As a result, the CBR partnership provided the shelter with the means to capture and interpret information themselves on a regular basis that is used to monitor and assess the program's operations.

CBR partnerships may also improve the ability of community groups to make more strategic decisions about their operations. David Beckwith, a community organizer from the Center for Community Change, refers to this as "helping us get ahead of the curve" (Beckwith, 1996, p. 167). In part, this stems from the fact that CBR projects can provide these groups with what they need to act more strategically: quality information, data, and analysis. In this sense, the needs of a grassroots group are no different from those of a Fortune 500 company, but the CBOs have no access to resources to pay for quality research and development.

Two essential areas where CBR can contribute to the work of nonprofit organizations are program development and program evaluation, according to Martin Johnson, executive director of Isles Community Development Corporation in Trenton. Describing the contributions of CBR to program development, he notes that many of program partners are forced to act on "anecdotes or gut feelings" when they work on developing new programs. One of his colleagues cites the example of an agency whose director chose a mentoring curriculum because it was used by her former employer, not as a result of any best practices research, which might have been the case if she had had a CBR team available. Because she had neither the time nor a compelling reason to question the choice of mentoring programs (she is one of only two employees), she chose the only program she was familiar with. In other cases, CBOs with strong professional staff or board often rely on their own, sometimes flawed or limited, internal knowledge to decide what programs to develop. Over time, they can become disconnected from the people they serve. A growing number of CBOs are using CBR teams to help manage focus groups, surveys, and community analyses to better connect, design, and execute plans.

Program evaluation is the second area cited by Martin Johnson where CBR can make a substantial contribution to the work of nonprofit organizations. He sees a shift in the ways that CBO funders and communities measure success: "Simply measuring the number of organizational outputs (houses, counseling sessions, events, and so on) is no longer adequate. Now we have to answer the 'so what?' question. What outcome has occurred because of your work?" This question requires new and better indicators and data collection methods than most organizations can manage. One of the program directors in his organization, who runs a program for high school dropouts, sought to improve their evaluation system because, like most other typical program measures, it failed to measure whether the participants were becoming more self-reliant, a core value of the organization. Instead, the data were limited to how many of the youth received a general equivalency diploma, acquired a job, or entered a training program. To develop a more focused way to assess their impact, the director helped a research methods class at the local college develop a new and more effective way to measure increased self-reliance in the program. Another colleague of Johnson runs a program that matches college volunteers with formerly homeless preschool children in an effort to develop their emerging literacy skills. In this case, the director worked with an education class to administer a pre- and posttest that served to clarify the effectiveness of this volunteer effort. Program evaluation, when it is done well, can lead to significant improvements in the way a program is designed or implemented. In this case, the results might indicate a need to increase the number of service hours each child receives or to change the way that tutors are recruited or trained.

In sum, CBR partnerships can be a useful tool for community organizations, helping them get more done in the short term and strengthening their capacity to plan and implement quality programs in the longer term. Such partnerships help these organizations complete concrete tasks that have a sense of urgency attached to them, think and act more strategically, develop skills, and establish more sophisticated internal systems. CBR partnerships have the potential, however, to do more than just enhance the capacity of community groups to achieve their programmatic goals. They also help position them to play a more active role in our democracy.

Effective Democratic Participation

Campus-community research partnerships might, finally, be seen as means by which we can help create what Barber (1992) calls a "strong democracy" in America. They do this by sparking interest in civic activism on the part of historically marginalized groups and, even more important, by removing some of the barriers that have long worked against real grassroots political participation. These barriers include lack of compelling information to engage policymakers, low credibility, and a dearth of feelings of civic efficacy and competence on the part of community groups and members. We discuss each of these in turn.

COMPELLING INFORMATION TO ENGAGE POLICYMAKERS. Community groups working with academics typically devote their greatest effort to developing projects whose results can help them accomplish their primary mission. The information, data, or analysis that they obtain often can be used to help sway government officials and other key decision makers at all levels as they draft legislation or develop budgets that may have an impact on CBO constituencies in long-range, powerful ways. CBOs seldom have the financial resources with which to hire expensive lobbyists. This means they must resort to other strategies, and one basic but potentially effective one is to inform the policymaking process with compelling information whose aim is to influence presumably well-intentioned and rational decision makers. This was the aim of the director of a transitional housing agency for homeless families when she asked her local CBR center* to help her design and carry out a survey of those whom the agency had helped in the past. She hoped that the data would demonstrate the effectiveness of her program and thus help convince state officials to create

---

* A CBR center is typically a centralized office that coordinates an institution's CBR activities, including soliciting community projects, matching institution personnel and resources with projects, conducting trainings and outreach, and other related activities. Such centers can range in size from a single staff person or faculty member to large operations managing numerous programs.

an exception under the new welfare law for transitional housing programs. Although she was not entirely successful at influencing state legislation, she was able to use the results to convince a reluctant funder to provide continuing financial support for her agency.

CREDIBILITY IN THE EYES OF DECISION MAKERS. Sometimes it is the message combined with the messenger that makes a difference when it is time for officials (public and private) to make an important decision. Community groups and their causes often acquire additional credibility when the reports they are disseminating are authored or coauthored by someone with an advanced degree who is affiliated with a university or college. David Beckwith (1996), of the Center for Community Change, calls this "using your priestly power for good" and recognizes that many professors working with community groups may be initially reluctant to highlight their credentials (p. 166). "You may not like to put that 'Ph.D.' after your name," he advises academic researchers working with the community. "But a letter from Professor Jones, Ph.D. can convince people that [the community] really has 'somebody' on their side. In life, that matters." He cites a market study of Ohio nonprofit housing developers that was produced from the Urban Affairs Center at the University of Toledo. The content of this report *and* its connection with the university made it legitimate in the eyes of the state legislature, which later passed an appropriation to support community development.

HIGHER LEVELS OF CIVIC EFFICACY AND COMPETENCE. We previously noted that community members who participate in CBR projects often develop research skills. Such participation can also develop what political scientists call civic efficacy and civic competence. People who actively participate in a research project that addresses a local problem become more confident that they can make a difference in their own communities. If the process eventually leads to action, such as writing a letter to an elected official or organizing a meeting with that official, the participants begin to learn the rules of the game. In short, they are learning how to make a difference.

At an even more fundamental level, when CBOs empower individuals by enabling them to acquire skills or resources necessary to engage in effective political participation—for example, literacy, access to transportation, and computer skills—they help create a stronger, more participatory democracy. The Day Labor Center in the city of Pomona, California, illustrates how the creation of a community organization established to serve the needs of a disenfranchised group has enhanced their ability to participate in the larger community (see the Pomona Economic Opportunity Center case). Students experience the same development process and acquire the knowledge and skills attached to learning how to participate in the political process while they also develop a sense of empowerment and personal efficacy.

In sum, CBR partnerships provide what Ansley and Gaventa (1997) call "social capital" (p. 51), which they see as consisting of connections between and among groups and individuals through which various resources flow. It is such connections that enable grassroots organizations to develop linkages and relationships with others, in the community and on campuses, who control important assets that can have a tremendous impact on the social change and advocacy efforts of these groups. The collaborative teams of community members and academics that form around CBR can serve as important incubators of social capital (Ansley and Gaventa, 1997).

Principles of Successful Community-Campus Partnerships

Now that we have considered the benefits of CBR to the community, answering the "why" question, we examine ten essential principles of successful CBR partnerships—the "how" question. We present them in a

---

Pomona Economic Opportunity Center

The Day Labor Center of Pomona, California, was created from a participatory style of community-based research. It was established in response to a city ordinance passed in July 1997 that prohibited "the solicitation of work on any street or highway, public area, or non-residential parking areas in the city of Pomona." Those caught in violation of the ordinance would face a fine of up to a thousand dollars and six months in jail.

When the ordinance was passed, a group of Pitzer College students in Professor José Calderon's class, "Restructuring Communities," worked with various community activists to research day laborers, organize them, and pack city hall for demonstrations. With the help of this class, a funding proposal was written, and a nonprofit organization, the Pomona Economic Opportunity Center, was formed. Subsequently, the city council allocated fifty thousand dollars to this nonprofit organization for the purpose of developing a day labor center. The council also appointed a board of directors that included city commission members, representatives from the community, and students and faculty from Pitzer College. This campus-community collaborative has resulted in research on immigration, health, language, conflict resolution, and leadership development that involves the workers in all aspects of the decision-making process.

---

more or less sequential framework (see Exhibit 2.1). The first three principles relate to the approach or perspectives that potential partners from both campus and community bring *into* successful partnerships. The next four help us understand the process of conducting CBR projects, with particular attention to the kinds of interactions that govern successful partnerships. The final three principles relate to the outcomes or desired results of projects and partnerships. Because all of these principles are interrelated, this framework should be viewed not as a rigid categorization but rather as a conceptual tool that can help us identify and understand some of the key features of successful community-campus partnerships.

Entering Partnerships

The first three principles help us to understand more clearly what motivates community and campus partners to undertake CBR projects together and delineate some important orientations toward one another that successful partners either bring with them or develop jointly in the course of their work together:

1. Partners share a worldview.
2. Partners agree about goals and strategies.
3. Partners have mutual trust and mutual respect.

PARTNERS SHARE A WORLDVIEW. In successful CBR partnerships, the key players share important elements of a worldview, including basic philosophical assumptions about people, communities, society, and how they connect with one another. One such assumption, well articulated by Benjamin Barber (1984), is that "every human being, given half a chance, is capable of the self-government that is his or her natural right, and thus capable of acquiring the judgment, foresight, and knowledge that self-government demands" (p. 13). This idea—that we can and should trust ordinary men and women with power to make more decisions that affect themselves and their communities—dovetails neatly with CBR's commitment to collaboration. Academic and community partners who share it will work more easily together to promote shared authority and the participation of community members in all aspects of the research process.

Another important element of a shared worldview is an understanding of what constitutes *community.* Who is "the community" whose interests the researchers represent and work for? Is it a geographical community— that is, one that is spatially bound, such as a neighborhood? Or is the community a more dispersed one, identified by shared status or identity or

---

Exhibit 2.1. Ten Principles of Successful
Community-Campus Partnerships.

Entering partnerships

Community and campus partners
1. Share a worldview
2. Agree about goals and strategies
3. Have trust and mutual respect

Conducting partnerships

Community and campus partners
4. Share power
5. Communicate clearly and listen carefully
6. Understand and empathize with each other
7. Remain flexible

Outcomes of partnerships

Community and campus partners
8. Satisfy each other's interests or needs
9. Have their organizational capacities enhanced
10. Adopt long-range social change perspectives

---

other interest? Community-based organizations typically address such core definitional issues as they are formed, so that their notion of the community they serve is captured in their mission statement or incorporation papers. From the campus side, this can be a bit more of a challenge. While faculty members and students entering a partnership assume the partner's perspective regarding the particular community they serve, the issue might be more problematic at the institutional level. Here, the college or university—faculty members, CBR center staff, and administrators—must make some decisions about the community or communities with which they will work. Where should they commit their limited resources, and why? What are some of the political and ideological ramifications associated with working with some groups as opposed to others? The faculty at the College of Public and Community Service at the University of Massachusetts–Boston addressed this question by committing to work with groups "that do not have political power, or that have less economic power or fewer opportunities" than others in the Boston area (Kennedy and Stone, 1997, p. 120). As a result, teams of students work under the direction of professors to assist "under-funded, grassroots community, labor, and advocacy organizations serving the interests of low-income communities . . . in the greater Boston area" (p. 124). The Washington, D.C.-based network of campus and community partners engaging in community-based research has adopted similar language for its CBR clearinghouse operations and is the basis of the meaning of *community* set out at the beginning of this chapter.

PARTNERS AGREE ABOUT GOALS AND STRATEGIES. Another important principle of a successful partnership is agreement about the desired outcomes of the joint endeavor, along with similar ideas about the best strategies for achieving those goals. At a minimum, all CBR partnerships seek to ensure that colleges and universities are a useful resource to local community organizations, and hence mobilize faculty, students, and other campus-based resources to complete research and planning projects that the community groups have identified. Somewhat more sophisticated than this *resource model approach* is an *empowerment* or *capacity-building model* (Reardon, 2000), when CBR partners share the additional aim of using the collaborative research process to build various capacities of community members, perhaps including both residents and staff from community organizations. Here they work to equip community members and organizations with new skills, tools, practices, and systems that make it easier for them to achieve their goals and gain control over their own neighborhoods.

Equally important are shared ideas about strategies to achieve those shared goals, including the different roles and contributions of members of the CBR team. A partnership committed to building the capacity of community members, for example, is likely to stress the participatory nature of CBR at every stage of the project and to work with the same group of community members over an extended period of time. Furthermore, if the goal of CBR is to empower communities, there must be a process through which community members shape and control elements of the partnership. Thus, our shared assumption is that the community must articulate the questions that the research will address, whereas the faculty members bring the expertise to address the questions. Similarly, the community organization determines the social change agenda that it will pursue, whereas the faculty and students align themselves with the change agenda with which they are most comfortable. This discussion of these larger philosophical issues must be an ongoing process among the partners, from the first discussion of the possibility of establishing a specific project partnership to a continuing conversation that becomes part of the partnership between academics and CBOs.

Sometimes conflicts of organizational policies or values make a partnership inadvisable. An example was when the Denver chapter of the Boy

Scouts of America contacted faculty members at the University of Denver wanting help in determining why such a small number of Latino boys were enrolling in their programs. Although several University of Denver graduate students were interested in and even had some research expertise around the issue of Latino participation in school-based and community programs, they determined that the Boy Scouts' gay exclusion policy clashed with the social justice orientation of the university's CBR initiative, and they declined to partner with the Boy Scouts.

This example illustrates the tactical and moral dilemma that exists when one chooses to partner with an organization whose policies conflict with the social justice principle of CBR. The University of Denver might have taken a different stance and accepted the CBR offer with the Boy Scouts in the hope of developing a partnership that over time might lead the organization to reconsider its stance on homosexuality and hence to advance social justice. Often there is no single answer to such dilemmas. A more common dilemma that several of us face in our work is partnering with social service organizations that may disempower community members through the treatment models they employ. In these cases, we may choose to work with such partners in the hope that an effective CBR project that insists that clients become participants in the CBR project may also open up the agency to more empowering practices.

PARTNERS HAVE MUTUAL TRUST AND RESPECT. Strong CBR partnerships exhibit and nurture trust among the participants in two important ways. First, each partner trusts that the other can be counted on to "do the right thing"—that the partner will know what that is and ultimately will make a genuine effort not to compromise the other's interests. Second, the partners share, or at least work to develop, a faith in the collaborative process itself.

Trust among partners does not emerge instantly in a new working relationship. The community and campus partners start by sharing their goals and discussing the constraints within which they operate. Over time, an understanding develops about what the primary objectives are for each of the partners, which of the outcomes and processes cannot be compromised and which are flexible, and the contextual factors that will influence the dynamics. During the course of a successful collaboration, each partner comes to trust the other to act in good faith, keep in mind the interests of the other as well as their own interests, and refuse to sacrifice the other's important objectives in favor of one's own lesser ones.

Successful partners trust not only each other but also the process of collaboration. They have confidence in the partnership: that it will produce meaningful results even as it faces hurdles of various kinds along the way.

The partners share the often implicit assumption that although any particular short-term project may fall short of expectations in some way, the relationship is worth maintaining because of the promise of fulfilling important joint interests of the partners over the long term.

Lydia Santoni-Lawrence, the executive director of the Community Service Action Center (CSAC) in Hightstown, New Jersey, illustrates this sort of trust. In the midst of her first CBR project, it became clear that the research team of students from the local college was on track to deliver a mediocre product at best. The students had lost their focus, their professor was not engaged enough to alter their project trajectory, and the young agency staff member who was most directly involved in the project was proving to be too inexperienced to assert leadership to affect the process. As the unsuccessful project drew to a close, Santoni-Lawrence shared her concerns with the organizer who initially brought the team together. But she also added: "Don't get me wrong. I am committed to working with you to form these partnerships. I am convinced that these types of collaborations can have a substantial impact on our agency's efforts to improve the lives of the local immigrant population and the poor as well as on the students. And I know that we will eventually get what we need. This is just a natural part of the process." Since that time, Santoni-Lawrence has joined forces with a psychology professor who has worked with her students to complete two remarkable projects with the staff of CSAC. After the first project, this partnership has flourished as both community and campus partners have learned how to work together effectively.

Trust must be nurtured and sustained if it is to last. In the CSAC case, the campus liaison that brought the partners together in the first place spoke frequently with the community partner during the course of the project. In these conversations, he reiterated his commitment to the community's needs—that her agency would receive a quality product even if it meant finding another team (additional faculty members and students) to build on the work of the first group and complete the report during the winter break. (The significance of effective communication is examined in the next section.)

Mutual respect goes hand-in-hand with trust as essential orientations that campus and community partners bring with them to the CBR relationship. When all members of the CBR team recognize the value of each member's knowledge, mutual respect prevails, and the partnership is far more likely to be successful. Here, the respect is predicated in part on the assumption that in CBR, multiple sources of knowledge are both valid and essential to address community needs. To be useful, CBR projects must draw on both the expertise of the academics and the valuable experiential knowledge of community partners and members. Thus, a professor's years of experience in survey research design are of little value without community members' insights about how to approach people and pose questions in ways that will secure their cooperation and participation. A graduate student's technical knowledge of how to measure levels of industrial pollution is only one piece of the knowledge needed to bring legal action against a company with a longstanding and complicated history in a community. Community members are indispensable sources of information about themselves, their lives, their community's history, and the workings of the local political and economic institutions. For their part, students and professors bring technical research expertise along with analytical and conceptual perspectives that can enrich community efforts in myriad ways.

The Process

The next four principles describe some patterns of interaction that characterize successful campus-community partnerships:

4. Partners share power.
5. Partners communicate clearly and listen carefully.
6. Partners understand and empathize with each other's circumstances.
7. Partners remain flexible.

These patterns typically emerge over time. They also tend to be self-perpetuating, such that effective interactions among members of the CBR team fuel further effective interaction.

PARTNERS SHARE POWER. At the broadest level, this notion of shared power is akin to the assumption that all people, even the poor and marginalized, have the right to participate in the decision-making processes that affect their lives. In the context of CBR, with its commitment to collaboration, shared power means that campus and community partners participate fully in shaping decisions about their work together. In general, the balance of power should tip toward the community when it comes to the most basic aspects of the CBR project, especially identifying the research question in accordance with community needs and shaping and implementing change strategies that might emerge from the research. When community members are afforded less authority than their academic colleagues, the research is likely to be of far less value to the community than otherwise would be true. Moreover, CBR partnerships that mirror conventional notions of academic expertise and authority end up perpetuating the sort of inequitable power structures that they ultimately seek to challenge and change. This makes the goals of shared power especially compelling. There are cases, however, when the community may not be organized enough to participate in these decisions during the earliest stages of a CBR project. In such situations, an academic with effective community organizing skills may be able to bring together community members so that they can participate and take charge of the next stages of the project (Stoecker, 1999a; Brydon-Miller, 1993).

Shared power could mean that all parties participate equally in making decisions that govern every stage of the research project: identifying the research question or topic, designing the research, collecting data, analyzing the data, formulating the report, and taking action on the findings. In reality, such uniform power sharing across every step of the project is neither achievable nor always desirable. Community partners may prefer not to be involved equally, or even at all, in decisions about such matters as sample selection, instrument design, or analysis strategies because they have more limited expertise in those areas or because such discussions require time away from their other obligations. Students do not always participate in decision making about what projects will be undertaken and what the research question might be, also because of their relative lack of expertise or—in many cases—because such decisions must be made by the professor and the community partner prior to the beginning of semesters when the work will be completed. And some discussions about the research might well occur in settings such as coalitions or staff meetings when no one from the academic side of the partnership is present.

Deciding which decisional points each party will control requires common sense as well as ongoing frank and friendly give and take about everyone's particular interests, strengths, and weaknesses. This is where trust and mutual respect become crucial: each member of the CBR team must be comfortable deferring to others in the interest of improving the project, respecting each other's commitments, and supporting the wider aims and principles of community-based research.

Sometimes issues emerge about which compromise is impossible. One issue may have to do with standards of practice that cannot be compromised without jeopardizing the results of the study. From the community side, such an issue might be related to protecting the rights and dignity of community residents. Here, again, patterns of openness and honesty in interactions among members of the research team mean that these sorts of claims will be articulated, understood, and respected.

As partnerships evolve, they may involve sharing of significant resources, such as grant funds. Presumably, a partnership that has reached this point will have developed patterns of shared decision making that are well grounded in trust and goodwill. However, some partnerships have also developed concrete mechanisms that facilitate this sharing of power and resources, among them memoranda of understanding, legal agreements, or representative steering committees charged with making key decisions. (These are discussed at greater length in Chapter Three.)

PARTNERS COMMUNICATE CLEARLY AND LISTEN CAREFULLY. Community-based research brings together people from very different worlds—the academy and the community—and requires that they engage in a series of conversations aimed at carrying out a challenging and complex task: designing and carrying out a collaborative research project that meets a community need. To accomplish this, both partners must work to avoid the dangers of what Paulo Freire calls "alienating rhetoric." He observed that educators and politicians often "speak and are not understood because their language is not attuned to the concrete situation of the people they address" (1970, p. 77). When academics speak in abstractions, rich with disciplinary jargon and institution-driven imperatives, they not only exclude community members to whom the jargon is unfamiliar but also run the risk of sounding cold and dispassionate, thereby alienating community partners. Similarly, from the community side, communication rife with blame, "guilt-tripping," and staking out the moral high ground has the potential to alienate faculty and students. To be understood, all participants must avoid the inaccessible language of their discipline or community, take care to clarify meanings and assumptions that may be obscure to outsiders, and otherwise work to develop a common discourse that will ensure inclusive and fruitful subsequent interactions among participants.

The second and equally important element of effective communication is careful listening. Professors are used to having captive audiences—for fifty to ninety minutes or more at a time—and as a result, their listening skills may be underdeveloped. Recently, one of our community partners asked us to intervene and cancel a meeting with a local professor. She sent us an e-mail saying she could not waste any more time with him: "He does not listen." For their part, community partners accustomed to "rallying the troops" through public speaking or running woefully understaffed agencies that never allow them to have a real conversation may also be challenged when it comes to good listening skills. Students occasionally report a similar experience with community partners. One group of traditional-age female undergraduates came back from a meeting of the local coalition for the homeless complaining that "they didn't seem to care about anything that we had to say." The effective dialogue that CBR requires relies on clear communication and good listening on all sides.

PARTNERS UNDERSTAND AND EMPATHIZE WITH EACH OTHER'S CIRCUMSTANCES. Some communication problems in campus-community partnerships are the by-product of bringing people together from dramatically different professions and institutions. And just as successful partners learn how to communicate with each other across these sociocultural divides, they also learn how to recognize and work around the various institutional constraints that affect their partners and may stand in the way of accomplishing the group's goals.

Community organizations and colleges and universities are very different institutional structures in terms of factors such as the size of their operations (for example, staff and budgets), the degree of financial stability and cash flow, internal organizational structure and accountabilities (for example, academics at universities are separated by discipline on campus and rarely work together), levels of bureaucracy, interorganizational relations (for example, CBOs in the same community that work on the same issue seldom coordinate efforts), schedules, and reward structures. All of these can frustrate the growth of strong CBR partnerships.

Among these institutional incompatibilities, the differences between academic and community calendars are perhaps the most fundamental. The community partner may operate from the assumption that a true partnership means that both parties are available for each other on an as-needed basis—and in particular when an urgent need arises—because that is how the organization itself operates. That means that many projects are put together without extensive planning and continue based on the schedule of the problem they address. In addition, the community organization may need the report in time for some political hearing, media event, or other external purpose that does not coincide with the end-of-semester due date. In contrast, academic schedules are sometimes planned a year or more in advance, and students schedule their classes months in advance, often making them unavailable to pick up a last-minute project. In addition, most faculty members and students are not on campus during midsemester breaks, holiday weekends, and between semester breaks. Faculty members need to turn in grades for students at the end of the semester, so projects must be ready to be evaluated at that time, regardless of any complications that may have interfered with the project's schedule.

In the next chapter, we detail some of the strategies to facilitate this cross-institutional understanding and to work around the potential conflicts that different institutional constraints produce. Here, again, partnerships that are built on trust, honesty, and mutual respect—and in which partners are informed and empathetic about each other's institutional constraints—are able to work around such constraints for the benefit of the CBR project. Also, creative solutions are more easily forthcoming when parties remain flexible, the principle to which we turn next.

PARTNERS REMAIN FLEXIBLE. In successful CBR partnerships, the partners are flexible. Flexibility is a crucial element given the challenges of discovering how to begin to work together. There are important tensions in such partnerships, and an array of challenges and constraints exacerbates these tensions (Nyden and Wiewel, 1992). The need for flexibility is implicit in much of what we have discussed thus far. Here, we raise a few additional points about why flexibility is prerequisite to strong campus-community partnerships.

One of the inherent tensions we note is that the partnerships are product oriented, meaning that they are committed to producing a research product by a certain date (usually the end of the semester). At the same time, these partnerships are developmental; they are designed to promote student learning and, often, to build capacity of community members as well.

The tensions created by these different goals may be exacerbated by other constraints imposed by both the campus and community members of partnerships. We have already noted the problem of fluctuating intensity—the result of incompatible schedules that make students and faculty members unavailable during academic breaks. Staff and residents on the community side live in an environment that is far less predictable than the typical college campus, which means that they, too, may have shifting priorities that require flexibility on the academic side of the partnership. An example of this occurred when the Central American Center, a long-standing partner with one of our universities, was preparing a grant proposal and a report on the impact of a local piece of legislation on the city's immigrant population. The professor involved, new to CBR but knowledgeable about the community, met with the center staff and worked out a plan with them to have a group of his students work with the staff in doing background research for the grant proposal.

During the course of the semester, the priorities of the center shifted, requiring the group to focus more of their energy on completing the report in a timely manner and to defer their work on the grant proposal. Because of inadequate communication between the professor and the staff,

staff asked students to help work on the report, whereas the professor insisted that his students complete the draft grant proposal, as originally planned for the students' group project. Both the professor and the center staff were upset, and the students were caught in between, pleasing neither the professor nor the staff. Only at the end of the semester did the changed situation at the center—and the need for flexibility—become clear to the professor. During the ensuing semester break, he agreed to help the staff by working on the report, writing a summary for the report, and editing the draft for the center.

OUTCOMES OF PARTNERSHIPS. The final three principles of an effective partnership have to do with desired outcomes or results of partnering that go beyond producing useful research:

8. Partners satisfy each other's primary interests or needs.

9. Partners have their organizational capacities enhanced.

10. Partners adopt long-range social change perspectives.

PARTNERS SATISFY EACH OTHER'S INTERESTS OR NEEDS. Beyond its central goal of producing a high-quality and relevant research study, CBR typically brings together campus and community partners whose needs and interests diverge in some important ways. Recognizing and helping each other meet these differing needs is important to strong CBR partnerships.

On the academic side, the priorities are to offer students an effective learning experience and, in some cases, to produce publishable research that can advance the faculty member's career. The campus partner may also look to CBR partnerships as a way of improving the image of the college in the community, helping students identify postcollege career opportunities and contacts, bolstering the institution's experiential learning opportunities, or improving recruitment and retention of students. Community partners who are sensitive to all the different needs of their academic partners might help out in a variety of ways. They are sensitive to students' limitations, assume the role of teacher at appropriate times and in patient and effective ways, and are understanding of instructors' need to conform to academic requirements and restrictions. They may attend and even speak at college-sponsored events where they vouch for the value of campus-community collaborations and for the quality and importance of the work that students and faculty members do. At institutions where faculty members are required to produce publishable research reports, a community partner might support such efforts by being generous with permission to use data that the research produces; providing agency data, records, and other information that support the professor's goals; and otherwise sympathizing with the multiple demands on faculty members as they juggle the teaching, service, and scholarship aspects of their CBR work.

Similarly, a good campus partner appreciates that the partnership must produce a concrete benefit for the community agency and perhaps even for the individuals with whom they are working. Reports have to be of sufficient quality and usefulness to advance the agency's social change agenda. In addition, strategic or program recommendations must make sense in terms of where the organization is and what it is capable of doing. This ensures the continuing support of administrators and funders for the partnership and the agency staff involved in it. Campus partners also must be cognizant of more subtle interests, such as inter- and intra-agency politics and issues related to funding and outside funders.

PARTNERS HAVE THEIR ORGANIZATIONAL CAPACITIES ENHANCED. A common shared goal of CBR partners is to enhance the capacity of community partners to undertake additional collaborative work and use whatever is gained from the partnership to improve the effectiveness of the organization. The most successful CBR partnerships, however, are those that increase the skills and knowledge of participants on both sides of the partnership—campus and community—so that everyone is better prepared, at the end of a CBR project, to make subsequent partnerships even more productive.

When both CBR partners work to strengthen the capacity of the other party, they find it easier to continue working together over time and increase the likelihood of successful subsequent collaborations. This is true for faculty and students who, as they acquire familiarity with the community and technical skills, are able to do more and better work on their next project. Similarly, community organization staff members who develop a solid understanding of the research process and learn various strategies for working effectively with students can use that knowledge gained to make the next CBR project even more successful. Some partnerships have gone far beyond individual CBR projects to a program of capacity-building activities.

The Trenton Center for Campus-Community Partnerships, a citywide consortium of four higher education institutions and nonprofit agencies, is a good example. After limiting its activities to small CBR projects for their first two years, the consortium developed a series of capacity-building workshops by tapping into the expertise within its own network: professionals and nonprofit staff who offered seminars and training sessions on strategic planning, advocacy, participatory neighborhood planning, indicators of success measures, geographical information systems, and a number of other topics. During the first day of workshops, nonprofit staff led four of the six seminars, and a number of academics joined other community workers as students.

This sort of mutual capacity building can also be brought to bear on financial issues, as some successful partnerships have found ways to collaborate in raising funds to support CBR (see Joint Development of Fundraising Capacity Financing case).

Another technique that has been widely used is for CBR teams to engage in collaborative grant writing. Successful grant getting can provide substantial support to the ongoing operations of the CBO and CBR-related infrastructure of the university.

PARTNERS ADOPT LONG-RANGE SOCIAL CHANGE PERSPECTIVES. Finally, an important principle of a successful CBR partnership is developing and sharing a long-term perspective. Certainly an important incentive for this work in the short term is the hope that the research can be used

---

Joint Development of Fundraising Capacity Financing

CBR can be an area where competition and conflict prevail. However, campus and community partners can both gain by working together to identify and nurture sources of financial support for their collaborative work. In one case, the Perth Amboy (New Jersey) Housing Authority decided to pay the Trenton Center for Campus-Community Partnerships six thousand dollars to conduct a survey of its residents. The staff was influenced by the fact that the center's seed grant was about to expire. If it ran out of funds, it could not continue its CBR work with local nonprofit organizations. Because the housing authority had funds from a grant, it decided to pay for the survey in order to support the center's overall operations.

In another example, Georgetown University's Partners in Urban Research and Service-Learning participants discussed funding opportunities and identified some tensions over the community partners' concern that the university was soliciting grant funding from local foundations that were already funding the CBOs' programs. To complicate matters, in order to apply for several different national foundation or federal grants, the university needed to be the primary applicant with demonstrated community partners. What they created over time is a symbiotic relationship through which the CBOs serve as the lead agency and fiscal agent for grant applications sent to local funders, whereas the university tends to be the lead agency and fiscal agent for national level grants. This arrangement has prevented the partners from competing with each other for limited funds in a particular pool and has instead expanded the possibilities for funding for both community and university partners.

---

to bring about some improvement in the quality of life of the community in the near future. This is a particularly important motivator for students, who nonetheless are typically not around long enough to witness even the short-term benefits of their CBR efforts. Effective long-term partnerships are the ones that keep a collective eye on long-term goals and recognize that each short-term CBR project can make an incremental contribution toward the larger goal of changing social arrangements in a more fundamental way.

CBR promotes long-term change in three areas. The first is higher education, where the aim is to help colleges and universities become more relevant to the wider community and society and to make more effective their preparation of students to be engaged citizens. The second area of long-term social change is in the balance of power in local communities, to help traditionally marginalized groups gain more influence than they currently enjoy. This captures a central aim of CBR: to empower community groups so that they become better-organized and more proficient advocates for themselves and their constituents, as well as better able to control the resources that will contribute to their further development.

The third area of long-term social change is in society at large. CBR partnerships are sustained and empowered by the shared faith in democracy: the commitment to the belief that the more people who are engaged in the process of shaping the larger forces that influence their lives, the better off we all will be. CBR models participatory democracy in a powerful way. Moreover, every successful partnership and project helps to create—in students, community members, faculty members, and other participants— citizens who are both predisposed and equipped to be active, engaged, and effective. Thus, although the concrete and somewhat more immediate aims of CBR projects are to effect changes in policies, programs, or practices in local communities, a longer-term aim is realized when participants carry their knowledge, skills, and commitments to other projects, organizations, classes, jobs, and communities throughout their lives.

There are practical and more immediate arguments for assuming a long-term change perspective as well. One is that to expect institutional, let alone societal, change in the short term is unrealistic and leads to frustration and burnout (Marullo, 1996). Also, many community groups wish to partner only with others who adopt a long-term perspective for more practical reasons. In a cost-benefit sense, it is not in their best interest to invest the time and energy in a partnership that promises to produce only one project; that is not a large enough return on their investment. When the college or university is willing to make a long-term commitment, community groups are sometimes far more willing to invest scarce resources.

Summary

In this chapter, we have addressed the two important questions about campus-community partnerships: How can they benefit communities? and What are the features or principles of successful ones? CBR partnerships can be of value to community-based organizations by helping those organizations access new resources and better mobilize the ones they have, enhance their capacity, and contribute—in a long-range sense—to a democratic political system. The benefits of such partnerships for both parties depend in large part on the strength of the partnership. Strong partnerships are those in which partners—both when they enter the partnership and over the course of their collaboration—share a common worldview, goals, and trust and mutual respect. Successful campus-community partnerships require that partners, in the course of their work together, share power, communicate clearly and listen carefully, understand and empathize with one another's circumstances, and remain flexible. Finally, the most successful partnerships have outcomes that satisfy both partners' primary needs or interests, develop the capacity of both partners, and contribute to longer-range social change. In the next chapter, the focus expands from examining benefits and principles of strong partnerships to considering how these principles can be turned into effective practices.

3

COMMUNITY PARTNERSHIP PRACTICES

IN THE PREVIOUS CHAPTER, we examined the benefits of community-based research partnerships and principles that govern successful partnerships. We now move to the nuts and bolts of CBR partnerships, or how to turn the ten principles of successful partnerships into practice: strategies to establish productive partnerships, practices that lead to successful outcomes, and processes that contribute to the long-term sustainability of effective partnerships for social change.

Finding and Starting a Partnership

The first two principles—sharing worldviews and agreement about goals and strategies—concern fundamental characteristics of the two potential collaborators that are not likely to change in the short run. Thus, our practical suggestions concern finding the right partner for collaboration. The element of trust grows as a result of partnering effectively, starting with clearly articulating interests, operating with openness and transparency, and establishing good communication. We thus focus here on how to find and select partners—from among the potentially large number that exist in any community—with the greatest possibility for developing into an effective CBR collaboration.

There are two basic approaches to finding a CBR partner. The first, and in some ways the more desirable, is to build from an existing campus-community partnership and expand that relationship to include one or more community-based research projects. This approach is especially useful for academics who are forming CBR partnerships for the first time.

Working with a community organization that already partners with the college or university in some other capacity—for example, through service-learning, community education programs, job training grants, or direct service programs—contributes to the likelihood that some important requirements for a successful collaboration have already been met. These include things such as like-mindedness about goals and strategies, mutual trust and respect, familiarity with the constraints imposed by academic institutions, appreciation for the challenges and opportunities offered by working with students, and experience with modes of effective cross-institutional communication and collaboration. This is especially true when the faculty member seeking to do CBR has worked with the community partner previously. Often, faculty members know an organization from having volunteered there or having helped it with other projects on a consulting or volunteer basis.

In other cases, CBR projects emerge as a result of students' involvement with an organization as volunteers, through service-learning courses, or in professional training placements. For example, Georgetown University's Community Outreach Partnership Center is an indirect outgrowth of a student-run tutoring program that had operated in the community continuously for more than twenty-five years before the faculty and staff started to locate service-learning and research projects at the Perry Community Service Center. The University of Denver's primary CBR partners are located in the northwest and southwest areas of Denver, where the university's Center for Service Learning and Civic Engagement has a long-term relationship through its outreach efforts. Even serendipity can play a role in sparking a CBR partnership. In one case, a sociology major who was a long-time volunteer in the Salvation Army's after-school program learned, through a casual conversation, that the board was exploring the possibility of expanding its services to low-income seniors in the immediate area and wished to have some hard data about what sorts of services they might wish to have available. The student expressed some interest in helping, talked to her professor, and subsequently worked with the Salvation Army board of directors in designing and carrying out a small needs assessment survey of senior citizens in a nearby housing project.

A somewhat different approach is required when partnerships with potential for CBR do not currently exist. Finding new partners for campus-community collaboration may require a bit of effort and creativity. One initial strategy is to conduct or access an asset mapping of the community's nonprofit sector to identify CBOs in the community and their missions, perhaps with a focus on those that are known to, involved with, or operating in a neighborhood near the university. Because many community development corporations and subsidized housing developments value citizen participation, they may be good organizations to contact. Public schools and school-based or -affiliated organizations are also potentially suitable and eager partners.

Some potential partners can be problematic, such as government or nonprofit agencies that do not involve their constituents in program decision making or small and underresourced organizations that may lack the capacity to undertake a CBR project. In these cases, a number of different strategies might be used: organizing the community, convincing the agency that it should include community members in its decision making, starting with small projects, or offering to help begin building the organization's resource base.

Sometimes people from the campus identify prospective partners by making a blanket solicitation of community organizations and agencies. This kind of cold contact may be initiated by the CBR center staff or by individual faculty members, with an announcement that briefly describes what they can offer in the way of research collaboration to a targeted list of potential community partners. The easiest way to do this, but one with limitations, is to send out mailings announcing interest in collaborating.

For several years, one faculty member at Hood College blanketed community organizations and agencies with the following invitation to submit research proposals each summer (see the sample letter). Eventually partnerships developed, and most of this professor's CBR work now is within ongoing collaborative campus-community partnerships. Web sites to solicit project profiles and research services have been developed by some centers to solicit potential collaborators on an ongoing basis. (See, for example, coralnetwork.org or linkresearch.org for examples of a citywide and a nationwide CBR solicitation Web site.)

One urban university's CBR program sends students out each summer to survey area CBOs and ask them about their research needs, which results in a CBO profile book. Princeton's Community-Based Learning Initiative interviews staff from a select set of CBOs, solicits research ideas, and compiles project profiles for its Web site, which faculty and students then use during the academic school year to find CBR partners.

As another variation, an academic researcher, either independently or in connection with a course she or he is teaching, reaches out and asks whether anyone in the community could use particular professional skills and knowledge. When one psychology professor arrived at his new position, he asked local elementary and high schools if they would have any use for his expertise in psychological diagnostic testing. The schools were immediately open to the possibilities, and everyone collaborated to put in

---

Sample Letter

Dear Frederick Community Member:

I am writing to invite you to submit a research project proposal to Hood's Center for Community Research. A proposal form is attached; this year's deadline for submission is June 30th.

The Center for Community Research, which is described in the enclosed brochure, gives organizations and agencies in the Frederick community access to some of Hood's resources to undertake collaborative research projects that meet community-identified needs. For the coming year, we hope to be able to work with groups in the community on at least one substantial year-long project as well as some smaller semester-long projects. Proposals tied to a variety of disciplines—social sciences, environmental studies, and humanities—are welcome.

Project proposals will be carefully reviewed by the Center's Advisory Committee, using the criteria of feasibility, perceived usefulness to the community, and fit with interests and resources of Hood students and faculty. The committee will identify promising proposals and notify applicants by late August or early September. In some cases, we will accept proposals contingent on finding faculty or individual students who wish to take them on. In every case, the next step will be to meet with you to talk about how we might work together to develop your idea into a workable research project that will be of use to you.

We are delighted by the interest and support expressed by so many in our research center, and we look forward to working with you. We encourage you to submit a research project proposal and, in other ways, to keep us informed about your needs and how we might work with you to help meet them—if not this year, then in years to come. If you have any questions, please feel free to contact me (strand@hood.edu or leave a message at 301/555–1234). We look forward to hearing from you.

Sincerely,
Kerry J. Strand, Director
Center for Community Research and
Professor of Sociology

---

place a preschool diagnostic testing program conducted through his "Psychological Tests and Measures" course. The faculty member worked with the local school system to address a perceived problem that it lacked resources to address. The school system had free access to his expertise, and students in the class applied their new knowledge and sharpened their skills at administering and interpreting psychological tests.

From the community side, finding an academic partner to help with a research project can be a bit daunting. If CBOs do not already partner with the college or university, knowing which office to call to solicit support can be quite confusing; the local telephone directory may list dozens of university offices with words such as *service, volunteer, community out-reach,* and *research* in their names. In such cases, it might be most effective to start at the top, contacting an office such as a university vice president for community relations, explaining one's interests, and asking for a referral to an appropriate office. Once a university establishes a CBR center or office and it becomes known on campus, referrals will be made quickly. Ideally, as the community learns about the university's CBR work, the CBR center will become a first point of contact for interested community partners. Nonetheless, prospective community partners should be wary of offices or individuals who seem disinclined toward or unknowledgeable about CBR, as they may end up wanting to control rather than collaborate or otherwise might think of the community as little more than a laboratory for the principal purpose of advancing students' learning or advancing their own research agenda.

CBOs that are already involved in some type of partnership have it easier; they can ask the person from campus with whom they interact most for suggestions about which professors might be interested in collaborating on a research project, or they might invite one or more student volunteers to take on a project with the guidance of a faculty member. Faculty members whose students are already doing some sort of community-based learning might be the best to approach first, as both the students and faculty may be enthusiastic about having the students get involved more deeply with the initiatives of the CBO. Faculty who are teaching research-oriented courses or supervising graduate theses are also potential partners, especially, perhaps, those in graduate programs in areas such as urban studies, public policy, architecture and planning, education, social work, environmental studies, sociology, and political science.

Another resource for matching up prospective CBR partners is a clearinghouse. Although these seem most often to be located in university centers or offices devoted to CBR or service-learning, there is no reason that such a resource could not also be maintained, separately or jointly, by community-based organizations. The Web sites noted above also serve the purpose of maintaining a listing of project ideas seeking collaborators or of willing collaborators seeking out new projects. Another strategy is to have someone serve as a community-campus liaison (whether formally designated as such or not), in which capacity she or he helps to identify potential partners and plays an explicit role in introducing the partners or arranging for such introductions to take place.

A somewhat different approach to finding good new community partners for CBR projects is to develop them. One strategy is to organize "Introduction to CBR" workshops and invite both campus and community members who might be interested in community-based research. The participants learn about the core principles of CBR and how it differs from traditional research, share information about their own work and research needs, and hear from successful practitioners about their experience with CBR, including its potential value for community organizations, students, and faculty members. In Trenton, a series of these workshops led to the idea of creating a community center that could serve as a focal point through which all the groups would channel their research requests. This was established and has evolved into the Trenton Center for Campus-Community Partnerships. In Denver, a two-day workshop led to the creation of several new collaborations among Denver CBOs and faculty from the University of Denver and Regis University. Such workshops can take many forms: a half-day workshop, an intensive two- or three-day conference or retreat, or an ongoing seminar or learning circle. The most intensive and deliberate of these is the joint seminar, where faculty and community members work together in a course or seminar over several months developing collaborative research projects. The Partners in Urban Research and Service-Learning (PURS) at Georgetown University is an example of this intentional partnership development process.

Academics who approach community organizations should also be prepared to be tested on the extent of their commitment by those organizations (and community organizations should be prepared to determine this commitment). The first time one of us (Randy Stoecker) offered to help a neighborhood organization, he was directed to clean out a storeroom. His willingness to help in this way provided an early indication on how cooperative and reliable a partner he could be. The storeroom cleaning was a success, and he continues the partnership with this neighborhood organization almost twenty years later.

Finally, the University of Michigan's Center for Community Service-Learning has articulated a set of questions for potential partners to ask themselves as they consider engaging in community-based research. We include them here because they provide a helpful starting set of considerations to reflect on for community and university members who are contemplating undertaking CBR together:

1. Does what you want to investigate require the community-based research paradigm?

2. Do the research and community partners have shared goals and time line?

3. Have norms been set for working together and for making decisions?

Partners in Urban Research and Service-Learning

At Georgetown University, several faculty engaged in CBR sought to create a mechanism for deepening working partnerships between faculty and community service agencies. They recruited other interested faculty and a comparable number of agency staff and community members in order to establish an ongoing seminar through which they would develop common understandings of community issues and priorities; deepen their understanding of collaborative, community-based research; and raise funds to support their collaborative projects. The community partners were drawn from neighborhoods and agencies with which the university already had some working relationships, several of which were based in ongoing community service programs. Thus emerged PURS, which would meet biweekly, develop collaborative research projects, attain funding for them, and carry them out.

PURS established community data centers, youth empowerment programs, a community development certificate program, and entrepreneurship development training through funding raised from a Community Outreach Partnership Center grant sponsored by the U.S. Department of Housing and Urban Development. A faculty cofacilitator and two community cofacilitators were hired part time (at .20 full-time equivalent) to administer the PURS project, with initial funding provided by internal university discretionary funds. Working groups of faculty and community partners met outside the PURS seminars in order to develop additional research projects. In addition, two faculty and two community partners created a year-long research seminar that they jointly teach, "Project D.C.," through which students learn the methods of and participate in community-based research, undertaking projects in collaboration with the PURS community partners.

4. Where will the data that are collected be housed? Who owns the data?

5. Have roles and responsibilities been clearly delineated for all partners?

6. What is the understanding about sharing and using knowledge produced from the research?

7. How will conflicts about the research be addressed or resolved?

8. How will community participants be compensated for their time?

9. Where will grants be housed, and how will grant money be used?

10. Have important political considerations been addressed?

Facilitating the Collaborative Process

Once a suitable partner has been identified, maintaining an effective CBR partnership requires modes of organization and communication that promote shared power and resources, mutual respect, and a free and comfortable exchange of information, concerns, and ideas. The best partnerships are also flexible, in part because of the inherent tensions in this work. In addition, CBR as pedagogy is still in its infancy, and there is much we have yet to learn about how to do it well. We share some of the effective partnership practices here that have evolved from our own projects, centers, and the experiences of our colleagues engaged in similar work around the country.

Sharing Power and Resources

The best CBR partnerships are organized to promote true collaboration throughout the process. This means that academics do not monopolize power and expertise, but neither are they mere tools used by community groups. In addition, resources, including money, are shared and controlled by both campus and community representatives.

SHARING THE POWER. One strategy that facilitates the sharing of power is to establish a project steering committee. This group may include everyone involved in the project if it is a fairly small one (for example, a couple of CBO staff members, a professor, and a few students). When the project involves more people, the steering committee consists of a small group of representatives from each project constituency. The committee meets regularly and makes decisions at each of the key stages of the project. At various meetings, one partner may take the lead or have more influence in decision making. For example, when the partners come together to identify the research question, the community representatives typically and ideally have a louder voice, but when it is time to review the proposed research design, which is usually prepared by the professor and students, their suggestions and leadership may prevail. Nevertheless, every member of the committee should have a vote in the final selection of the question and decision about the overall research plan.

The project steering committee may wish to formalize the agreed-on understandings and division of labor by writing a memorandum of understanding (MOU). An MOU can be useful not as a legally binding document but rather as a vehicle for talking through the entire project and anticipating how future decisions will be made and who will be responsible for them. The form and content of MOUs vary substantially, but all should be constructed with the understanding that no project unfolds exactly as anticipated and that all the partners will have to respond flexibly as conditions and the process unfold. The collaborative process of creating an MOU is itself valuable; it enables the participants to lay out their vision for the process and hence to establish clear understandings of where each other stands on various important decision points and resource and power-sharing issues. The MOU also serves as a tool for holding each other accountable because key markers, activities, and time lines are likely to be spelled out in the document so that each of the partners has a written obligation to each other to make a good-faith effort to fulfill their commitments.

Some useful administrative mechanisms can facilitate real collaboration in CBR partnerships on an institutional or regional level as well. Many campus-based community research centers have advisory boards that include members from the campus and community. In addition, some citywide consortiums are governed by a board of trustees that includes both campus and community representatives, with a majority of voting members from the community. These boards exercise a broad range of powers, with tasks that include developing the menu of programs that the center or consortium office will offer to community groups, designing plans to coordinate activities across campus or among institutions, raising funds, establishing criteria that will be used to determine what projects will receive support, and developing short-term and strategic plans for promoting CBR in their area.

The research process itself provides a vehicle for sharing power and leads to increased trust and shared understandings. From a methodological point of view, such collaboration strengthens the validity of the data. The different life experiences and backgrounds that community and university partners bring to the research play a role in how data are interpreted and presented. For example, how words are interpreted—the meanings that respondents assign to them—must be decoded by the researchers. The community research partner may have a better sense than the academic researcher of how such responses should be interpreted. To avoid interpretation problems, the researchers may develop participatory data-gathering methods that enable the community residents to process and clarify their own meanings. Sometimes, however, the academic researcher may be less influenced by particular vested interests and may provide a less biased interpretation of responses. Such collaboration, through open communication and operating from a premise of equality, strengthens the partnership and improves the quality of the research.

One issue warrants special attention and needs to be addressed openly and continuously through the collaboration process: the different and potentially contradictory vested interests of the stakeholders. Two "poisonous suspicions" are especially common. The first, held by the academic partner, is that the community research partner may interpret data in such a way as to serve the interests of a particular set of constituents or may suppress information that is not self-serving. On the other side is the commonly held view of the community partner that the academic researchers' real priority is conducting research that will serve their own career interests—that is, to publish and thus earn academic credit—rather than bringing about needed change in the community. Open discussion about each partner's aims and intentions allows students, faculty, and community partners to share the power to define reality, strengthen their partnership, undertake better research, and enhance the capacity of each.

An explicit and deliberate way to share this knowledge construction process is to build community training components into each project step. Such a practice may even be built into the requirements of a center's request for proposal (RFP) process. Training need not take place at the same time that the research project is being completed; a professor can recruit strong students to train community members during winter or summer break, after the project has been completed, so they learn how to conduct the research themselves. We have found that some community partners who are too busy to attend a few eighty-minute class sessions will sign up for a three-hour training if it is scheduled well in advance. In addition, some practitioners deliver these training sessions at the offices of the community agency to make it easier for them to participate.

Sharing the capacity to undertake such work is also a means of sharing power. One practice that some teams are exploring takes advantage of the ongoing need of community agencies to explain their evaluation strategy to almost every funder. Because most of these funders ask the community applicants to budget for these evaluations, it may be possible to build in their local CBR center or citywide consortium office as the evaluator. There is some precedent for and history of nonprofit organizations completing fee-for-service projects or work on a contractual basis. Conversely, as more universities establish service programs, the training component that such programs should include is strengthened by the contributions of community members, who bring invaluable wisdom and experience. Finally, many colleges offer grant-writing courses that teach students how to raise funds, and the professors can create learning opportunities that help community partners without the resources to hire their own grants officer. Some have even approached their own college grants officers about adopting a community partner. This simply means taking a few moments each week to scan their regular sources of information and identify potential funding opportunities for the partner.

Another strategy that promotes collaboration is to conduct joint evaluations of CBR projects. Often it is helpful to conduct this evaluation while the project is still in motion, using a debriefing model favored by community organizers. In community organizing, after each important event in the life course of a project, the group meets to assess what has worked well and not so well up to that point. In some cases, however, there may be an opportunity to evaluate the project only when it concludes. Even when projects are less than wholly successful, the likelihood of future successful CBR collaboration is increased when academics and community partners jointly evaluate the project—what worked and what did not—and thus end up working together to see to it that their next joint project will better satisfy their interests or needs. If collaborative evaluations are not practical because of time constraints, or if one believes that they may not be objective enough, some CBR practitioners have turned to outside evaluators. This may be another academic or community partner who was not involved in the project who can independently interview those who were directly involved.

SHARING OTHER RESOURCES. If a CBR project has a steering committee, its members can develop the budget together, usually at the first meeting about the project. Even when the project is a very low budget one, which is often the case, collective decision making about spending needs and priorities underscores the shared authority of all partners, as does some effort to get partners to share costs wherever possible. Where to hold project funds—that is, who will be the fiscal agent for a project—is an issue that requires honest and open discussion about the relative advantages and disadvantages of each of the partners taking on this responsibility. The faculty member may wish to control the funding and make use of the university's budgetary and accounting resources. However, a good reason to allow the community partners control of the project funds is the notorious slowness of the fiscal bureaucracies of colleges and universities. The CBO partner may be capable of the sort of fiscal flexibility that enables the research team to spend money quickly for supplies or unanticipated expenses that might arise during a project.

The budget development process should ideally include ways to support community members (with stipends, if possible) as well as faculty members (with release time) and students (such as stipends for teaching assistants or as work-study employment if done outside a class). One practice is giving honorariums to community members who organize site tours, deliver guest lectures, or engage in other activities to make the project work. Especially if faculty unions require that academics be compensated for spending time on projects outside the classroom, it is only fair that the time of community partners is honored in an equal fashion.

At the institutional or citywide consortium level, there are many ways to share resources. Some citywide consortia have earmarked a pot of funds that only community groups can apply for to develop and implement CBR projects, with or without an academic partner. This fund is separate from the funds available to the campuses to institutionalize CBR on campus and support faculty efforts to integrate projects into the curriculum. Citywide centers may engage in collective fundraising on behalf of several partners engaged in common projects, with the expectation that common evaluation procedures will be used to assess the impacts of the projects funded. Staff members of the citywide center can serve as project facilitators or even undertake particular roles to help keep a challenging project running smoothly.

And lest we think that CBR projects must operate from a zero-sum splitting of the funding pie, it is possible to use CBR projects to increase the funding for both the community organization's work and the academic partner's involvement. Funders such as the Sociological Initiatives Foundation now provide up to ten thousand dollars for CBR projects that can help support the organization's program budget (when it is part of the CBR project) and provide for the costs of the research. The federal government's Weed and Seed program also recently provided up to twenty-five thousand dollars for evaluation research that can be used to develop locally based Weed and Seed efforts and free up the program budget to do actual programming.

Communicating Effectively

Effective communication is critical to successful partnerships and the successful completion of any CBR project, and it requires both goodwill and effort. Nevertheless, barriers to good communication include constraints that are rooted in the contexts and circumstances of members of the research team: students who are shy or intimidated by talking with agency personnel or professors; professors who are tied up with committee work, research deadlines, or other teaching demands; staff members for whom the CBR project is but a small and relatively low-priority part of the demands of running overburdened and understaffed agencies. Nevertheless, a number of strategies can be used to achieve ongoing, open, and productive interaction that makes partnerships work and helps to produce useful research.

EFFECTIVE TALKERS AND GOOD LISTENERS. It is important that all the members of the research team work to be effective talkers and good listeners. For some, this means avoiding language—academic jargon and street slang alike—that may be immediately clear only to those within one's own profession or community. And it may require a concerted effort to give equal voice to everyone at the research table, including those people who, because of age or social status, are not used to contributing equally to discussion or to being listened to. As we have already indicated, this may be a particular challenge for professors and community leaders who are accustomed to running meetings, shaping discussion, and otherwise assuming a dominant role. Talking frankly about these communication challenges, perhaps at the first meeting and thereafter when necessary, is one important step. Drawing up ground rules that explicitly state that all members of the team have a right to be heard and keeping them permanently displayed in a meeting space is a simple device to remind all the participants of their right and responsibility to give voice and listen on each issue. Another simple device is to make sure that every person at the research table is sufficiently introduced and drawn into discussion wherever it is possible and useful.

MEETINGS. Providing sufficient opportunities for interaction is critical as well. Although regular meetings are a must, there seem to be no hard-and-fast rules regarding how often a committee or research team should meet; schedules are (and should be) driven by such matters as the nature of the project, its time frame, and the personal styles and preferences of the partners. The first meeting might be scheduled before the beginning of the semester, unless student involvement from the very beginning is considered to be vital; in that case, the first meeting must be held after students have returned to campus.

This first meeting typically includes the following purposes:

- To become acquainted with one another (name tags, more lengthy introductions, and icebreakers all work here)
- To formulate agreed-on ground rules for the work of the team
- To set up the broad terms of the project, including aims and research design
- To explain and review the principles and aims of community-based research

- To establish a schedule of deadlines
- To determine the division of labor and responsibility
- To identify limitations and constraints

At the first meeting, participants usually begin shaping a set of general questions and research aims into a manageable and focused project. Even if the work is being done primarily by students, the faculty member should be present at this meeting, which typically requires two hours or more. The professor's presence at subsequent meetings depends on the nature of the project and the partnership, the professor's availability, and the capabilities of students if they are going to be involved in doing the work. Three or four meetings during a semester, supplemented by occasional telephone calls to the community partner, may be sufficient for many instructors, especially when students are rather closely supervised during the research process.

Some steering committees meet more frequently—as often as once a week or once every other week if the project is to be completed within a semester. Meetings are best held at both campus and community sites, perhaps alternating locations. If possible, lunch or refreshments should be provided, especially when community members and agency staff are giving up valuable time during the day and may find it efficient to meet during lunch. Some partners prefer more frequent meetings, which can keep the project moving along and also help partners avoid misunderstandings. However, such frequent meetings are often burdensome for one or both partners and may actually get in the way of the research getting done.

E-MAIL AND THE INTERNET. E-mail can be a tremendously useful way to ensure ongoing communication among members of a CBR team, especially when community partners are included in the communications that are increasingly common among professors and students. Many professors now make the exchange of e-mail addresses the first order of business at the initial meeting of a steering committee or research team, and everyone is subsequently included on the e-mail list for every correspondence relating to the research project.

Faculty members who use Web-based software such as Blackboard, which provides a Web site for course-related materials and interactions, should also make sure that community members have access to the site. This site provides a useful central place for sharing information about the research project, including written materials such as drafts of research instruments and meeting schedules. This recommendation is contingent, of course, on community members' having access to computers and the Internet and feeling comfortable using them. And even when that is the case, there is no substitute for regular face-to-face meetings.

PROJECT DEVELOPMENT WORKSHEETS. Another administrative tool that promotes effective communication is a project development worksheet. These worksheets are especially useful when a partnership is in place but the CBR project has yet to be clearly defined. The worksheet can provide information that both defines a single project and helps to shape a larger research agenda for the organization or agency.

On the worksheet, the community partner describes what the organization does (its mission and activities, such as operating a food bank or providing adult education to clients of the food bank), what problems or issues it is currently working on (such as trying to determine if a mobile food unit is necessary to serve other parts of the city or finding out if a particular training program is meeting the needs of clients), and ideas about how to go about acquiring the information needed to proceed (for example, conducting face-to-face interviews with clients who have completed the training program or compiling data from other area food banks). This information provides the basis for the beginning work of the project committee: formulating a research question, articulating goals, choosing research methods, and developing plans for putting into place the social change agenda that the research might suggest.

FORMAL AGREEMENTS AMONG COLLABORATORS. Once the leaders of a team have been assembled, some CBR practitioners also use an agreement such as an MOU to increase the likelihood that all participants will be satisfied at the conclusion of their collaborative work. These agreements serve a number of functions. First, they delineate the expected products or results of the project. It is always a good idea to establish clear and concrete objectives at the start of any project, especially if the partnership is a new one. Second, written agreements help clarify the roles and responsibilities of each of the key players. In fact, some successful partnerships do not formalize their discussions by capturing them in a written document. What is most important, however, is that the partners discuss and agree on the expectations, goals, and roles before the research begins, and a project agreement helps to ensure that the discussion has taken place and consensus has been reached. This exercise is likely to reap other rewards as well. As the parties begin to articulate collectively the details of the planned project, they are able to identify areas of concern, such as additional resources that are needed and how those resource needs might be met.

WORK PLANS. For the ongoing project, it is helpful to maintain a work plan that keeps track of the various tasks that need to be completed, who is to do them, and deadline dates. This can be done on paper with pencil, on a large newsprint page that is kept posted in the project work area, or on-line through project management software (assuming that community partners are able to access materials on-line).

At each meeting, this document serves as the basis for checking progress and revising the plan as needed. The course Web site might also serve as the repository of this work plan, with a time line posted and updated regularly. For projects that continue from one semester to the next, an ongoing document is even more important because it allows new students to pick up where the previous class left off, without having to start anew. Some of us have also used project diaries: a group of students documents the steps that they have taken to develop the project and outlines the next steps they would plan to take. The incoming group reads this document to become acquainted with and grounded in the project's development— again, picking up where the previous group left off.

INFORMATION SHARING AT THE CENTER LEVEL. At the center level, a number of communication tools and practices can help facilitate the sharing of information among projects, at times indicating where resources might be shared effectively—for example:

- A regular center newsletter to share updates about ongoing projects, inform its readers of upcoming events, and detail project development opportunities.
- An e-mail list through which more timely matters, such as funding opportunities, might be shared quickly.
- A regular forum for interested stakeholders—project participants, policymakers, and community members—to share information and findings from their projects. The Policy Research Action Group in Chicago holds weekly one-hour breakfast meetings for the purpose of enabling representatives from all the funded projects to keep informed about each other's work and share other kinds of information.
- A less frequent but longer meeting, with a focus on strategic planning and center decision making rather than detailed reporting about ongoing projects.
- A Web site to facilitate effective communication by posting notices about projects, training opportunities, and job opportunities. The

site might also serve as a repository of data and project reports that are available to the public and to make available technical assistance forms and research protocols.

Developing Empathy with Partners

A previously discussed strategy for identifying potential community partners is to develop them by means of an "Introduction to CBR" workshop. These workshops can also be valuable to newly formed partnerships by helping all the collaborators in a CBR project understand the roles, constraints, and expectations of the others. The workshop can provide new partners with a common vocabulary as well as a forum in which to address their particular concerns and expectations about participating in the project and partnership.

We have conducted several of these workshops and have found them to be exceedingly valuable; they allow community members, faculty members, and students the opportunity to express their concerns and to hear them echoed through and responded to by the other participants, each from their respective positions. Two features of these workshops have been especially remarkable. First is the degree to which the concerns of the three different groups—community, faculty and staff, and students—parallel each other. Second is how many creative and valuable strategies for dealing with these concerns emerge from the discussion. The success of these workshops depends in part on having attendees who are truly interested in and committed to forming effective campus-community CBR partnerships.

An important means to develop empathy with one's partners, as well as to achieve equality and mutual respect and to build capacity, is to ensure that the community partners and residents, the students, and the professor all assume the roles of both student and teacher. A number of different strategies might help accomplish this. One is to provide the means for community members to be actively involved in students'—and often the professor's—education about the community as well as about the problem, issue, or social change goal that drives the proposed CBR project. Toward this end, community partners might assume any of three different roles: table setter, guest lecturer, and co-teacher.

• *Table setter.* The table setter visits the CBR class early in the semester to explain the community's research need, share information about the social problems that the organization is seeking to address, and describe the organization's mission and the program—current or proposed—designed to address this problem. This table setting may include taking the students on a tour of the facility or area (for example, a homeless shelter or neighborhoods adjacent to a polluted river) or organizing a training session in the community for professors and students. These training sessions may vary in their focus. If a class is conducting a project in the north ward of a city, for example, community leaders from that area can ground the research project by explaining the historical, social, and economic dynamics or history of that area. Another kind of training session might introduce students to the issues, programs, policies, and people that will be an integral part of the CBR project that they will undertake. Although this sort of introduction may take place outside the classroom, bringing the community members into the classroom and making this introductory material part of the course content is especially effective as it neatly underscores the equal value of experiential community knowledge to more conventional academic knowledge found in textbooks, monographs, and professors' lectures.

• *Guest lecturer.* The guest lecturer plays a somewhat more active role in the classroom: the community partner not only introduces students to the community and to the issues that their CBR project will address, but visits the classroom during the semester and helps to make clear the connections between the CBR project and the learning objectives of the course. The guest lecturer and the professor collaborate on setting the learning goals for the class for those periods during which the guest lecturer is taking on leadership of the class.

• *Co-teacher.* The community partner who becomes a co-teacher assumes a central role in the classroom by becoming a team teacher with the professor. The co-teacher takes charge of a number of classes, delivers lectures and other presentations, helps with the design of the syllabus, and participates in the evaluation of students at the semester's end. The co-teacher role is an ideal because it clearly represents the full equality of campus and community expertise in the educational process. At the same time, it is the most difficult of the three roles to realize. Because community members are likely to find it difficult to take time away from their own work to prepare for and attend classes, they should be compensated for their work. This not only assumes there are funds available but also probably requires some validation of the expertise of the community member on the part of the employing institution—this despite the likelihood that community members lack the formal credentials that are often prerequisite to employment by the college or university. This co-teacher role also requires close collaboration with the professor, who must be willing to acknowledge the expertise of the community member, relinquish some control over the course, and give the extra time and attention that such team teaching typically requires.

Community partners can educate students, but in some important ways, they can also become students. Sometimes this takes a fairly conventional form, with community partners enrolling in college classes. Milt Sharp, a CBO director, audited the research methods class taught by his academic partner at the College of New Jersey so he could play a more meaningful role in their ongoing CBR project. In another case, Latanya Webb in East St. Louis was involved in a CBR project as a high school student, and the professor subsequently recruited her to study at the University of Illinois. After graduating from college and attaining a master's degree, she is employed by the university as a community planner and works in East Saint Louis in the Neighborhood Technical Assistance Center.

Some colleges have established innovative education programs that are tailored to fit the needs of their community service or CBR partners. The University of Illinois established the Neighborhood College, which enrolls community leaders in a variety of classes that relate to their interest in community development, such as fundamentals of state and local government, grassroots fundraising and development, and nonprofit management. Some universities offer nondegree certificate programs with reduced fees or free, through their continuing-education program, allowing CBO partners to enroll in such programs in exchange for their collaborative work.

Practicing Flexibility

Up to this point we have described and promoted ways to structure partnerships and CBR projects with the aim of achieving equity, efficiency, openness, and clarity in the operation of the partnership and toward the successful completion of CBR projects. Nevertheless, problems and challenges often occur. Effective response to them requires, above all else, flexibility: the willingness to alter course in order to deal with any of a variety of unexpected turns of event. In our experience, these include circumstances as diverse as changes in personnel (as a result of job changes, health problems, personal or family circumstances, reassignment, or dropping a course or out of school), severe weather that impedes data collection, personal animosities and conflicts that arise within or across campus and community, flaws in or unanticipated problems with the sampling design, irresponsibility on the part of someone (students, faculty members, community partners), or any of a number of other impediments to smooth discourse, goodwill, or completion of the project in a timely manner. Sometimes the changes are not negative. New directions or opportunities might arise, such as interested parties who learn about the project and want to contribute or unanticipated ease and success in the collection of data.

No matter what the nature of the change, partners will have to be flexible and creative with things like their original design and allocation of resources. Open and effective channels of communication are critical here as collaborators continue to meet, talk, and revise their project agreement in midcourse.

At the project level, having a living work plan or MOU helps to maintain flexibility and avoid disastrous consequences. The work plan reminds all the parties of each of the steps and interconnectedness of the project as a whole. By forcing the team to reexamine the work plan in light of the changed circumstances, the project steering committee can make a better decision about revisions. What might at first blush make sense to change in response to changed circumstances might, when considered in its full consequences, be better left unchanged. Should such changes be desired, the living work plan will force the collaborators to revise each of the subsequent steps and expectations, and perhaps revise the time line as well.

On a more structural level, one way to build in flexibility is to plan for adequate resources and time in anticipation of the need to make changes during the research process. The primary aim, of course, is to produce quality research at the end of the course or collaboration. One way to ensure that the students do a good job is to have two teams operate in tandem with each other—that is, to have *shadow teams*. Here, a professor organizes the class into small teams such that two teams have overlapping assignments on the same project. The expectation is that between the two teams, the combined quality of their work would be an excellent product that could be passed on to the community partner. By having the two teams shadow each other's work, the quality of both teams' work is likely to be enhanced. A similar idea is to have a research "backstop" ready to put on the finishing touches of a project at the end of a semester. This person may spend the semester break or the first month of the following semester weaving the best papers produced by the class into a coherent, polished report. A paid graduate assistant might fill this role, or the professor might recruit the most exceptional students from the CBR class itself to do this. Or, although it is less than an ideal alternative, the professor may end up doing the editing and rewriting of students' reports in order to produce a useful product for the community partner.

Depending on the nature of the project, another strategy is to establish a working relationship with the direct service programs on campus,

The Importance of Flexibility

A university professor teaches a Washington, D.C.-based internship program, designed to provide students with an understanding of how government operates and interacts with constituents. Prior to the beginning of the semester, she worked out an interesting CBR project with the staff of the city's alcohol prevention and recovery agency to survey community-based alcohol prevention and recovery programs and compile a directory for the city's use. Her students would identify these organizations from various directories, verify that they were still in operation, and identify some of their basic features through telephone interviews. Then they would visit a number of the programs for in-depth interviews about the strengths and weaknesses of each and their need for city support. The broad outlines of the project were agreed to in advance, and the professor and her students drafted interview schedules at the beginning of the semester, to be approved by the city agency before implementation.

Week after week passed, with no approval of the instruments forthcoming from the city. The professor had her students keep reading about these programs and sort through various directories to compile lists for calling. Soon the agency staff member working as liaison to the project stopped returning telephone calls. Frustrated, the professor went to the person's office to find out what had happened. Awkwardly, the agency staff member admitted that her superiors, based on their fear that embarrassing information might be documented, would not approve the study. Now, more than midway through the semester, the professor had to reexamine the learning goals for the course and try to figure out how the students' research to date could be used in some sort of alternative project that might be of value to the students. Thinking creatively, she turned this challenge into the focus of the group project: examining how the project had been derailed and exploring with some community-based alcohol prevention and recovery programs their particular challenges in working with this city agency. The students revised their interview instruments and interviewed a number of program staff, focusing on the problems they faced in working with the government. They also interviewed staff members at the agency to find out what issues they were concerned about that had led them to cancel the study. In the end, they wrote a report and presented it to the agency staff and the community program directors, documenting the several types of miscommunication and misunderstanding that characterized their relationship. Although the students did not produce the directory that they originally intended, they received a valuable learning experience about the challenges of CBO-local government relationships.

especially those that are organized like a team and can be mobilized with some level of supervision. This might be helpful if a community group asks the CBR team to complete a survey that requires a significant number of interviews. A direct service team can join students in a class to conduct interviews as well as enter the data into a statistical analysis software program. In addition, since many of these direct service programs seek to enroll a diverse group of students, they can be a source of bilingual interviewers, while the class involved in the CBR project may not be as diverse.

In addition to these practices that can add some flexibility to a team working on a single project, there are also some ways to make campus-based centers or citywide consortium offices a bit more nimble. One idea is to hire floating project coordinators who can quickly move from one project to another to provide support as needed. These can be students, and they may receive credit or pay for their efforts. This practice is attractive, especially to those who are about to embark on their first CBR project, because often many unforeseen needs and challenges emerge during the research process. This project coordinator may assume a number of responsibilities, such as gathering information, recruiting volunteers, or coordinating and organizing meetings. Again, the time constraints that pose so many challenges to integrating CBR into classes make it wise to have a variety of resources available that can be drawn on as needed.

Achieving Long-Term Outcomes and Goals

Clearly, the aims of CBR are multifaceted: to acquire information and create knowledge that will help the community achieve its social change goals, enhance the capacity of the community organization or agency and the university, fulfill the university's goals of contributing to the public good and educating students, and set the stage for further successful collaboration between campus and community partners.

Satisfying Each Partner's Primary Needs or Interests

The various partners in CBR participate because they believe it is an effective mechanism to meet some of their primary interests. These partnerships provide excellent opportunities for students to learn, professors to apply their knowledge, and community groups to develop their capacity to effect change. Thus, all of the practices discussed so far contribute to this goal of ensuring that the primary interests or needs of all parties are satisfied. We also suggest some additional practices. Some of them increase the likelihood of meeting everyone's needs, and others have to do with assessing how effectively the project is doing so.

From the CBO's perspective, the organization may draw up several safeguards or guidelines to ensure that participation in such partnerships is constructive and in alignment with the organization's overall goals. These guidelines might refer to such matters as the appropriate use of CBO resources, the participation of community members or clients in the research process, or the protection of participants' privacy. The CBO should ensure that resources, especially staff time and funding, are not being drawn away from other essential organizational goals defined in the organization's mission statement. Sometimes CBOs develop their own internal review board to ensure that projects and partnerships serve their interests.

Those on the academic side may wish to establish a parallel set of safeguards to guide their work. At one level, traditional offices of sponsored research or institutional review board (IRB) protocols serve to guide university-based researchers, ensuring that research is done in accord with ethical practices, uses resources properly, and does not coerce or exploit research participants. When it comes to undertaking CBR projects, this might include quite different guidelines that may in fact clash with traditional institutional definitions of research, as we will see in later chapters. An IRB, for example, may not approve a research project that has nonacademic co-researchers (more discussion of IRB-related issues can be found in Chapters Five and Nine).

On the community side, some CBR organizers primarily recruit faculty members who are willing to assume the role of consultant and take on professional responsibility for the final product. These are likely to be academics who are not as interested in student learning as they are in contributing their own efforts as community organizers or public educators. Indeed, they may not involve students at all in their CBR work, but may act more like project facilitators or directors who organize community member research teams, sometimes conduct the research themselves, and even write the final report.

Involvement with CBR has all kinds of implications for assessment of faculty members, particularly in relation to the institution's rank and tenure policies. For faculty members to be rewarded—or at least not punished—for investing time and effort in campus-community partnerships and CBR, the institution's guidelines must make provisions for how such work will be evaluated. Just as traditional research is evaluated according to principles of excellence as defined by national standards and disciplinary bodies, so too should CBR professional work be evaluated in accord with such standards of excellence. Several institutions have expanded their guidelines for rank and tenure to consider work in the scholarship of engagement and the scholarship of teaching and learning, in addition to the more conventional importance assigned to the scholarship of discovery. Operationally,

this means that alternative publication forms (beyond traditional disciplinary journals), expanded conceptualization of peers (beyond other academics in parallel departments in other institutions), and additional
mission-based goals (not just discipline-driven questions) serve as bases for
assessing faculty excellence. Three institutions' guidelines have been held
out as models for this expanded notion of scholarly excellence: Indiana
University–Purdue University (Indianapolis), Portland State University
(Oregon), and California State–Monterey Bay. In addition, the American
Association for Higher Education and the Campus Compact have devoted
considerable energy and time promoting and developing such expanded
concepts of the scholarship of engagement, dating back to the publication
of Ernest Boyer's *Scholarship Reconsidered* (1990). We deal with these issues again in Chapter Nine.

For students, learning is the main goal of community-based research.
Faculty members routinely assess student learning by means of graded assignments and project work, and students' CBR work should be treated
no differently. Student learning can be evaluated by how well students have
achieved the course's learning objectives, as demonstrated by their written
and oral presentation of their work. Students should be provided a venue
for offering feedback on the process, both during the course and at its completion. Chapter Seven discusses some strategies for student evaluation.

Enhancing Capacity

Enhancing capacity refers to the process through which the community and
university partners increase their abilities to undertake CBR over the long
term. This comes about through enriching the knowledge and skills of the
particular people involved, putting into place the people and systems for
undertaking such research, and setting up processes for feeding into these
activities. At the individual level, *enhancing capacity* refers to the intentional
educational processes through which the community partners and university partners learn the skills and principles of CBR and acquire the practical
experience to undertake an ever-widening range of collaborative, participatory research. This may be accomplished by finding people skilled in such
research and having them teach others through workshops or on-the-job
training while projects are under way. At a more systematic level, this capacity building may take the form of courses on how to undertake various
types of collaborative research that are offered through the university, the
CBO, or a nonprofit technical support organization.

Even more formal institutionalization may be sought as a natural outgrowth of the success of individual courses and in response to the desire
to ensure longer-term structural change, which would entail establishing a

formal training and education program for members of the community and university. This could take the form of continuing-education certificate programs, or even degree programs, that provide information, skills training, and experiential learning opportunities for interested parties to undertake such work. The best example of this model is the East Saint Louis Action Research Project. In response to some constructive criticism from their community partners, professors and university officials at the University of Illinois, Urbana-Champaign established a number of programs, including the East Saint Louis Neighborhood College, which enabled local community leaders to take a variety of tailored-made courses (see the East Saint Louis Action Research Project). They also created the East Saint Louis Neighborhood Technical Assistance Center, where residents can find planning professionals as well as other community-building tools. While any good CBR project (for example, undertaking a neighborhood survey with residents serving as interviewers) helps build the capacity of communities and community groups, because it provides them with more knowledge, this capacity-building process seeks to institutionalize this activity and reflects a long-term perspective and commitment by all parties.

Another means of institutionalizing capacity building is by putting in place the positions to ensure that there are people whose job it is to undertake and coordinate this work. Better-established centers have positions for research coordinators or directors who will oversee or manage others who are doing particular research projects, ensuring that the CBR projects meet the organizations' needs. Such positions also include responsibilities for establishing and maintaining quality standards for the CBR work being done. They might also have responsibility for ensuring adequate funding streams to sustain this work over the long term.

At the most advanced level, community organizations and higher education institutions understand the need for such positions and programs such that they build in permanent funding to ensure their long-term sustainability. At the university, this would take the form of creating centers with endowment monies to ensure the long-term survival and flexibility of the CBR unit to respond to the needs of the community and continuously enhance both the university's and community's ability to engage in such work. At the community level, such a commitment would be found in funders' long-term commitment to creating and sustaining a CBR center with adequate staffing to ensure its ability to thrive. In either the university- or community-based center, such well-established initiatives will have the staff and partnerships to enable long-term strategic planning, collaborative fundraising strategies, and development of ongoing assessment procedures.

East Saint Louis Action Research Project

The East Saint Louis Action Research Project (ESLARP) has evolved over the years in response to the requests and constructive criticisms of community partners. After a few years of work, it became clear that the residents wanted more out of their partnership than the receipt of CBR and planning projects, as valuable as they might have been. Community members wanted the partnership to place more of an emphasis on the development of their own skills and to have access to resources that would improve their ability to influence local decisions. ESLARP then moved toward a highly participatory and reciprocal model that embraced residents as co-investigators and co-teachers. The residents were strongly encouraged to participate in all aspects of the projects and given opportunities to contribute their knowledge about the social, economic, and political life of East St. Louis. These informal or project-related efforts to build the capacity of residents were followed by more formal initiatives. The East Saint Louis Neighborhood College was established to offer a variety of courses to build the capacity of residents in such areas as state and local government, community-based crime prevention, grassroots fundraising, and development and nonprofit management.

Although projects and courses are not constant, ongoing support is available at ESLARP's Neighborhood Technical Assistance Center. This one-stop site for technical assistance can provide community groups with help in a number of areas, such as grant writing, financial management, project management, needs assessment, and volunteer recruitment. In addition, at the center or any other location, residents can use an array of Internet resources that make it easier for them to play a meaningful role in local decision making and planning. EGRETS, for example, allows residents to review geographical information system maps that convey detailed demographic and land use information for each neighborhood. Also, USM (Urban Systems Model) allows them to predict the impacts of proposed developments on the city in terms of employment, income, pollution, and public finances.

Developing a Long-Term Perspective

Many of the practices discussed in this chapter contribute to developing a long-term perspective, particularly the joint fundraising and strategic planning processes, development of educational programs, and establishing assessment practices. An explicit practice that combines many of these elements is an intentional grant-making process to be housed within the center for undertaking collaborative research, targeted to support strategic priorities. The center raises funds explicitly for this purpose, maintains an ongoing process for determining priorities, and periodically issues RFPs to support CBR projects. The center might provide ongoing support by offering technical assistance, training, or project facilitation. It would also evaluate the quality of the work being done and the impact of the work on the community.

One specific suggestion regarding the RFP process is that the center reserve some funds for applicants that wish to develop a multiyear agenda. Such a strategy might yield several positive benefits. If a community partner's top research priority cannot be addressed immediately for one reason or another (perhaps the professor's class that is best suited to work on that project is not offered until the following semester), the team can take steps to prepare and organize resources that will eventually be used in undertaking the project. In addition, developing a multiyear agenda gives the partners some time and space to be more creative with respect to bringing in other assets and resources to help each other. They may, for example, consider how the direct service program on campus can respond to the results of the research and establish a new relationship between the community agency and another key player (such as the service-learning coordinator) at the college.

Thinking beyond the boundaries of the college and community helps to identify additional ways that the two can help each other establish a long-term relationship or perspective that is mutually beneficial. A campus-based center or citywide consortium office, for example, can go beyond inviting community partners to sit on advisory and other governing boards. They can include community partners in strategic planning sessions that chart a road map for their collaborative efforts. Along those same lines, the accreditation processes and reviews that colleges must periodically endure often lead to the formation of committees and a return to fundamental charters and other planning documents, such as college mission statements. Community partners could receive invitations to participate in these discussions. The point here is to recognize that there are often other discussions that take place—at a level that is higher than the project level—that can either encourage or discourage people "in the trenches" who wish to work together on an ongoing basis.

The Campus Compact, in its useful handbook for community service-learning directors, *Establishing and Sustaining an Office of Community Service,* enumerates several characteristics of sustainable service-learning centers (Torres, Sinton, and White, 2000). These characteristics seem to apply equally well to sustaining a CBR center, so we adapt them here to apply to community-based research. For a CBR center to achieve long term sustainability, it should have the following characteristics:

- Clarity of mission/vision—ensuring that the CBR center formulates and articulates its vision collaboratively with the community

- Community demand for and quality of research—ensuring that the research projects are needed, are undertaken carefully, and provide useful information
- Organizational leadership—characterized by both technical quality and interpersonal relationship building skills
- Appropriateness of organizational structures—. . . to realize CBR principles through everyday operational practices
- Strength of human resources (internal and external)—requiring continuous mobilization and enhancing of capacity
- Strength of financial resources (internal and external)—building diverse sources of support
- Willingness to assess, improve, and change—establishing ongoing evaluation processes to assess partnership practices [p. 23].

The successful CBR center needs to build in a self-reflective process so that it periodically considers how well it is achieving these aims. This is done by undertaking strategic planning, process and empowerment assessment, center staff and board reflection, and soliciting external reviews. Each of these practices helps to build shared beliefs and perspectives among the participants and expands the cadre of people committed to the principles and practices of CBR. Each center needs to develop from its own trajectory, however, taking into account the resources, capacities, investments, and pressing needs of the immediate community and interested stakeholders. The practices we have suggested here will help to advance a group to establish itself as a more permanent presence, capable of undertaking and achieving more and better community-based research over time.

Summary

This chapter discussed strategies for establishing and sustaining effective campus-community partnerships for community-based research projects. We started with the principles of effective partnerships developed in Chapter Two and detailed some of the many ways that such principles can be turned into practice. To this end, we outlined a large number of concrete strategies for finding—or, in some cases, developing—prospective partners, facilitating positive collaboration within relationship, and seeing to it that long-term outcomes and goals are met by campus-community CBR partnerships.

4

METHODOLOGICAL PRINCIPLES OF COMMUNITY-BASED RESEARCH

THIS CHAPTER EXAMINES the ways that the principles of community-based research—collaboration, demystification and new ways of discovering and disseminating knowledge, and social change—shape the way we approach the design and conduct of this kind of research. In many respects, CBR draws on conventional methodological protocols and procedures as they are defined within each discipline, and we detail how these are brought to bear in CBR. We also consider how the essential differences between CBR and conventional academic research translate into new ways of thinking about every aspect of the research process.

Collaboration

Collaboration is essential to CBR because it:

- Ensures that the research focus is one that community members identify as important to their own social change agenda
- Enhances the quality of the data collection methods, including the validity of measures, by incorporating the language, perspectives, knowledge, and experiences of the participants
- Encourages greater involvement of the community at large in the study, thus leading to higher response rates and richer, more valid data
- Empowers all sides of the research team by giving every member access to one another's expertise: research skills from the academic

Collaborating Through the Process

Isles, Incorporated, a community development corporation in Trenton, New Jersey, is engaged in a systematic effort to develop success measures for all of its programs. Over the 2000–2001 academic year, Isles partnered its YouthBuild job training program with Matthew Lawson's advanced course in sociology research methods at the College of New Jersey. To provide standards, Lawson assigned Martin and Kettner's guide to human service program evaluation (1996) as a supplemental text for his students and gave copies to agency executives.

In the first semester of collaboration, five students worked with the program's executive staff to review program materials and existing data collection forms to report on the relative merits of particular measures of program impact on clients. Between semesters, program staff reviewed this report and finalized a set of indicators, and in the spring Lawson divided seventeen student volunteers into four groups working on the project. YouthBuild's assistant director audited the class and supervised a group of students doing follow-up telephone interviews with former clients. The program's social worker supervised another group gathering data from clients' case files. Isles's director of research supervised a third group of students, who conducted an ethnographic study of the program in operation. Lawson trained and supervised a fourth group, which expanded YouthBuild's Student Tracking Application in Microsoft Access. Groups periodically presented their work to other groups to share their findings, and each group drafted sections of a final report. At the end of the year, YouthBuild paid two students to polish the report and test the revised computer program, now fully loaded with client information.

In reflecting on the project, Lawson reports that students have expressed excitement and pleasure to have worked on a project that so clearly benefits a worthy program, and YouthBuild USA is interested in the project as a pilot for its national effort to develop program success measures.

side and local knowledge and lived experience on the community side

- Underscores the democratization of the entire knowledge-creation process

- Ensures that the results are owned by the community as well as the researchers and thus have real consequences for guiding social action, policy, or program change

Barriers to Collaboration: Doing CBR "in the Middle"

In some respects, projects such as that of Isles, Incorporated, represent an ideal form of community-based research because students and their professor are collaborating directly and extensively with the community part-

ner throughout virtually every stage of the research process, from instigating the research, to sharing in the data gathering, to engaging in some
sort of action based on the findings. In part, this was made possible by
the nature of this organization: a service provider that employs staff members eager to participate fully in the research, help train students, and
learn new skills themselves.

In reality, this level of collaboration is not often achieved. One reason
is that often the communities that are most in need of CBR partnering are
unorganized ones, and few academics are equipped to work directly with
a grassroots community. An academic who takes on this kind of research
in an unorganized community needs to have some knowledge of community organizing and to be working with people who are engaged in organizing. In order to achieve real collaboration, they also need to be skilled
popular educators, or partnered with such people, so that community
members both conduct and learn from the research. These are skills that
few academics and students possess. Indeed, based on our own training,
we suspect that traditional preparation for undertaking research in most
graduate programs would have discouraged doctoral candidates from participating in such organizing and popular education activities, viewing
them as a distraction from completing the candidate's dissertation.

Most academics also lack the ongoing ties to local communities that are
prerequisite to partnering with grassroots groups, and so most end up
working with organizations such as Isles, Incorporated—groups that might
be thought of as one step up from the grassroots and also include volunteer groups, social service organizations, community development corporations (CDCs), and government agencies, such as the state department
of social services or a branch of the local health department. Partnering
with these kinds of organizations—what we might call *doing CBR in the
middle*—has obvious advantages; these are already organized groups with
staff and leadership who are easy to identify and contact, unlike the case
with unorganized communities. However, there are disadvantages as well.
One is that they may put distance between academic researchers and community members and, hence, fall short of the ideal of true community
collaboration. The other disadvantage is that some social service and other
helping organizations may in fact pacify or disempower the community—
those at the bottom of the stratification order—rather than working for
real economic or social justice. For that reason, we agree with McKnight
(1995), who cautions that the "primary directive" of community-based research is, first and foremost, to "do no harm" to the community (p. 101).
We refer here not to some evil-intentioned CBR practitioners who might
purposefully harm community members through their insensitive research

protocol or ill-intentioned reports or recommendations. Rather, even CBR that is undertaken by academics with intentions of improving conditions or enhancing social justice in a community may inadvertently or unintentionally harm the intended beneficiaries if their work supports agencies or organizations that disempower community members.

McKnight elaborates this point in *The Careless Society* (1995): that sometimes service organizations and professionals, despite good intentions, may undermine their clients' sense of competence, commodify and commercialize the services they offer, and create "counterfeit communities" that control people rather than liberate them. When applied to CBR, this suggests that we must be wary of working with organizations that treat community members as devalued subjects, promote policy recommendations that commodify the community's problems and approaches to addressing them, and encourage policy and action recommendations that surrender control and community to agents external to the community. It is for these reasons that we have stressed a practice of CBR that is truly collaborative in design and execution, characterized by acknowledging and building on the community's knowledge and its capacity to increase its knowledge, research methodologies and policy and program analyses that are specific to the community context, and the integration of such research into larger community-developed social change action plans.

At the same time, we caution the current or would-be practitioner against becoming paralyzed by imperfections from these ideal principles, acknowledging that no CBR practice is perfect in its design and execution and that at some level, we need to do the best we can under our current circumstances. In fact, CBR with midlevel organizations and agencies may have any of a number of positive results—for example, identifying shortcomings or injustices in the agency's work, previously unrecognized needs in the community, problems in the delivery of services, gaps in public information about the organization's work, or other kinds of information that might be the basis for some sort of change that benefits the community.

Also, there are things that we can look out for when choosing community partners and projects. Doing CBR in the middle is most likely to conform to the basic principles outlined in Chapter One when the organizations or agencies have demonstrated a real commitment to their constituent communities. One indicator of this commitment is that they make ongoing and concerted efforts to be community based—for example, by having constituents on their policymaking boards or by working with community-based grassroots groups. Another is their willingness to recruit constituency members to be involved in planning and carrying out CBR projects, along with expressing real commitment to using research results to bring about improved services to the community—in other words, their commitment to the important principles of community-based research. Sometimes this requires that the academic researchers insist that some community representatives be invited to join the CBR team and that they pay careful attention to ensure an equitable participation of constituent representatives throughout the project. Finally, even organizations or agencies that seem relatively distant from or unresponsive to their constituencies might be willing to involve constituency members in the project once they have a model that shows them how it can be done. A CBR project done with such an organization can both empower the constituency and transform the organization. And in many cases, carefully integrating participation of constituency members into the steps of an actual research project can give organizations and agencies an alternative model for how to work with and for their constituent groups.

Other Barriers to Collaboration

Other barriers to achieving true collaboration in CBR have to do with the nature of the project and the community with which one is working. A defining feature of CBR is that the research focus, if not the question itself, always derives from the needs of the community rather than the theoretical interests of the discipline, as is the case with traditional academic research. Equally important is that decisions about how and if the results will be used must also always be determined not by the academic researcher but by community members themselves. Hence, the need for involvement of community members at these two stages of the research should be considered nonnegotiable, and every effort should be made to give priority to the voices and interests of the community.

True collaboration at other stages of the research is often more problematic, however. Sometimes community members' involvement may take the form of reviewing and approving some aspect of the research design without having a hand in its development and implementation or, similarly, reading and perhaps suggesting changes in the final report without actually having helped to write it. Some community groups have neither the interest nor the time to participate in the development of the research instrument or the collection and analysis of data. In other cases, the community is dispersed and unorganized, while the CBR partner is an agency or organization serving or advocating for that community's needs. In that case, the agency personnel or organizational leaders are the ones who will likely be most involved—at least as "reviewers"—in different stages of the project, and researchers must make special efforts to solicit constituent input.

One strategy for ensuring community involvement at different stages of the research process is to conduct one or more focus groups with community members at an early stage of the project to provide a forum in which members can suggest issues and actual questions to be included on the questionnaire. This method has the additional benefit of sensitizing researchers to the community itself—its language, worldview, and so on—as well as providing an opportunity for researchers to get ideas about how best to reach prospective participants and how to gain their trust and help with the study (Lynch, 1993). For example, before a small group of undergraduate students developed an interview schedule to assess the day care needs of low-income mothers, they held a small, informal focus group, with lunch included, for a half-dozen mothers participating in a job training support group at the local department of social services. During an hour and a half of lively discussion, the student researchers learned a great deal about the wide variety of child care arrangements that women use, the difficulty facing mothers with jobs when their children are sick, and (if they were not aware of this already) the overriding importance of their children's well-being to young mothers struggling with myriad economic pressures. This same group of students met with yet another small group of mothers once the interview schedule was in draft form. They administered the interview to pairs of women and took into account their comments and criticisms as they developed the final interview schedule.

Occasionally, the nature of a CBR project is such that the community group—for political or strategic reasons—does not wish to be affiliated with the project as it is being carried out. In an example described in Chapter Six, the local human relations commission requested that a college's community research center investigate the existence of discrimination based on sexual preference in the county. Their purpose was to marshal empirical support—to share with the board of commissioners—for their proposal to add sexual orientation to the county's antidiscrimination statute. This was a case where a formal advocacy organization requested that academic researchers—in this case, a student doing a senior honors thesis and her adviser—conduct a study on behalf of an unorganized constituency (gays and lesbians in the county) for the purpose of effective legislative change. Moreover, although the human relations commission proposed the research question and took responsibility for disseminating the results, they adamantly refused to be involved in any way with the ongoing research project so as not to be seen as somehow biasing or influencing the findings. The student and her adviser developed the research design, and members of the gay and lesbian community, as well as some sympathetic heterosexuals, participated as paid testers in the collection of data, which involved a matched audit study of housing discrimination. The gay and lesbian community in this case did not collaborate in the identification of the research question or in the implementation of results. The point here is simply that while the ideal may be full collaboration of grassroots community members at every stage of a CBR project, this is seldom achieved and on occasion may be at odds with the best interests of the community served by the research.

Collaboration is essential to the goals of CBR not only because it makes the research project better and more valuable, but also so that everyone involved in doing the research has the chance to grow from the process. This means that some of what the community stands to gain from the project lies not only in the research results but also in the process through which the community members increase their capacity to undertake research independent of outside experts as well as stronger organizational, strategic, and other skills that empower the community. The more limited is the participation of community members in the research, the less the potential is for such capacity building.

The Creation and Dissemination of Knowledge

The second principle central to CBR has to do with its distinctive approach to issues relating to knowledge—what counts as "real" knowledge and how it is best acquired and disseminated. As we explained in Chapter One, CBR recognizes and validates sources of knowledge that are often not legitimated within the context of more conventional research approaches. It also requires greater flexibility in methods of data collection and dissemination and, most important, calls for different criteria in making a whole host of methodological decisions. In CBR, the measure of the value of the research is not just the quality of the data, but also its usefulness to the community to help bring about social change. This has multiple implications for the way we go about designing and carrying out research projects, particularly as our thinking must deviate from the conventions of the academic research with which we are most familiar. It also influences the mechanisms through which we disseminate our findings because of the primary objective of advancing the community's social change initiative.

The implications of this second CBR principle regarding the democratization of knowledge creation and dissemination can be seen in choice of methodologies, disciplinary perspective, and the practice of the profession. It also challenges traditional conceptions of expertise and objectivity. We explain each of these below.

For those used to being quantitative or qualitative researchers, CBR is both and neither. In the real world, philosophical differences over whether cold statistics or richly detailed stories provide better information are irrelevant. What matters is what information is needed to contribute to the social change effort, and this often calls for multiple methods of data collection. For example, when the residents of a rural area in Kentucky became concerned that an upstream tannery was dumping pollutants into a nearby river, killing both fish and livestock, they ultimately initiated legal proceedings to get the tannery to stop discharging toxins into the water. They worked with epidemiologists from a nearby university in order to compile the quantitative data that would help them win their court case. At the same time, they relied on qualitative approaches—stories shared by members of the community affected by the pollution—to do battle in the popular press and bring needed attention to the environmental hazards that the tannery posed (Williams, 1997).

Certainly some CBR projects use only one method of data collection. But getting useful data is the key, and that means being flexible and willing to employ a variety of data collection methods to accomplish that.

For those used to working within their discipline, CBR neither recognizes nor respects rigid disciplinary boundaries. The problem or need drives the research, and problems in the real world are rarely just sociological or biological or economic. Indeed, researchers often find that they must develop expertise about a range of topics that lie at least somewhat outside their area of training, and in some cases, a project may require technical expertise from a number of different disciplines. For example, a North Carolina community group attempting to create a nature preserve on their community's highest mountain ended up working with professors and students from four different disciplines at a nearby college: the business department on a cost-benefit analysis on the project's ecotourism potential; the recreation department on designing and building hiking trails; the biology department on long-term research on the ecosystem of the mountain; and the history department, whose students helped conduct oral histories of longtime residents who lived on and near the mountain.

For those in the academy used to compartmentalizing their teaching, research, and service roles, CBR is all three combined. CBR both provides services to the community and promotes long-range broad visions of the collective good. It educates students, community members, and even professors if they are sufficiently open to learning about what is beyond the narrow confines of their disciplines. And CBR makes professors, community members, and students all researchers and knowledge producers. At Middlesex College in Edison, New Jersey, the initial connection with

Using Multiple Methods

In a study of the strengths and needs of people living in the rural areas outside a small city, five undergraduate students worked with the local Community Action Agency and interviewed over one hundred people at food banks, clinics, senior centers, and in their homes. They focused on three areas—transportation, housing, and health—and developed an interview schedule consisting mainly of short-answer, forced-choice questions, for example, "Do you have health insurance?" "Are there any things in your house that need fixing right now?" "What would make it easier for you to get around in the county?" But many people whom the students talked to had important opinions to share and stories to tell—about the difficulties of raising a child with a disability, the history of the old house that has been passed down through their family and is now falling apart, their mixed experiences with the county's social service agencies. The student interviewers listened carefully, wrote fast and furiously in the margins and on the backs of the questionnaires, and finally decided to teach themselves to use software that analyzes qualitative data along with the statistical package that took care of the quantitative data. They learned a great deal. More important, their final report speaks with numbers, but also with rich and powerful human voices that bring the data—and the people in those rural communities—alive.

the community was through the establishment of an America Reads program, where college students tutored at-risk children. The college built on the trust established through that program to do needed research projects. Some colleges and universities began to build relationships through service projects with area organizations, as well as through regular meetings between faculty and CBO representatives, before attempting serious research projects. In this case, the division between research, teaching, and service broke down quite totally and became irrelevant to the work of the partnership.

For academics used to being the expert, CBR is challenging because it recognizes multiple sources of expertise: the abstract, generalized knowledge of the academic, the detailed hands-on experiential knowledge of community members, and the fresh perspective brought by students, whose eyes are unencumbered by community traditions or academic canons. Some of what academics bring to CBR that is most valuable is, of course, their research expertise—a knowledge of sampling theory, experience developing questionnaires or using other instruments of measurement, the skills (and resources) to compile and analyze data and to produce a well-organized and clearly written research report—all of which can, among other things, greatly increase the credibility of the research in the eyes of policymakers and others with whom it is ultimately shared. And as Nyden and others point out (1997, p. 5), the "outside perspective" that faculty members and students bring to the community may reveal trends and patterns that are not at all apparent to people who are immersed in the community's social world. At the same time, community members can enhance the value of the research in innumerable ways, providing language, perspective, history, and practical information that strengthen the study and enhance the validity of results.

For those used to objectivity and scientific distance, CBR insists on connectedness and relationship building. CBR does not assume that objectivity automatically leads to accuracy and in fact raises the concern that distance *increases* inaccuracy. In this way, CBR shares with interpretive paradigms an emphasis on the importance of what is meaningful or relevant to the research participants and the goal of understanding a social setting and seeing it from the perspective of those who experience it (Neuman, 2003). Building trust with community-based participants who have access to valuable information is absolutely crucial, particularly when dealing with difficult and controversial social issues. CBR is premised on the assumption that uncovering quality data requires both commitment to a cause or issue and engagement with the people. So although CBR often relies on both qualitative and quantitative data, the importance of engagement means that even when the aim is to gather and present purely quantitative data, it is important to keep in mind that people cannot be reduced to statistics. Careful statistical research may be important in a social change struggle, but if the process takes the humanity out of the research and makes the research distant from the people, it will ultimately undermine the social change mission of CBR that attempts to empower ordinary people as information producers

In short, doing CBR requires shifting perspectives. It requires understanding what the community wants as the source of research questions: Safer streets? An expanded child immunization program? Better services for senior citizens? Or does the community want to know whether a social program is working? When we think about these questions as research projects, we recognize that already the ground has shifted. These research questions do not come from theoretical disputes or disciplinary empirical debates. They require choosing methods that serve the needs of the community rather than the inclinations of the researcher. They require producing and sharing knowledge with the community that is seeking change, rather than sharing and producing knowledge within a disinterested professional association.

Community-Based Research as Social Change

The ideal form of social change that CBR seeks to contribute to is to alter some aspects of the political, social, or economic institutional operations or cultural context that give rise to a problem. In this respect, it stands in contrast to other forms of direct service whose aim is not to challenge the status quo but to ameliorate its negative consequences. However, the effectiveness of any CBR project at achieving real social change is limited by at least two factors. One is that CBR must always be seen as one item on a larger community-based social change agenda. Although the information that a CBR project produces might be useful to a community or organization trying to effect change, most typically it is one small piece of a larger effort that relies on more than just information to succeed. Put another way, whereas research may be the focus of the researcher, to the community the research is probably only one part of a bigger project.

From the community's vantage point, research looks very different from how it looks from an academic vantage point (see Figure 4.1). In many communities, community-based organizations are becoming somewhat

---

Creating Social Change

When Mary Brydon-Miller began her doctoral dissertation, she wanted to do it as community-based research. As an activist working with a Gray Panthers chapter, she became involved in helping to manage a conflict between senior citizens and younger people with physical disabilities living in the same public housing development. Those efforts led to her spending time volunteering with the independent living center in town that served people with disabilities; she drove the van that transported residents. She developed relationships with many of the people with disabilities and as a result decided to do a CBR project with them.

She began by interviewing people about their experiences with problems of accessibility and discrimination. Eventually she held a meeting with the independent living center staff and residents to discuss some of the issues she had uncovered in her interviews. At this early stage, her plan was to help residents organize to bring in legislators so as to have an impact on local and state laws. But residents rejected this idea in favor of taking on a local shopping mall and fighting to make it accessible. They eventually won, after fighting all the way up to the state supreme court. Prior to Mary's arrival, there was no organized disability group. Her research process contributed to the community's building one, and the group that formed quickly took over the process themselves. Her dissertation turned into a documentation of their organizing and their struggle (Brydon-Miller, 1993, and personal communication, 2000).

---

wary of researchers who approach them and want to "do research." As one CBO member put it, "We've turned down research because of the way the academics want to do it. Our first responsibility is to our service population. Our rules are that one, if it will help, do it; two, if it will neither help nor hurt, do it only if we have time; three, if it will harm, don't do it." In other words, community members are, by virtue of their very different situation and perspective, inclined not to put as much importance on the research effort as do academics.

The other limitation to the social change impact of CBR is the real limits of any single social change effort and the difficulty in effecting social change of any kind. The scope of change that CBR seeks to produce varies widely, from the individual-level improvement in the quality of life, to intermediate-level group change of access to opportunities, to the structural level, where real change involves basic institutions and a shift in the distribution of economic and social power to enhance the life chances of oppressed groups. As a rule, the greater the level of change that is sought, the greater are the resources—power, knowledge, money, effort—that need to be mobilized to achieve the change. And although knowledge is an important resource, clearly other resources and institutional power relations need to be altered to achieve social change.

On one level, a CBR project typically focuses on using research in the service of furthering some change in some segment of society. Whether it is to create a better program, build a more effective organization, make a safer neighborhood, enhance public health, or change a law, CBR is about action. It is about changing social conditions, whether on as small a scale as a single family (Miller and Brydon-Miller, 2000) or as large a scale as

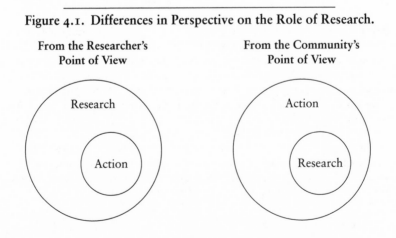

Figure 4.1. Differences in Perspective on the Role of Research.

From the Researcher's
Point of View

From the Community's
Point of View

Research

Action

Action

Research

the global economy. This social change focus of CBR is a particularly difficult transition for academic researchers to make.

For most academics, trained in the ideology of scientific objectivity and belief that scholars should be disinterested with respect to outcomes of their research, moving to a model that insists they not only care about the impact of their work but participate in translating research findings into action can be paralyzing. Academics who get involved with CBR must adopt a new paradigm of research that assesses the value of the research findings, not only on their validity but also on their relevance, and that argues that the validity of research results is dependent in part not on how distanced academics are from their research but on how connected to it they are. This is what it means to adopt a paradigm that values usefulness alongside validity, and experiential knowledge as much as abstract knowledge.

Although social action and social change are the ultimate purposes of CBR, academics must take care not to take on a CBR project thinking that academic knowledge or research alone will make the difference to the community. If the community partner is an established agency or community-based organization, even the most compelling research results are likely to bring about at most a minor change in policy, programming, or service delivery, and perhaps effect a relatively minor transformation in the organization itself. Successful social change at the grassroots level, especially in a disorganized community, is even more of a challenge, as it requires other kinds of experts who are more important than a researcher: community organizers who can recruit and mobilize people around a cause, leaders or "animators" who can express the thoughts and feelings of the people, and popular educators who can help people understand their circumstances. Only once these needs have been met is CBR likely to be of much value. One failed CBR project illustrates this.

Two colleagues at a midwestern university agreed to help a community organization do research on a program involving parents in their local school to show its outcomes and write proposals for more funding. Not understanding the importance of these multiple roles in CBR, they trained some parents to interview other parents about their school involvement. But they did not recruit neighborhood leaders to promote the importance of the research, they did not do popular education with parents to analyze the information they were obtaining, and they neglected to realize how important the group's organizer was to keep the project on track. Some interviews were collected, but the project died without producing any results. Here again we see that CBR is only one ingredient in a larger social change project, and that project entails far more than just research. Because of the constraints that can face CBR practitioners, one of the most popular models of CBR, developed by the Policy Research Action Group in Chicago (see Chapter Eight), consciously splits the roles of research and action so that academics need be responsible only for the research itself, and community leaders and community-based organizations assume the responsibility for making action happen from it.

Another mistake is made when academic researchers who take on CBR with disorganized and resource-poor communities attempt to fill all of the social change roles themselves, especially at the beginning of projects. These initiators face daunting challenges: they will be the ones who must bring people together for meetings, reach decisions, and make everyone feel like a real participant. They need to be seen as legitimate leaders, and they will need empowering pedagogical skills (see Figure 4.2). Some academics think that because they are good at technical research tasks, they can perform all of these other tasks as well. In fact, organizing, leadership, and popular education are difficult to learn because they cannot easily be reduced to a set of textbook rules and because they require sophisticated interpersonal skills.

More commonly, community-based researchers serve as consultants, particularly when they are working with already organized communities that know what research they want. Consultants provide limited services for community organizations in much the same way as other consultants provide limited services for corporations or government agencies. This is the model often used by CBR researchers working from the middle with social service or government agencies. In some respects, the most effective

---

Figure 4.2. Roles of the Researcher in Social Change.

→ Community organizer

→ Animator-leader

→ Popular educator

Action researcher ⟩	Types of Action Researchers
Initiator:	Manages the social change project as well as the research
Consultant:	Manages the research only, and from a distance
Collaborator:	Is a full participant in social change project, but primarily as researcher or educator

type of community-based researcher is the *collaborator.* This is an academic who is engaged with the community over the long term as a true participant. This person is probably not playing leadership or organizing roles—or typically involving students in their community-based work—but is attending all the meetings and offering perspective and knowledge along with all the other participants.

Steps in Social Change and CBR Projects

Because CBR should be seen as part of a social change project, it is important to distinguish the differences between the stages of a social change project and the stages of a research project, depicted in Figure 4.3. At each of the steps of a social change project, complete research projects can be completed. For example, a single CBR project could be devoted exclusively to helping a community group choose a problem, and an entirely different CBR project could begin by identifying resources. This section will explore some of the kinds of CBR projects that can take place at each of the social change steps.

Step One: Choosing a Problem

Choosing a problem is different from finding a problem. In many historically oppressed communities, there is no shortage of problems; thus, doing research at this stage of a social change project often involves specifying what the range of problems might be or what the extent of a particular problem might be. Research at this stage often also has a hidden, or not-so-hidden, agenda. In disempowered, disenfranchised, and disorganized

Figure 4.3. Steps in a Social Change Project.

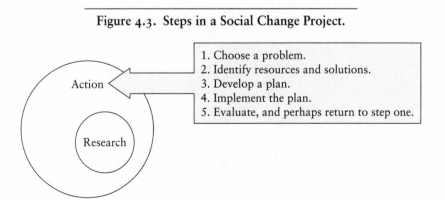

communities, CBR may serve as a "front activity" for community organizing. Most community organizers know that one of the best ways to build a community organization is to find a hot issue that can motivate large numbers of people to participate. That issue might be getting a stop sign on the corner, improving the neighborhood school, shutting down the crack house on the block, getting better jobs, or any number of other things. Often, the only way to have a chance of picking the right issue is to knock on people's doors and ask them what they care about and what they are willing to do about it.

When community organizers and other community workers have access to research assistance, that informal door-to-door research process can become more systematic and produce more benefit. The most common research model used at this stage is the needs assessment. In this model, the research focuses on documenting or measuring the gap between reality and community desires. In its pure form, needs assessment can be an extremely sophisticated methodology, with intricate procedures for identifying stakeholders, planning the needs assessment, conducting it, and then setting goal priorities based on it (Witkin and Altschuld, 1995). But in practice, there is wide variation in how needs assessments are conducted. The closest to a pure model is an approach that involves a constituency in a research project in determining its own needs. Often, however, agencies conduct needs assessments on behalf of constituencies, with constituents serving as participants and "informants." This is illustrated by the project already described in this chapter, where students and their professor worked with the child care liaison person at the local department of social services to identify the practices, problems, and successes of low-income women in attaining informal and formal child care. Another project in the same community started with the local Coalition for the Homeless (an advocacy group) requesting a survey of the local homeless population to ascertain, among other things, what needs they had that were and were not being met by local services providers. Such a model has the advantage of getting the research done with the involvement of the people who can implement the program and may sometimes involve mobilizing the constituency itself to take action.

In other cases, the community is fully aware of the extent and even the causes of a problem, but needs official documentation in order to get funding or other support to address the problem. From a cynical perspective, this is the "here are the conclusions; now get me some data" approach to research. However, while those who object to an engaged research model may see it that way, research conducted to document what people already know is not so different from replication research testing the validity of previous research findings. Another way to view such research is that it is really hypothesis testing, with the hypothesis being the belief of the community or agency personnel as to the nature of the problem. In any case, advocates cannot go to court, or even to the media, without careful documentation of the problem. An example of this issue was when a local organization knew there was a serious gap in services between the juvenile justice system and simply releasing probationers into the community. Because they wanted to develop and get funding for a step-down program for juvenile offenders, they contacted the local college for advice on how to do the necessary research that would show the need for the program. This version of a needs assessment has the advantage of focusing resources on an already strongly felt need, but has the disadvantage of sometimes putting the solution before a careful definition of the problem. In one particularly difficult case, a community organization was not happy with research done by one college that did not show a need for their program. They went to another nearby college to do the research again, only to receive the same findings.

Step Two: Identifying Resources and Solutions Around a Problem

Once the community has defined and chosen a problem, they move into a process of trying to solve the problem. If they made the most of the problem definition stage, they have already moved on to organizing a constituency that can begin to plan and take action. Those committed individuals are the first resource needed in any social change effort. Other resources are time, money, skills, equipment, and even political leverage. Some of those resources may come from within the community, and some of them are likely to come from outside the community. Often, groups trying to change themselves, their circumstances, or their society adopt a strategy of simply getting all the resources they can find and work with what they are able to mobilize.

When a group is ready to begin gathering resources, however, there is also the opportunity to do research on what resources already exist. In some ways, this is the opposite of needs assessment. While needs assessment identifies what is missing, this approach, commonly called *asset mapping* (Kretzmann and McKnight, 1993), which is the most common form of resource identification research, identifies what the community already has. In asset mapping, researchers survey community members to learn the skills they have, the community work they have done and are willing to do, and the interests they have in developing new or different skills. They may conduct a similar survey for local businesses, organizations, and institutions. The resulting *capacity inventory* then becomes a basis from which to build programs.

Asset mapping often works best when the community does it for themselves, since one of the goals is for neighbors to get to know each other. As an example, a youth outreach worker at an urban university began partnering with youth and community organizers in the local area who were attempting to keep their high school from closing. They jointly developed a community asset-mapping curriculum for youth in the community to learn how to do the research, and thus find resources in the neighborhood to support their campaign. The curriculum component is now used in the community high school's social studies classes each year as a vehicle for integrating youths into local community organizations. On the heels of this effort, they have taken on issues such as housing displacement, economic redevelopment and gentrification, access to jobs and housing opportunities, and safe spaces for youths.

An asset-mapping activity may take on the form of survey research—asking people questions about their own background, skills, and experiences and soliciting information about other resources in the community. However, it is likely to serve as an organizing tool as well, with the interviewers distributing information about the sponsoring organization and the priorities around which they are organizing. They may even invite people to attend already planned events, such as rallies or popular education forums, or to join their organization. In one of our classes, our students helped to undertake a needs assessment survey of community residents facing displacement due to gentrification of the neighborhood. The CBO sponsoring the project insisted that the students always be accompanied by a member of the community, all of whom were recruited through the housing residents' associations that it had helped to create during the previous years. The organizing community residents handed out brochures about their associations and encouraged the respondents to attend upcoming meetings or events. The students gathered and compiled the data and wrote a draft report, which was altered substantially by the community to highlight the vibrancy of the community. By this simple division of labor, pairing a community resident-organizer with a student to undertake a door-to-door survey in the targeted neighborhood, it is easy to see how both an organizing and information-gathering function were accomplished through what appeared to be a survey research process.

In other cases, research at this stage of a social change project involves studying potential resources beyond the boundaries of the community. One example is a professor who was approached by a local CBO to do an analysis of all the philanthropic foundations in the metropolitan area to assess which ones would be most likely to fund community-based development or to amend their giving patterns to include it. It was not glamorous research and involved hours spent going over microfiched foundation tax records and tabulating numbers. But at the end of the research, the professor had compiled a listing of all the area foundations with a description of their giving patterns. The professor claims that this has turned out to be the most requested research report he had ever written and has since been used repeatedly by groups looking for resources to help solve their problems.

Solutions are another type of resource that research can help identify. Indeed, information about possible solutions is one of the most important resources. But in contrast to research that identifies resources, which is often guided by some knowledge of what is wanted, research exploring solutions is much murkier. Often this kind of research involves identifying and surveying all possible similar solutions used in other places and evaluating them for fit with the current group's situation using a comparative case study methodology (Yin, 1994). In one such approach, the group decides what the relevant characteristics of the problem or need are and then looks at how many of those characteristics were present in other places where a particular solution worked. After learning what other people in other places are doing and looking at how their circumstances compared to the task at hand, the group can work on adapting one or more of the strategies.

One project along these lines involved students from Middlesex County College working with area CBOs to identify and research important state issues. Students compiled thick binders of pending legislation custom-designed for each organization that each one could try to influence. The strategy of the project was to match the characteristics of the CBO with the characteristics of the bill, looking for those most important to the particular organization's work so that they could organize their own local campaigns to work for pertinent legislation. In another project, a newly formed advocacy group wanting to make the Toledo, Ohio, city government more accountable conducted a study of cities with strong citizen participation processes to see which could be most readily adapted to Toledo. Volunteers went out and collected information on the citizen participation programs, as well as on characteristics of the city such as population size, types of economic activity, and type of city council.

Much of the information that communities and community organizations want at this stage is not technically difficult to acquire. Often it simply involves counting things—how many service programs there are in a neighborhood, how many residents in a rural county have access to health care, how many children have up-to-date school immunizations. Consequently, it may not look like research the way academics define it, and it is certainly not the kind of research that typically gets published in journal articles. But it is often the kind of research that attracts the attention of the media and instigates change.

Step Three: Developing a Plan

With a clearly defined need and an inventory of possible resources and solutions, those involved in a social change effort are ready to develop a plan. Much of the literature on community-based planning looks at it as a holistic process that begins with a need and asset analysis and ends with proposing solutions to defined problems. But there are aspects to any planning process, particularly if it is a strategic plan for a community organization, that involve yet other kinds of research—that is, introspective research, where the group analyzes itself. One of the most popular forms of introspective planning research is a SWOT analysis, that is, an analysis of strengths, weaknesses, opportunities, and threats (Mathias, n.d.). Strengths and weaknesses involve an assessment of a group or organization's internal capacity. Opportunities and threats shift the focus to conditions external to the group or organization. A typical SWOT analysis is like an introspective focus group, as members meet to build a collective list of strengths, weaknesses, opportunities, and threats. Often, themes emerge from the process that help the group in its strategic planning. When the Coalition to Access Technology and Networking in Toledo was trying to develop a mission statement and goals, it conducted a SWOT analysis at one monthly meeting and in the process found that one of the most important strengths the group had was strong volunteer commitment. In setting goals, the group emphasized programming around volunteer trainers, and over the next year trained dozens of new computer users in publicly supported housing to use the Internet and various office computer software. A similar form of research, developed by the action researcher Kurt Lewin (1947), is force field analysis, which differs from SWOT primarily in that it focuses on conditions external to the group. When members do a force field analysis, they list the forces supporting their goals and those impeding their goals and then develop a plan to maximize the supportive forces and minimize the impeding forces.

Sometimes a plan might not require research on its face, but the plan itself might point to more research. For example, a community organizing group trying to stop an unscrupulous developer from wrecking their neighborhood might want to take action against the developer's investors.

To do this, they need to find out who the investors are. The research would identify the investors, their community ties, and their potential response to community action. Then the group might pick one of the investors as a target and picket that person's home or business. The Youth Action Research Group, organized through the Georgetown University Volunteer and Public Service Center, provides one example. As part of a campaign to improve neighborhood housing, the group members did a study of absentee property owners in the neighborhood. They decided to target their organizing actions in part based on the negative record of absentee owners—selecting owners who owned multiple neglected properties and considering the number of city citations against the owner.

While SWOT and force field analysis are appropriate when the group already has adequate information about itself, that is often not the case. Groups or organizations doing programmatic planning often need research that may look like a more specific form of needs assessment or asset mapping. At one college, the dean of students approached a faculty member about surveying students on campus regarding at-risk sexual behavior to feed back into student services programming. One of the findings of the research was that students were not interested in attending public meetings about at-risk sexual behavior, so the plan developed to build a Web site where students could educate themselves in private.

At Georgetown University, the Partners in Urban Research and Service-Learning collaborative decided it wanted to enhance the community's capacity to understand itself and conduct its own research, so it created the Center for Technical Cooperation as a joint university-CBR enterprise. To determine its programming priorities, the CTC codirectors spent the first six months meeting with partner agency staff to determine their priorities and interests. This led to the creation of a continuing-education certificate program in community development, which the university offers free to the community, staffed by volunteer faculty and community experts and leading to a certificate in community development.

Step Four: Implementing the Plan

Regardless of how carefully the problem is defined, how effectively the resources are inventoried, and how completely the plan is developed, no social change will occur without action. It might seem odd to think of the action phase of a social change project as involving research, since it is the action phase where people protest, or lobby, or change their organizational chart. In contrast, research—the way we normally think about it—is seen as a separate, static activity rather than a dynamic intervention.

This comes from our historical association of research with the myth of scientific objectivity, where the cardinal rule was *not* to affect the system. In community-based research, just the opposite is the case: the goal of the research *is* to affect the system. Hence, there is nothing strange about the research being not just preparation for the action, but the action itself.

Research as action has a long, venerable, and unrecognized history in the United States. When the Congress of Racial Equality sent an integrated group of "Freedom Riders" on interstate buses through the South in 1961, they were engaged in action research—in this case, to determine whether new federal legislation outlawing segregation on interstate buses was being followed. The torching of the bus and beating of the Freedom Riders created research data more profound than any survey of the bus companies could have revealed.

When the East Toledo Community Organization was trying to get a fair share of the city of Toledo budget for its neighborhood, it undertook a massive study of the budget itself. Ultimately, the group developed a set of proposals that it took to city hall during the holiday season and sang to the tune of "We Wish You a Merry Christmas" but with a new title: "We Wish You Would Fix the Budget!" Union research into corporations, community research on discrimination in police treatment or city service provision, and many other forms of action research have produced wide-ranging changes.

Research done at this stage also might be designed to build an organization. A group doing an asset-based assessment in its neighborhood might be trying to recruit people into the organization at the same time it tries to find out what resources and skills people can bring to the group. One faculty researcher did a community-based research project with local CBOs that led to a local conference where funders, CDCs, and government officials discussed the findings of the research and formed the Working Group on Neighborhoods, which helped bring over $2 million to begin filling the needs identified in the research.

In an interesting twist on this model, a university sponsored a group of high school students to conduct participatory action research projects on issues in their neighborhood ranging from housing to employment to health. They sometimes worked with a youth adviser from the university and sometimes with university students. In this case, the research itself—and particularly the participation of the students—was one of the most important goals of the program. Doing the research was empowering for them, and everyone was very pleased that all thirteen high school students from the first two cohorts of participants went to college when they graduated.

Step Five: Evaluating

Evaluation may seem like the end of the process, as is the case when researchers determine whether a program worked, an action was successful, or an intervention had the desired impact. This is also the most feared form of research. Typically, evaluation is done by the powerful against the powerless and is used by administrators and funders against programs and organizations, especially in a time of budget cuts. But that is the case only when we think of evaluation from the traditional research model. When evaluation is done as community-based research, two things about it are quite different.

First, rather than being controlled by the powerful against the powerless, community-based evaluation research is more often done by the powerless against the powerful. Of the examples in the previous section, many of them fit into a community-based evaluation model. When the Lagrange Village Council, a Toledo, Ohio, neighborhood organization, did a community-based evaluation of garbage collection, the group carefully documented what garbage was left behind on trash collection day, what streets were skipped, how many garbage cans were dumped over without being picked up, and a number of other measures. They presented the director of the division overseeing city garbage collection with their research findings and got both an admission of bad service and a signed commitment to improve. Another variation on this form of evaluation research occurs when researchers evaluate programs already implemented in the community to see if a problem might still exist. In one example of this form of research, students undertook a study in conjunction with a division of the local health department to explore why the rate of African American women participating in cancer screening programs was so much lower than that of white women. Although the health department officials assumed that the reason had to do with attitudes or lack of information on the part of the client group, the students did not find either to be true.

Second, and even more important, when a group wants to know whether what it is doing is effective, it is increasingly turning to new models of evaluation called *participatory evaluation* or *empowerment evaluation* (Fetterman, 2000; Patton, 2002; Stoecker, 1999b). In this model of evaluation research, the people running the program control the evaluation process; many groups even develop their program with an eye to evaluating it. Consequently, in the planning phase, they set goals and decide how to measure those goals in preparation for the evaluation. In this way, the planning phase is not just planning for action but also planning for further research, and the audience for the evaluation is not the funder or the administrator but the people running the program. In addition, rather than doing an evaluation at the end of a project when the results will have little impact on outcomes, the evaluation is done as an integral component of goal setting, and research findings are fed back to the group on a regular basis so that the group can make midcourse corrections. In one case, a faculty member with a group of students did an evaluation of one of their service-learning programs with a local partner that had a long-term relationship with the college. The community-based evaluation research became an integral part of a service-learning program where college students acted as mentors for youth with emotional troubles. The results of the evaluation were used to set up new goals and training programs for the student mentors.

This perspective on evaluation clearly differs from a traditional approach that would have an outside evaluator measure outcomes and declare an intervention to be a success or failure. The emphasis on collaboration, especially over the long struggle for social change, leads the CBR evaluation researcher to be more likely to intervene in the process being evaluated for the purpose of improving it. Clearly, however, it is not the role of the academics in CBR to impose such change, nor would the researchers have the authority to do so. Rather, the researchers would present their findings, along with suggested explanations and possible alternative program or organizational responses, to the clients, constituents, and leaders for their response and reaction. One possible response is that the research has missed the point, misunderstood the evaluation objectives, or misinterpreted the data so that it is the research process that needs major revision. Were the researcher merely to drop off the research report to the interested parties at this point, the whole effort would be seen as a waste of time from both the researchers' perspective ("the community is ignoring our report") and the community partner's perspective ("the researcher just doesn't understand"). Unfortunately, this may happen all too often when short-term consulting relationships are established for the specific purpose of creating a program evaluation (even in CBR collaborations, let alone a more traditional research framework). However, when the researchers and community partners are committed for the long term and in the context of a larger social change effort, the evaluation takes on a quite different purpose. If the instruments are not providing useful information to assist in guiding program change, then the research process can be changed. If the results do indicate that improvements can be made or program changes are less effective than desired, then the program can be altered and reevaluated in the light of the new operations. Even if the change initiative is meeting all of its goals, there are still likely to be areas that can be improved, and the evaluation process can provide guidance as to what form the improvements might take.

Summary

In this chapter, we have seen how the principles of CBR are embodied in the research approaches and methods used in campus-community partnerships. True collaboration is valuable for ensuring not only that the methods address the community's pressing issue, but also that the research results are useful and applied throughout the social change process. The methods of knowledge creation, discovery, and dissemination employed in CBR are typically an eclectic mix of traditional and nontraditional techniques, selected and employed based on the value of their contribution to the larger social change agenda. This typically leads to academics' becoming learners alongside community members, as new techniques are applied, adapted, and developed in the course of the research. Seeing research as just one item on a larger social change agenda forces us to deal with the power and resource differences that exist between the change advocates and the structures of the status quo. Within the larger social change process, community-based research takes on different forms, to achieve different purposes, at each stage in the process. Thus, whether the community partners with which the university partners are allied are at the initial stages of choosing a problem and identifying assets, developing or implementing a plan, or evaluating programs or policies, different types of methods are employed.

5

RESEARCH PRACTICES IN COMMUNITY-BASED RESEARCH

IN THE PREVIOUS CHAPTER, we considered different ways that CBR might contribute to an organization's planning, implementation, and evaluation processes, as well as how the distinctive features of CBR influence overall decisions about the design and conduct of research. In contrast to the breadth of coverage in that chapter, this chapter strives for depth, focusing on strategies and techniques at each stage of the research process. Whether a community is doing needs assessment, developing a plan, conducting an evaluation, or taking on any one of the myriad of other kinds of research projects discussed in Chapter Four, some common steps are involved (see Figure 5.1). On the face of it, these steps seem to be fairly clear-cut. First, CBR partners must identify a research question. Then the research team—community members, students, faculty member—must make decisions about the kinds of research design and methods that will most effectively answer that question. The data are then collected and analyzed, and results are reported.

These are the basic steps in any research project. However, the process of doing community-based research is not as straightforward as it appears. As a consequence of taking collaboration seriously, seeking to demystify knowledge creation, valuing community knowledge, and disseminating research for public application and social change, familiar research methods may need to be modified and new methods used. At each stage of research, the questions may be far from straightforward and the answers far from obvious—for example:

- What should the research question be? Should it be, "Why aren't Latino parents more involved in their children's schools?" or "What beliefs do school staff and administrators hold about Latino/Latina students

Figure 5.1. Steps in a Community-Based Research Project.

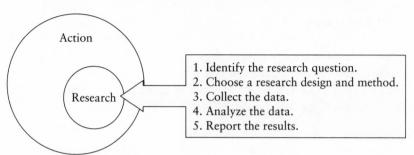

1. Identify the research question.
2. Choose a research design and method.
3. Collect the data.
4. Analyze the data.
5. Report the results.

and their parents?" Should the research focus on the levels and forms of air pollution produced by the local mill, or on the political strategies that might force conformity to environmental regulations?

• How—and where—should the data be collected? Will statistical data speak more powerfully than the voices of community residents about the consequences of welfare reform? Is it only old people who can provide perspectives on the roots of the Native American community here? Is this population literate enough to complete a self-administered questionnaire? How can we be sure to protect the anonymity and privacy of illegal immigrants while we collect information about their community's problems? Will we be able to gain access to the school [detention center, company records, former clients, current employees, health clinic clients]? Are the small businesses in the central city representative of businesses across the more rural parts of the county?

• Who should collect the data? How involved does the community want to be? Can we count on teenagers from the local community center to use the instruments carefully and correctly? Will members of the tightly knit Croatian community here be willing to talk to our African American students? How do we identify community members who might be interested in helping us administer interviews? How much do we need to train them? Should we pay them, and if so, how much? Will we be given access to school data about ethnicity and suspensions? Which is more important: validity or a high response rate? Highly standardized data collection or a focus on rapport and relationship building? Are there community organizers who can gather the information we need in the course of their normal door knocking?

• How should the data be analyzed and presented? Can undergraduates do justice to the rich personal accounts of Holocaust survivors? Should we teach community members to use Statistical Package for the Social Sciences or geographical information systems software? What would have the greatest impact: Neighborhood residents organizing a community theater project to express the results? A demonstration, protest, or barrage of letters to the local media? A professional-looking report full of statistics about needy schools? Who should make the presentation to the local management board: The students? Community partners? The professor? Which would have greatest impact: a lengthy report or an executive summary? How many and which people should review the final draft?

Some of the options from which to choose at each step of most CBR projects sound familiar because they are the kinds of decisions that researchers make no matter what the nature of the research is. However, many of them are not as familiar. Thinking of ways to involve community members in the collection of data, for example, or helping a community theater project report the research results takes researchers quite beyond the alternatives they normally consider in their research decisions. Perhaps the most basic difference between CBR and traditional research is that in contrast to traditional research, whose single overriding goal is to get meaningful data as defined by disciplinary norms, the central goal of CBR is acquiring data that are useful to the community to help advance its social change agenda. From the CBR perspective, research data that are collected in isolation, plugged into inscrutable formulas, and used to inform theoretical, jargon-laden debates in scholarly journals are likely to be worthless to the community. Truly useful information acquired through a process in which all the participants are empowered by their participation is the ideal to which CBR strives.

This chapter is about how to accomplish the twin goals of producing good research that can contribute to social change while working effectively with students and community members in the context of a campus-community partnership. In the following sections, we explore the options available at each stage of the CBR process, some of the distinctive challenges that come with this kind of research, and how researchers might go about pursuing strategies and making decisions in line with the principles of community-based research.

Getting Started: Identifying a Research Question

The first step in the effort to identify a research question in a CBR framework is to establish a connection with an organization or agency that wants some research done. This connection can be initiated in different ways, some of which are detailed in Chapter Three. Even when a potentially fruitful partnership is established, however, the community group may have only the vaguest idea of just what it wants to know, what is possible to find out, and how it all might fit with their larger mission or social change efforts. Many community groups have never thought about what research they would like done because they have not had anyone ask them before. In other cases, a CBO may have a clearly defined research question along with a definite sense of how the research findings can contribute to their work, which is more likely to be the case when the research partnership results from a response to a request for proposal. More often than not, the reality is something in between: community partners have some idea of what they want to know and why but need the expertise and outside eye of trained researchers—or researchers in training, in the case of students—to help them articulate the research question and shape it into a viable project.

Collaboration at this stage is essential. Ideally this means meetings of the entire research team where participants get to know one another; learn about the particular skills, knowledge, and other resources (for example, time) that each can bring to the project; and come to an understanding about what the partner needs to know and how that need can be clearly stated. In reality, the demands of an academic schedule might mean that some of this important groundwork is laid without students present, perhaps by the professor meeting with community partners prior to the beginning of the semester to identify and define projects for students to work on during the academic year. What is most critical is that the research question emerges from the community's needs, as it defines them.

The biggest challenge in identifying a research question might well be translating a large, ambitious, all-encompassing research agenda into a single, focused, manageable question. Community groups have the best knowledge about what their own problems, issues, and needs are. However, they might not have the technical expertise to frame a researchable question, so the researcher's role is to help the group think through how to make the question researchable. A group that wants to evaluate whether its adult literacy program is successful, for example, may need to start with a project that helps it determine just what the aims of the program are—that is, what is meant by *success*. When the dental unit of the local health department wanted to learn as much as possible about the quality and quantity of dental care that low-income children in the area received, the vision of a huge, comprehensive survey of all low-income parents and dentists had to be tempered by the realities of limited resources—in this case, two undergraduate students available to take on the project for a course that lasted only one semester. The group worked with the professor and the students to carve out what turned into a very researchable question: What do low-income parents see as the major barriers to their children's dental care? A community group that starts with the question, "How do we reduce crime?" can be pressed to think further about what is underneath that question. Was there a particularly heinous crime in the community that has mobilized people? Do they know the kinds and rates of crimes that occur in the community? Sometimes a community group may approach the researchers wanting to implement a program when what they really need to do is study the problem so they can make an informed choice about what sort of program is likely to be effective in their community.

Although it may seem obvious, the research question or questions, once they are identified, ought to be clearly written and shared. One professor has students who undertake collaborative CBR projects type and post the research question or questions in a common area to serve as a visible guide throughout the work of the project. In this way, everyone is quite literally "on the same page" with regard to the basic directions and purpose of the CBR project.

Choosing a Research Design and Method

Most of the criteria that govern choices of a research design and method in a traditional research project also apply to CBR:

- Resources (time, money, people) available
- Population characteristics
- Population accessibility
- Orientation and skills of the researcher
- The nature of the research question

Additional criteria assume primary importance in CBR, and they make decisions about research design and data collection more difficult and challenging than in traditional research. The first of these is the purpose of the research. All CBR is intended to contribute to positive social change, directly or indirectly, and this aim must affect decisions about research design. What kind of study will have the greatest impact? A study aimed at determining if discrimination against gays and lesbians occurs in a county in Maryland was undertaken to inform county commissioners' decision about whether sexual orientation should be added as a protected class to county antidiscrimination legislation. A largely conservative, and even reactionary, group of people, including groups from the community, would be reading and responding to the study, looking (or so one might assume) for ways to discredit it. What sort of research design would be least discreditable? A matched audit design—a highly controlled form of field experiment that allows the researcher to isolate the test variable and thus establish causality—was used to test for discrimination in rental housing. In the end, this research design had a far greater impact on the county commissioners than the second part of the study, which consisted of semistructured interviews with self-selected gays and lesbians who described incidents of discriminatory treatment in their everyday lives and which was more easily dismissed as "subjective" and "unscientific" by its critics.

Similarly, an assessment of services for abused women might document what kind, location, indicators of need, and outcomes by means of statistics, graphs, charts, and maps. When the aim is to influence policymakers with persuasive data, quantitative information often works best. But such a study also might aim to document the personal stories of victims by means of qualitative data, which serves both to dramatize the problem for the media (often a vehicle for change) and to mobilize sympathy and support on the part of community members themselves, to whom numbers and charts do not speak as compellingly.

Another important purpose of CBR is not just to produce useful results but rather to make sure that the process of designing, implementing, and presenting the research mobilizes and empowers the community. This might mean paying special attention to research designs that invite the active participation of community members as both researchers and involved respondents or even that effectively blur the two roles. For example, a study that organizes focus groups of low-income parents around issues of child care can serve not only to highlight concerns but also to develop connections among people that persist long after the particular CBR project is completed. And when the participants of the focus group are also asked to critique the draft of a questionnaire and make suggestions about how other low-income parents can be contacted and recruited to participate in the study, they become both participants and researchers. A questionnaire that is worded such that respondents are asked to comment on the questions themselves and to serve as important informants rather than objects of study may serve to involve community members in the study long past the interview itself. These are all effective and important ways to realize collaboration and to eliminate conventional hierarchies in the research process.

This kind of community involvement in the process of planning the research can also help to educate community members in meaningful ways. Community members who are involved in discussions about the technical aspects of research design become less dependent on academics, consultants, and other experts. In one program, parents received a small stipend to do assessment research of a social service program serving their children with training and support through the local college. As a consequence, the parents developed a range of research skills and knowledge that they were able to use in subsequent assessments. By understanding the logic involved in designing research, community members are also better able to evaluate the research findings with which they are bombarded by the media on a daily basis, which is empowering for them.

There are other considerations in the design of research and choice of method:

- The skill levels of students and community members. Unlike traditional academic research, which typically involves one highly trained researcher and perhaps a research assistant or two under the researcher's

---

Juvenile Voices

In 1999, the Richmond (Virginia) Juvenile and Family Court invited Richard Couto and his students at the University of Richmond's Jepson School of Leadership Studies to undertake an ambitious project: a study to identify gaps in the court's services and the needs of at-risk juveniles and their families that services might effectively address. As Couto (2001) explains it, the original plan was to speak with service providers, stakeholders, and staff of different agencies within and connected to the juvenile justice system. However, at the suggestion of the Citizens Advisory Council, he and his forty-four students decided to talk with detained juveniles as well. They did so in gender-separate groups of three to six, each run by two university students using a methodologically creative strategy that involved sharing a short story about a young person, Shorty or Denise, who was caught up in a violent incident. Then members of the group were asked to fill in what they thought was true about the main character's experiences with family, school, neighborhood, and the juvenile justice system. The young offenders responded enthusiastically, thoughtfully, and analytically. They talked about the character's background, compared themselves to her or him, and provided rich insights into their own lives, dreams, and experiences with the court system. The result is an array of compelling reflections, narratives, and even some heart-rending paintings that add immeasurably to the more objective interview and statistical data that comprise the final report (Couto, Stutts, and others, 2000).

---

authority, a CBR research team consists mainly of community members and one or more students, all of whom are assumed to be teachers as well as learners, are of essentially equal status, and possess for the most part minimal research skills. The research design must take this into account. What sort of data collection method is within everyone's abilities? And what sort of training will have to be built in to ensure that everyone has or acquires the necessary skills?

• The academic time crunch. Often the biggest challenge is tailoring a research topic so that a quality project can be completed within the time frame dictated by the academic schedule, while also taking into account other limitations (number of students, workload of the faculty member, time commitments of community partners).

Learning Goals in Community-Based Research

The central aim of CBR is community betterment and social change, but another aim is student learning, and sometimes professors must work with community partners to see to it that the research design meets not only the needs of the community but also the specific goals of a course and curriculum:

• A graduate course in ethnography in the College of Education at the University of Denver requires that students acquire and apply skills in field research. Consequently, the CBR projects that are part of that course must be designed to use at least some qualitative research.

• Students who complete group CBR projects in the advanced course in social research methods at Hood College typically use multiple methods so as to give them experience with both qualitative and quantitative techniques, an important learning aim of the course. A recent project involved interviews with homeless people that were designed to include a series of forced-choice questions—relating to demographic characteristics and respondents' ratings of area services, for example—and some less structured, open-ended questions that gave the respondents more voice and gave the students experience compiling and analyzing qualitative data.

• In an environmental biology course where students must learn instrumentation and measurement techniques, CBR projects might involve monitoring of local water quality and its potential impact on health in the surrounding community.

In cases where there is a seemingly irreconcilable conflict between specific course-related learning goals and community needs (a rarity, in our experience), the community needs must be given priority. However, it is usually possible to design a CBR project that meets the community's needs as well as student learning goals.

• Learning goals. How might decisions about research design and data collection methods help achieve course or curricular learning goals?

Collecting the Data

How we collect the data, as well as where and from whom, is central to all research and poses some special challenges and opportunities for people involved with community-based research. For the researchers on the academic side of the research team, implementing the research design is a way to begin overcoming the shortcomings inherent in outsider status. In areas where the communities in which the researchers work and the communities where they live are geographically or politically segregated from each other, doing the research work helps the community members to see the researcher as someone who is part of the community. Also, as students begin gathering the data—by whatever means—they become involved in the community and gain more intimate knowledge of its members' concerns and issues. Not surprisingly, students tend to like this stage most.

For community members as well, the implementation of the research plan can be a highly satisfying and engaging part of the research. This is especially true if they are able to participate directly in the collection of data, but it is also true if community members are kept abreast of what is going on in the field and otherwise participate as active and valuable members of the research team. Many CBR projects seem to involve interviews with specialized populations in the community—the homeless, low-income mothers, elderly African Americans, gays and lesbians, or employees of a certain industry, for example—who may be unable or unwilling to participate in data collection. Even when community members do not participate in the actual data collection, however, they often assume the role of gatekeeper by providing information and access to students who are collecting data. They may accompany students even when they do not actually administer the instrument. And finally, community members are an invaluable resource for ideas about strategies for getting others in the community to participate.

There are other reasons for getting community members to participate actively in data collection efforts. When the research requires that residents interview their neighbors, they get to know each other, and the research process itself helps build community relationships. In addition, for research involving specialized skills, training community members to do the research allows them to develop expertise that may enhance their employability and potentially reduce their dependence on outside experts, as is true when community members participate in each stage of the research.

Of the residents who spent hours upon hours doing research to understand the Toledo city budget and develop recommendations on how the city could change the budget to benefit neighborhoods, for example, a number went on to city council or city agency staff positions.

Given the value of involving community members in the data collection, what are some strategies for getting students and community members all working together to collect the data? Sometimes involving community members is not a realistic aim because they are not interested or are too busy to assist. When community members are willing but untrained, involving them in the collection of data carries with it the risk that the research will not get done on time or done well enough unless there are resources to support lots of training and supervision. Even when the community partner is a well-organized community organization or agency whose members or staff have some research expertise, the organization's resources might be stretched too thin to allow collaboration in the data collection effort. In fact, we have often found that such organizations expect that it is students who will provide the research labor, including the data collection. In situations where developing the residents' skills is not paramount, all the instructor's attention can be given to ensuring that students have the necessary training, while supervising and monitoring their work remain the central tasks for the faculty researcher.

Many CBR practitioners make concerted efforts to involve community members in data collection, which can be rewarding in many respects. One way to recruit community members to participate in data collection is to offer incentives for their assistance, which may take the form of money, academic credit, or simply the intrinsic rewards that come from contributing to a study that will, they believe, contribute to positive social change in the community. Prospective community researchers can be identified in different ways: a particularly vocal attendee at a meeting, an exceptionally interested and articulate respondent, a friend of a friend of a staff member at the collaborating organization or agency, or people who answer an ad posted at a neighborhood Laundromat or grocery store. Most data collection does not require high-level skills or knowledge, so that most community members can easily learn what they need to know to administer interviews or record observations in a short period of time.

Sampling

Selecting and reaching a sample can pose special problems for community-based researchers, particularly when—as is often the case—the sample consists of human beings (as opposed to, say, incidents, buildings, water

samples, or court cases) who are part of a population that is difficult to access. When the community is a geographical one, selecting a sample might
be a matter of going door-to-door at different times so that the sample finally consists of those folks who were home and willing to participate.
When the community is a more specialized group—mothers with young
children, the homeless, crime victims, immigrants, recent clients of a job-
training program, old people, ex-offenders—recruiting participants can be
a daunting task. And the challenge is made even greater by limitations imposed by the need to consider privacy and other ethical issues, lack of resources, and the constraints of the students' and institutions' schedules.
Here is where input from the community can be invaluable, and they are
frequently the most useful sources of ideas and strategies for reaching community members. When a professor and his students at Middlesex College
began discussions with a local transitional housing program about getting
information about former residents, they soon recognized the difficulty of
getting graduates of the program to complete a questionnaire or even to
make time for interviews. It was the community members on the research
team who suggested that they throw a big reunion party for all the graduates. By integrating informal interviews and focus groups into the party
atmosphere, they were able to collect rich stories as well as some basic data
about graduates' education, employment, and family changes since leaving the program.

The challenges of securing participants often mean that questions of
sample size and even of representativeness take a back seat to more practical concerns in CBR. After all, limited findings may be better than none at
all. At the same time, as with any other research, a seriously biased sample may make research findings useless or misleading so as to do a disser-
vice to the community. While the homeless who use area shelters are clearly
more accessible than those who do not, what is lost by talking only with
those people without homes who are currently using programs and services? Indeed, it is often the case that the people who are most accessible—
parents involved in the Parent-Teacher Association, women interviewed in
the lobby of a health clinic, children enrolled in after-school programs—
are not representative of the populations we most need to know about or
hear from. This is true, for example, when the study is a needs assessment,
in which case the views and experiences of people who are not currently
using programs and services might be most valuable.

Hard-to-reach samples also might require that researchers be somewhat
more flexible about data collection than they otherwise might be. When
two students began interviewing Latinos at a small reception following a
Spanish-language service at a local church, they were frustrated when they

realized how few interviews the two of them would be able to complete there. Their on-the-spot solution was to solicit the help of several Latinas who were not formally trained but were familiar with the study and eager to help. The result was many more interviews than the students alone would have been able to complete there, with some minor loss of control over the quality of the interview and a few more incomplete questionnaires than they might otherwise have had to tolerate. In other cases, students have developed abbreviated questionnaires for respondents who were unable or unwilling to complete the longer version—again, when available respondents are few and far between, and with the idea that some information was preferable to none at all.

Once prospective participants are identified and contacted, an additional challenge faces researchers: getting community members to participate in the study. Sometimes this is less a problem in CBR than in other kinds of research. In fact, community members may well be especially

---

Identifying Participants

Not all CBR involves asking people questions, but much of it does. Community-based researchers have used some creative strategies to recruit hard-to-locate participants:

- Flyers posted in public or semipublic places (grocery stores, Laundromats, church bulletin boards). Sometimes this approach is useful as a means to alert people that they will be approached by a door-to-door interviewer so that they are familiar, ahead of time, with the purpose of the study and are more likely to agree to be interviewed.
- Meetings that prospective participants are likely to attend. For one study, a student recruited participants for a study about local drug and alcohol programs by means of brief presentations at area Alcoholics Anonymous meetings. In another, a health care liaison at an African American church allowed students to attend a monthly women's meeting there to distribute questionnaires about breast cancer screening.
- Newspaper ads or articles. When a group is widely dispersed and invisible, as were gays and lesbians in one community, a newspaper article about the study was an effective means to recruit respondents. They were promised complete confidentiality and provided a telephone number to call to arrange an interview with a researcher about their experiences with discrimination.
- Word of mouth. This may work as a way to connect with respondents in tightly knit communities, particularly if researchers are in the community or otherwise easy to reach.
- Snowball sampling. This is where the researcher builds a sample by asking each respondent for the names of others that may wish to participate.

---

likely to complete a questionnaire or attend a focus group meeting when the researcher is from their own community, when they have a sense that their views and ideas are valued, when they are given a chance to talk about something that is important to them, and when they see the study as meaningful in terms of their own lives and communities—all of which are more likely to be true with community-based research. When community members know about and support a research project, they are far more likely to be willing participants and may even seek out researchers to volunteer their participation as respondents or even as researchers. But many times the opposite is true, and community-based research faces the same hurdles as does all other research that relies on people as participants: people find the whole business suspicious, bothersome, invasive, or simply a waste of their time and effort.

Much CBR relies on sources of data other than community members, of course. Researchers may interview service providers, legislators, teachers, judges, students, physicians, landlords, and others who can shed light on the research question. CBR frequently involves unobtrusive sources rather than, or in addition to, people: archives and agency data, public records, newspapers, Web sites, organizational charts, land use records, and so on. Their units of analysis might be water samples, court cases, classrooms, pieces of legislation, small minority-owned businesses, model programs, or firsthand observations of interactions.

Some kinds of data pose real challenges of the sort that are familiar: incomplete or incomprehensible records, bureaucratic regulations that limit

---

Incentives to Participate in CBR Studies

Sometimes the intrinsic incentives to participate in a study—a chance to have their views heard, to contribute to community improvement, to help out their friends—are not enough. The following incentives have worked for us (depending on the people recruited):

- A gift certificate for ten dollars at an area grocery store
- Money (a crisp five dollar bill)
- Candy or other small food gift
- A short break from work or school or—in the case of institutionalized people—a change in the routine
- A meal or dessert (for a focus group)
- Small toys or games (useful to entertain small children while mothers are interviewed)
- Magnets sent with mailed questionnaires that show the name and telephone number of the sponsoring CBR group

---

access, uncooperative or incompetent gatekeepers, bad weather, and so on. And some of these hurdles are a consequence of the nature of this work—that is, its goals of achieving social change and the threat to the incumbent powers can create subtle resistance or even outright hostility to data collection efforts.

Because of the many difficulties that might arise in relation to sampling and data collection—and unless a research plan is more or less foolproof—flexibility is essential to CBR. That means employing strategies such as having in place a backup plan for collecting the data, being willing to use a smaller sample than is perhaps considered ideal, and using multiple methods to ensure that when one research direction is blocked, efforts can be rerouted so that the entire project need not be abandoned.

Ethical Issues

Protecting the privacy and the dignity of respondents is a major consideration in any research involving humans, and it assumes particular significance when those people are powerless and marginalized, which is often the case with CBR. The principles of CBR impose an ethical imperative that is perhaps even more pronounced than in other kinds of research. Thus, particular attention must be paid to building constructive working relationships with institutional review boards (IRBs) and in adopting strategies for addressing ethical concerns in the design and conduct of CBR.

WORKING WITH IRBS. The distinctive time demands and other special circumstances surrounding CBR may require a closer relationship with IRBs than is typically necessary for academic researchers. Before embarking on CBR projects, faculty and students should be familiar with their institution's IRB procedures so that gaining approval to undertake the research project is not an insurmountable challenge but rather one that can be met smoothly. At the minimum, this means that prospective researchers should know the procedures for submitting IRB applications, including the specific forms and deadlines. These procedures can often be found on institutions' Web sites or in published materials. Campus IRBs usually meet regularly, and several professors from a variety of disciplines review proposals. Some institutions exempt research undertaken as class projects from IRB regulations, while others hold students to the same standards as professors. Regardless, the researcher—whether a professor or student—should plan ahead to ensure that there is enough time for IRB approval to be granted before the intended onset of the research project.

A useful strategy to build relationships is for researchers to meet at least occasionally with the campus IRB coordinator to get acquainted, discuss the kind of CBR projects being planned, and talk about CBR—what it is and how it is different from more conventional academic research. As the rate of CBR activity increased at the University of Denver, one of us (Nick Cutforth) invited Dawn Nowak, the IRB/human subjects administrator, to an all-day workshop on CBR held on the university campus. The workshop, which was attended by university researchers, community partners, students, and local foundations, was helpful to Nowak because it enhanced her understanding of the principles and methods of CBR. She was able to hear firsthand the challenges and benefits associated with CBR. The workshop served to establish a pattern of regular communication between Dawn and university researchers before and during their CBR projects, which has made the IRB process more efficient. Another way to improve understanding of CBR by IRB members is to work from within by becoming a member of the board and informally educating fellow members about the nontraditional characteristics of CBR.

The importance of good communication with IRB members is heightened because of the special challenge posed to the IRB process by the participatory and collaborative nature of CBR. To complicate matters, the IRB procedures that professors and students have to follow may seem rather strange and cumbersome to community partners, who do not operate under the same constraints as university researchers. Fulfilling IRB requirements will likely need to become a point of discussion or negotiation with the community partners because IRB procedures require the researcher to specify, in advance, the research design. However, when CBR projects are jointly developed by the researchers and the community partner, it is not usually possible to specify details of the full design in advance. Furthermore, due to the emergent nature of many CBR projects, the researchers cannot always predict the direction that the study will take even after it is under way, and changing conditions may require modifications of the research plan, a cycle that may be repeated often over the course of the project.

One solution to this quandary is for the researcher to ask for IRB approval in stages (Patton, 2002). For example, after meeting with the community partner to determine the focus of the study, the researcher should submit an IRB application prior to beginning the research. The application should describe the general framework of the study and clearly state the procedures for ensuring confidentiality and informed consent. As the study begins to take shape and the participants are identified, the researcher should update the IRB with an addendum that describes any modifications to the original design. These modifications can be minor or major. An example of a minor modification would be small changes in wording on a poster for recruiting additional research participants that is displayed in a community-based organization. A major modification would be when the decision is made to add focus group interviews to a recently completed survey design.

At the University of Denver, minor additions tend to go to the IRB chair, and major additions are usually taken to the full IRB review board for expedited review. Clearly, strong lines of communication between the campus IRB or human subjects administrator and the researcher ensure that IRB procedures are smoothly navigated during a study design without delaying the research. (Additional IRB issues, focusing on institutional and risk management concerns, are discussed in Chapter Nine.)

STRATEGIES FOR ADDRESSING ETHICAL CONCERNS IN CBR. States and institutions vary in their interpretation of the minimum standards required by federal regulations concerning the protection of human subjects. IRBs typically focus on three ethical requirements: that the research should not harm the subjects, that subjects should give informed consent, and that confidentiality should be ensured. In addition to issues of privacy, consent, protection from harm, and dignity, researchers doing CBR have to be careful about raising expectations about what such research efforts can actually accomplish. Community members' status in society may mean that they find it difficult to refuse consent when invited to participate in a research study, particularly when they are affected by the issue or problem under investigation, are dependent on the community program or social service being studied, or are led to believe that the research has the purpose of benefiting them or resolving the social problem.

The responsibility for securing consent may be especially important in CBR because the participants' powerlessness and vulnerability may mean that there are significant risks associated with speaking out. For example, juvenile offenders who complain about the treatment of the guards may receive backlash and repression, and welfare mothers might be subject to losing eligibility for benefits if they reveal certain information—or at least might fear that they are vulnerable. For these reasons, while participants such as these possess information that is critical to the success of the research at many levels, it is essential that they understand that they cannot be forced to participate. Also, they should know that if they choose to participate, they have the right to withdraw at a later time without repercussions. Of course, the mere act of producing an informed consent form and asking for a signature from community research participants may be awkward and threatening. To address all of these concerns, it is essential that consent forms incorporate user-friendly language and that community members are consulted throughout every stage of the research process about questions of privacy, dignity, and confidentiality.

A second ethical concern in CBR is confidentiality and anonymity. Confidentiality is when the researcher knows the source of information but the research audience does not know; anonymity is when neither the researcher nor audience can connect the source of information with an individual. CBR challenges anonymity norms in several ways. Because CBR is more likely to use methods that give voice to participants by relying on face-to-face interviews, anonymity is less likely. Traditionally, researchers disguise the locations of their fieldwork and replace the name of participants with pseudonyms in order to protect their identities. Sometimes protecting the anonymity of informants whose disclosures have been quite detailed or of individuals identifiable by their specialized roles or particular opinions becomes extremely difficult. Particularly in CBR projects involving small or closely knit organizations, changing names may not effectively disguise individuals. Also, researchers who establish friendships with community informants often gain access to all sorts of confidences, trusted and privileged information, secrets, and observations of unguarded behavior. The researcher may be faced with the dilemma of whether to report illegal activities or dangerous behaviors, which may be more likely with—but is certainly not limited to—CBR. For example, what should the researcher do if an HIV-affected individual reports that he or she is having unprotected sex? The most likely dilemma is when the researcher receives information that cannot be reported without revealing a source or putting a person or group of people affiliated with the organization at risk of reprisal.

This concern extends to the need for care in the development of survey instruments. A guiding rule here is to ask for personal information only when it is absolutely necessary or important to the study, paying attention to how questions are worded, how data are recorded, and whether raw data should be destroyed. Another issue is what to do with sensitive data, especially when participants may not want it reported or fear that it can identify them in ways that could harm or embarrass them. Furthermore, while research involving minors requires parental consent, there are some groups, such as gay and lesbian teens or runaways, for whom obtaining parental consent might be impossible or undesirable. In this case, participants could sign an assent form indicating their understanding of and willingness to participate in the research.

A third ethical concern has to do with sensitivity to privacy in how reports are written. Individual anonymity must be protected so that identification is not possible by other people in the community. One procedure that can be helpful in avoiding problems with publication is to have representatives from the community partner review the report before it is published or review sections in which their quotations are used. The purpose of this review is to protect the reputation of the community, not necessarily to change the data or alter conclusions that have been drawn from the data.

Ethical research requires adopting a particular frame of mind more than a set of specific, preestablished guidelines and techniques, and being sensitive to and anticipating ethical dilemmas involved in research is a continuous process. Often, ethical dilemmas and challenges have no simple answer. Rather, researchers doing CBR will have to rely on their own conscience, sensitivities, and sound judgment. Another resource is the Applied Research Ethics National Association, a national membership organization that serves as a resource for information about ethical and procedural issues related to the work of campus-based IRBs.

Analyzing the Data

Data analysis is another stage where community members, students, and academic researchers can all make a contribution and where the participation of community members, while not always feasible, nonetheless gives the projects extra validity and value. Academic researchers bring experience and training to the analysis and presentation of research findings, not to mention their access to the resources—computers, software, laboratories—for analysis. Similarly, students have much to contribute to this stage and typically are the ones to carry out the data entry and analysis. They also stand to learn a great deal from being involved in the analysis of real data and having to put the findings in a form that makes them useful and compelling. However, it is the community members' perspective, and their potential for acting on the analysis, that brings perhaps the most distinctive contribution to the collaborative research process. One way they do this is by providing an insider's view of research findings—an important means of bringing to CBR a level of validation that is often lacking in traditional research, where the meanings and interpretations of outsiders (in this case, students and professors) can lead to conclusions that are biased or ignore important nuances and information in the data. Also, community members are often positioned to make good decisions about how the findings ought to be organized and presented for maximum value and impact.

Having community members participate in the analysis brings to the fore the popular education methodology developed by adult educators such as Paulo Freire (1970) and Myles Horton of the Highlander Folk School (Adams, 1975; Bledsoe, 1969; Glen, 1988; Horton, 1989). The popular education model is unique among pedagogical philosophies in its emphasis on respecting people's ability to educate themselves, just as CBR is unique in its belief that people can guide their own research. As community members work with raw data, partially categorized data, or a rough draft of a research report, they begin to understand their own situation better. For example, community members who look at the data on home ownership in their neighborhood and draw maps showing where the home owners live will begin to ask other questions arising from their own experience in the community. They might inquire about the quality of housing where home owners are concentrated versus where absentee landlords own more property, or about the incomes of home owners versus renters. From the research, they may know of the blocks where home ownership is rare and correlate this with their own personal knowledge of the quality of housing in those areas, or the incidence of crime there, or the neighbors' perceptions of safety. As they ask these questions, they go back, or send the researcher back, for more information. Through this process, community members become more comfortable and more skillful at asking and answering their own questions. This can be an empowering experience.

As in the data collection stage of the research, overburdened and understaffed organizations, and those whose members are already skilled, may legitimately prefer that the researcher do the analysis. Academic researchers, including students, who have been engaged through the previous research steps should be prepared to do the analysis effectively and with the community's needs and interests in mind, which is best done by keeping the entire research team abreast of analysis strategies and findings. Because analysis is often an emergent process, community members and other participants should be consulted about additional directions for analysis that might be suggested by the data.

In situations where community members want to be involved in data analysis but lack the skills, the researcher's job includes training community members to do the analysis. Although there may be circumstances where time pressures and the complexity of the research require experts, most CBR projects can be done with basic training. Even quantitative CBR projects rarely involve analysis more complicated than basic descriptive statistics and can be done on a desktop computer using standard database or spreadsheet software.

Reporting the Results

Academics typically share the results of their research on panels at disciplinary conferences or in journal articles aimed at audiences consisting of others in their own disciplines who share their particular scholarly interests. Typically, their research garners little attention and has minimal impact. Communities trying to make change, however, know that much of the success of their efforts will hinge on the extent to which they can make reporting the results the most important part of the research. For this reason, decisions about how the research will be reported, where it will be shared, and who will present results are critical to the ultimate success of the CBR project.

Reports

The form (or forms) in which results are presented depends on a number of factors, including the purpose of the research and the nature of the community and the intended audience. More often than not, a written report is produced. However, compared to more conventional academic research reports, the CBR report is likely to be shorter, jargon free, and reliant on devices like eye-catching graphics and executive summaries that make the findings clear and readily accessible to a wide audience. The scholarly literature review is replaced by background information about the problem and the community or organization. The section that describes the research design and method needs to be detailed, especially when the report is intended for audiences—for example, skeptical legislators or agency officials—who may be inclined to question its legitimacy. And, finally, most CBR reports conclude with a section that outlines the recommendation or actions implied by the results—again, in contrast to conventional academic research reports, which likely conclude with suggested directions for further research.

When the CBR project is an internal evaluation or some other project not intended for consumption outside the group, the research team must think carefully about how to get its own members to pay attention to the research findings so that the group can act on them. A written paper is the least effective form of presentation one could make in communities whose members are more comfortable with visual presentations, gut-level emotional experiences, or oral communication. In these cases, a well-designed PowerPoint presentation, a skit, or colorful posters illustrating key results in graph or other form may be more effective. If the audience is external to the community, the results must be presented in a form to achieve maximum impact. A legislative or other decision-making body might be more receptive to something resembling a conventional research report, especially if it is clear and compelling and lends academic legitimacy to findings and recommendations.

Other Formats

When media coverage is the goal, the community may decide to supplement the written report, or forgo it altogether, in favor of more attention-getting formats or tactics: a press release, a conference, a theatrical or other more dramatic mode of presentation. This stage may not involve a presentation at all. Instead, it may be an action or demonstration, with the research results informing the strategy that guides the action. One community organization conducted detailed and careful research into the investors connected with a particularly unscrupulous housing developer. After researching the investors and their involvement with this developer, they began staging protests targeting the investors and making quite public their shady activities. In one case, the presentation of research results involved occupying a physician's office until he agreed to meet with the group and discuss the issues. Obviously, decisions to employ such unconventional tactics that involve students must be made carefully.

Often research findings end up being presented in more than one venue, in the community and perhaps on campus. At some schools with CBR centers and multiple projects going on each semester, an annual celebration is held where students, faculty, and community partner representatives get together to report research results and garner publicity for the projects, the partnerships, and the issues their research has addressed. Some faculty members take students, and sometimes community mem-

---

Using the Media

Media coverage is often the main goal of CBR and sometimes projects are specifically designed to produce findings to broadcast. The Community Media Workshop (CMW) in Chicago is one of a number of organizations whose purpose is to help nonprofit and grassroots community groups use the media to tell their stories and share their ideas. Since its founding in 1989, CMW has provided training and coaching to over eight hundred nonprofit organization in the Chicago area, including the Center for Urban Research and Learning at Loyola University. Other similar media-oriented organizations include Action Media in Minneapolis, Boston Media Research Action Project in Boston, and We Interrupt This Message, based in both San Francisco and New York.

---

bers as well, to present their findings at academic conferences—which not only is a rewarding experience but also underscores (for students and others) the legitimacy of community-based research as an academic enterprise and its value both as a teaching strategy and as a means for colleges to contribute to their communities. Campus-based presentations typically follow the initial and important sharing of results with the community, which might be with agency or coalition staff, county commissioners, a gathering of community members-at-large, media representatives, or other groups positioned to take action on the findings.

Finally, *who* should be involved in presenting research results depends on the nature and the aims of the research. When the research is primarily for the community, it may be best for community members to do the presenting. When the research has set its goal as effecting some sort of social change that requires action on the part of an external person or group, some community groups prefer to put the researcher out front in an attempt to establish the legitimacy of the research findings. In some cases where students have been integrally involved, they may be the best ones to do the presentations as they may have the most intimate knowledge of the research design and data. Also, when the research involves some politically charged issues, which CBR frequently does, students are often the most effective presenters because they are likely to be seen as without an agenda, that is, as comparatively disinterested. This alone can enhance the credibility of the project in the eyes of decision makers and perhaps the public. Finally, preparing and presenting research findings is an empowering process that brings benefits of all kinds to students and

---

Community Theater

Community theater is an increasingly popular and particularly creative way to report research results. In community theater, community members research their condition, or their history, and present the results in the form of a play. This format enhances the communication skills of community members who must develop their thespian talents, and it helps educate their neighbors using a method far more likely to attract attention than the average research report presentation. In one case of a disability community, community members researched and reflected on their daily experiences and produced a play depicting the discrimination they suffered, which was empowering for the community members and informative for outsiders (Lynd, 1992). The Youth Action Research Group produced skits for community theater performances and created a virtual tour of the neighborhood, using video and slides, which they took to community groups as part of an ongoing organizing campaign.

community members alike. For that and other reasons, including demonstrating the collaborative nature of the work, having students and community members present the research together has special value.

Summary

When a research project is community based, it is both similar to and different from conventional research. In this chapter, we examined some of the distinctive challenges and difficulties posed by CBR at each stage of the research process and detailed multiple strategies for dealing with those challenges and difficulties.

In identifying a research question, the community provides the major impetus for framing the question, balancing the academic disciplines' autonomy in defining questions. Methods are determined not in isolation or solely with respect to the academic researchers' capacities, but also in the light of the community's resources and social change strategy. Carrying out the research is likely to bring academic and community researchers into contact, cutting across social class and race and ethnic lines, thereby enhancing the skills and understandings of each of the parties and learning from the skills and experiences of the others. Analysis is likely to be strengthened as a result of the multiple forms of validation that are imposed on data and findings. Popular education techniques are likely to play a role in gathering and interpreting data and in presenting the data back to stakeholder audiences. Such presentations have as their primary goal contributing to the larger social change process and having an impact on a more immediate audience, rather than influencing a more diffuse, theoretically and disciplinarily interested body of experts. Finally, we saw how the process of undertaking CBR can be transformational for the actors participating in such projects—not only communities of disadvantaged people, but also agencies that purportedly serve them and institutions of higher education that strive to be more accountable to their own community service mission.

6

COMMUNITY-BASED RESEARCH AS A TEACHING STRATEGY

Community-Based Research and Student Learning

Latinos, mostly from Central America, are a small but growing population in a small mid-Atlantic city. When they began this CBR project, Amy and Melissa, juniors at the local liberal arts college, already had some limited contact with this community—Melissa through her tutoring and Amy through her work as a hostess at a local restaurant where many of the kitchen workers are Hispanic men. Both students speak Spanish. The county Hispanic Concerns Committee, comprising mostly local service providers and educators, a few of whom are members of the Latino community, wanted to know more about this community: how big it is, what its needs are, which programs are serving it, what its members perceive as the community's strengths and problems, and how service providers and other agencies might respond to those needs. Amy and Melissa agreed to work with them—and the director of the college's Center for Community Research, a sociology professor—to find answers to those questions.

What began as a project to meet requirements in two undergraduate sociology courses (research methods and ethnicity) turned into a year-long project from which these two young women gained immeasurably. Here are some things they learned:

- How to develop a quality interview schedule
- How to organize and conduct a focus group
- The challenges of translating a questionnaire from English to Spanish while retaining meanings and validity
- Some strategies for negotiating with professionals with conflicting agendas
- Policies and laws and issues relating to immigration
- Widely varying and subtle forms and consequences of institutional racism
- How to access and interpret population data using the Web
- How to use the computer to compile and manipulate and analyze survey data

- The value and uses of qualitative data
- The hurdles facing non-English speakers in the United States
- The fear that permeates the worlds of illegal immigrants
- The distinctive strengths and features of different Latino communities
- How to work in close collaboration with people whose styles and temperaments are very different from one's own
- The priorities and politics of local agencies and political bodies

And what did the community gain? Those who read their report—it was distributed widely and presented in three public forums—know now about the size and growth of the local Latino community, their social and cultural isolation, and their need for new services (such as interpreters) and better information about existing services to address their problems. Although the Latino community is no longer quite as invisible as it was, substantial gains have yet to be realized; neither the board of commissioners nor the Hispanic Concerns Committee has moved to implement much of the ambitious social action agenda suggested by the Latino community and proposed formally by the student researchers. However, the board of commissioners did hire a bilingual multicultural liaison staff person for the county—spurred, perhaps, by the students' report—and local service providers now have quantitative data that will help them justify additional funding for new services for Latinos.

However frustratingly limited are immediate benefits to the local Hispanic community, the long-range benefits of these students' involvement in community-based research are less dismal. Some community someday—and it may be a large one—will benefit from the work of Amy, who is interning this year with an immigration attorney while she applies to law school in hopes of pursuing a career in advocacy law. Melissa will pursue a career in social work, which will provide her a professional vantage point from which to champion the cause of Spanish speakers and other disenfranchised groups. Both students went into their CBR work with feelings of compassion, altruism, and concern for the welfare of others. They came out of it with much more than that: a range of skills, understandings, and capacities that prepare them for careers and lives of civic engagement and social action.

When community-based research is integrated into college and university curricula as a teaching strategy, it is a particularly effective form of service-learning, a form of experiential, community-based learning that involves students in carefully chosen, meaningful community service activities that are connected with course content through reflective discussion and class assignments. Evidence indicates that when it is done right, service-learning produces a variety of positive attitudinal, interpersonal, and academic learning outcomes. Nonetheless, some practitioners have suggested that some kinds of service-learning are better than others at effecting student learning. Specifically, service-learning that stresses collective action, advocacy, critical analysis, and collaboration for the purpose of social change—what some have called service-learning advocacy (Mooney and Edwards, 2001), and the category into which CBR seems to fall—may well result in greater curricular, academic, and personal benefits for students than other forms of service-learning without those features.

CBR is, we believe, an especially effective, powerful, and transformative kind of service-learning pedagogy—perhaps the "highest stage of service-learning," in the words of one sociologist (Porpora, 1999, p. 121). In this chapter, we explain why by showing how the promise of service-learning as a pedagogy can be truly realized in the principles and the practices of community-based research.

Service-Learning: Strengths and Limitations

Service-learning has gained a solid foothold in American colleges and universities as a pedagogy that is useful across a wide variety of disciplines and types of institutions. The growing popularity of service-learning has been a response, in part, to social and economic changes that have led higher education institutions to rethink their role and responsibility relative to their surrounding communities (Edwards and Marullo, 1999). But the other major impetus to the growth of service-learning has been higher education's renewed commitment to student learning. This, too, was inspired (or we might say required) by social and economic changes, particularly the great increase in the number and diversity of Americans enrolling in colleges and universities, changing skills and abilities required in the labor market, political pressures on higher education for greater accountability, and the call for graduates prepared and inclined to contribute in a meaningful way to civic life. Service-learning has been widely promoted as a strategy to help higher education assume a leadership role in addressing widespread social problems and to prepare students to meet the needs of a rapidly changing economy and democratic society (Boyer, 1990).

Educators have long known that students learn better when their learning is not bound by classrooms and textbooks and when they are called on to do more than memorize information so as to reproduce it on an exam to satisfy the instructor and earn a good grade. A plethora of research makes this same point: that the most effective learning takes place when reflection and practice are combined (Kolb, 1984). As service-learning has gained momentum, so too have efforts to document its value as a pedagogical strategy, particularly its impact on students and student learning. The result has been a rapidly expanding research literature on the contributions of service-learning experiences to a wide range of attitudes and behavioral outcomes.

The learning associated with service-learning is multilayered. It ranges from rather generic attitudinal changes—values, beliefs, and self-related feelings—to various kinds of interpersonal skills to very discipline-specific learning. These include indicators of personal development, such as personal efficacy, spiritual and moral development, and personal identity, as well as interpersonal skills, such as the capacity to work well with others, communicate effectively, and exercise leadership. Students who have engaged in service-learning show higher levels of cultural understanding, less racism, a heightened commitment to service, more confidence to engage in civic activities, and increased concern for the common good. Students also seem to like it. They report that service-learning enhances their interest in college, the course, and learning generally (Eyler and Giles, 1999; Eyler, Giles, and Braxton, 1997). Although we have less convincing evidence of service-learning's impact on disciplinary learning, there is some evidence to suggest that in courses in many different disciplines, students are able to grasp course concepts and are more motivated to learn course material when they can connect it to their activities and experiences in the community. Some researchers have found that service-learning experiences can also enhance the ability to understand and solve problems, use subject matter to analyze a problem, know the workings of agencies and the political system, and think critically.

Not surprisingly, service-learning experiences, not to mention the courses and disciplines and instructors with which they are connected, vary considerably. More recently, researchers and practitioners have begun to develop typologies of service-learning and to identify some of the differing benefits and limitations associated with different kinds of community-based learning experiences. One finding is that positive student learning outcomes, and especially academic learning, are directly dependent on two central features of the service-learning experience: the quality of the service-learning placement (including its relation to course content) and the degree of integration of the service experience with the course by means of well-designed reflection, discussion, and connection with course themes. Eyler and Giles (1999) describe a *high-quality placement* as one in which students can do meaningful work, exercise much initiative, have important responsibilities, engage in varied tasks, and work directly with practitioners or other community members—and where their work is clearly connected to the content of the course. A *well-integrated experience* is one in which the service experience is integral to the day-to-day activities of the course and allows students frequent opportunities for reflection—at its best, class discussion that goes beyond simply sharing feelings and experiences to analyze, dissect, and connect their service activities in ways that clarify course concepts, elaborate text-based information, and otherwise require them to integrate and process knowledge in ways that truly enhance academic learning. Most of the research on service-learning makes this same point: that a pedagogically effective service-learning experience requires quality reflection time, carefully crafted written assignments that require analytical connections to course material, and a placement that immerses students in meaningful, challenging, and rich service activities.

Others have distinguished service-learning experiences based on criteria such as how much time students spend in the community and how central the service-learning is to the course. Some of the most significant criteria that differentiate service-learning experiences have to do with the nature and aims of the community-based work itself. Is it mainly charity work, oriented toward meeting the immediate needs of individuals and families, or is it aimed at bringing about some real change? Are students required to examine the underlying economic, political, or social arrangements affecting the community? Does the service meet a clear community-identified need, and is it designed to empower or to disempower community members? Although service-learning of all kinds produces a variety of important learning benefits for students, some have suggested that justice-oriented or advocacy service-learning (Mooney and Edwards, 2001), emphasizing social justice, social change, real community collaboration, and critical analysis of the structural roots of problems, produces benefits that may be absent or deemphasized in more conventional or charity-oriented service-learning experiences. That is, students whose community-based learning requires that they collaborate with community members, critically analyze the sources of problems, consider alternative responses, confront political and ideological barriers to change, weigh the merits of legislative or other political strategies, and experience their own potential for social action are more likely to develop the leadership skills, political awareness, and civic literacy that represent developmentally richer form of service-learning. We think that CBR represents one of these more advanced forms of service-learning.

Community-Based Research and Student Learning

Students involved in CBR realize much of the same educational value as what students gain from more generic forms of service-learning . . . and more. For many students, community-based research involves much interaction with people who are very different from themselves in life chances, experiences, and worldviews. This enables some of them, in particular those who arrive from middle- or upper-class families, to learn about life outside the cocoon of their privileged lives. For students who come from poorer backgrounds, work on a CBR project can lead them to a different place; it can validate university-based research, since they have rarely seen it serve the needs of their communities. This is the view of Phil Nyden from the Policy Research Action Group, who cites the example of an African American student who grew up in a low-income neighborhood near Chicago. After participating in a CBR project during her senior year, she commented that it was the first time she saw anyone in the university doing something that was helpful to "her community" (P. Nyden, personal communication, 2002).

Students from all backgrounds also learn more about how different parts of the public world work (neighborhood organizations, activist groups, city councils, government agencies, schools, and so on). They experience an applied research process—the results of which matter—and they typically participate in most aspects of the study: research design, developing methods and gathering data, analyzing the data, writing up results, and assessing their significance for the issue at hand. And because the students see how the results will be used, they are all the more interested in the work and take care to ensure that their study is done properly and their findings are appropriately tied back to the original research questions.

The educational enrichment that students acquire goes far beyond those that are related to designing and conducting research to include a wide range of skills and experiences that broaden students in often unpredictable ways. As the case example at the start of this chapter illustrates, students in a typical collaborative CBR project are usually called on not only to "do research," but to take on a wide variety of other tasks that help them develop all kinds of interpersonal skills: make telephone calls, arrange meetings, explain the project to small and large groups, negotiate for access to information of all kinds, write letters, make posters, meet new people, settle disputes, give help of all kinds (a ride, child care), and otherwise venture into and interact in areas—cultural, social, emotional, intellectual, and geographic—where they have never been before.

Skills and knowledge of a more general academic nature are also developed through community-based research: critical analysis, the ability to develop reasoned argument, effective writing for different audiences, organizing and presenting information, and using computer technology for Web-based research, data compilation and analysis, community mapping, and public presentations. Furthermore, students acquire knowledge of matters as diverse as complex organizations, public and private funding, philanthropy and grant getting, social policy, legislative process, politics, interpersonal conflict, and community life.

Discipline-Specific Learning

Although our emphasis to this point has been on student learning that transcends particular disciplines and courses, CBR also has much to offer the achievement of discipline-specific academic learning. This is important in part because much faculty resistance to adopting service-learning approaches is rooted in the common view that service-learning does not lend itself easily to discipline-specific educational goals.

As Edward Zlotkowski (2000) notes, any efforts toward increasing the civic engagement of our colleges and universities "must begin with one incontrovertible fact: disciplinary perspectives and disciplinary identities—no matter how misguided or even counterproductive—really do matter to the vast majority of faculty" (p. 318). Add to that the fact that faculty members who teach are responsible for covering some component of their discipline's curriculum. This means that even those who are receptive to unconventional or progressive pedagogies and who are supportive of their use in, say, general education curricula are frequently resistant to introducing them into their own teaching because they do not see how service-learning can be successfully adapted to their discipline's and courses' curricular aims. Because of this, community-based research has a special appeal not because it is inherently interdisciplinary but because it links up readily with discipline-based learning as well. Through their community-based research, students come to understand the challenges of constructing knowledge from the perspective of the discipline.

One rather obvious place for CBR as a means to teach discipline-specific course content is in the social sciences and related fields: sociology, political science, psychology, anthropology, urban studies, criminology, social work, and education, among others. Here, CBR is a means to give students the valuable hands-on experience in the design and conduct of social research that is already a commonly used teaching strategy in required research methods courses at both the undergraduate and graduate levels. When CBR requires students to apply research-related skills that they have read about—develop a questionnaire, conduct a focus group, come up with a sampling plan, take field notes, track legislation, and write a report— their understanding deepens. Because CBR tends to rely on multiple and even unorthodox methods of data collection and analysis, including methods and approaches that are most accessible to community members and most responsive to issues of voice and local knowledge, students often get broader and more realistic experience in designing and conducting research than they might in more traditional research courses (Strand, 2000).

CBR has the potential to help take student learning far beyond conventional skills learning in research courses. With its emphasis on democratic participation in decisions about what we should know, how we should know it, and how knowledge should be used, CBR engages students with some important and interesting epistemological debates in different disciplines by modeling alternatives to conventional assumptions about the purpose of research, the role of the researcher, and who ought to control and participate in the production of knowledge. These are questions that are central to understanding modes of inquiry not only in the social sciences but in the physical and biological sciences and the humanities as well. By directing attention to these issues, CBR fits especially well with feminist, social constructivist, and other critical perspectives and pedagogies, a point to which we will return.

Motivation to Learn

Students involved with community-based research seem exceptionally motivated to learn. They are invigorated by their accountability and a heightened sense of purpose. They are doing the research and writing the final report not simply for a professor, but with and for community partners, as well as for others, whom they hope will be inspired by or pressured to take action on their findings. And their research has a purpose beyond simply their mastery of course material: improving a program, exposing an injustice, or documenting a need.

Those of us whose students do CBR are dazzled time and time again by their energy, creativity, and conscientiousness. Students subject their own and each others' work to extra scrutiny and care. Their questionnaires go through multiple iterations. They enthusiastically share suggestions and comments with one another. They listen carefully to community members who have understanding and suggestions that students lack. We have had students work together long into the night proofreading and perfecting a final report so as not to be embarrassed when the community partners read it. They ask for (and use!) suggestions about how to word questions, compile and present data, organize points, and develop action recommendations so as to be able to convince their audience—county commissioners, school administrators, funding agencies, politicians—of the validity and importance of their findings. They show remarkable sensitivity to the importance of involving community members wherever it is feasible and of

CBR and Academic Learning

In addition to research, CBR makes room for many other kinds of academic learning that fits with discipline- and course-specific content—for example:

- For a year-long senior honors thesis in her major, law and society, a student worked with members of the local gay and lesbian community to conduct a matched audit study to determine if there is discrimination in housing based on sexual orientation in the county where she lives and attends college. She conducted extensive library research and communicated with nationally recognized legal experts, government researchers, and activists and now knows a great deal about sexual orientation discrimination laws, how to conduct matched-audit studies and their role in discrimination and related court cases, and the process of instigating and promoting legal changes at state and local levels.
- Students in a course on community organizing at a southern liberal arts college researched issues of rural homelessness and housing in their county and learned much about the invisibility of homelessness—and reasons for it— in rural areas. The outcome was a community forum where representatives of agencies and organizations came together to work toward a partnership for an emergency housing facility for families.
- Students in an experimental psychology course at a historically black institution in a large city conducted a study with a local neighborhood to determine if there is a relationship between advertising aimed at African American males and their consumption of certain kinds of alcoholic beverages.
- A class in environmental science at a large liberal arts college in the Southwest researched U.S. industry practices in metals, plastics, and electronics. They hoped to produce information that would empower local Mexican community groups to pressure Tijuana industries to change their practices.
- In an undergraduate business course, students conducted a field audit to determine the need for a credit union to serve a Latino community (see Doing CBR in a Business Course).
- Graduate students in education at a midsize private university in the West had the option of meeting their research requirement by enrolling in an elective course, "Community-Based Research in Urban Settings." Recently the class CBR project involved working with inner-city high school students to conduct survey interviews with two hundred twelve- to fourteen-year-olds as part of an evaluation of three neighborhood after-school centers.

Doing CBR in a Business Course

A group of students in a business marketing class at a university in a large northeastern city worked with a local economic development corporation for Latinos. First, they surveyed the financial institutions near the Latino neighborhood and found few institutions serving the community. Then they worked with the corporation to conduct audits, sending English-speaking and Spanish-speaking "customers" into various nearby financial institutions. They discovered that Spanish-speaking customers were quoted higher fees to wire money abroad (to El Salvador).

The students' group project report described their methodology and documented their findings, which they learned to analyze statistically, and it was cited in testimony before the city council's licensing hearing. Largely as a result of this work, the corporation was granted a license to establish a credit union, which targets the Latino immigrant population as its primary customer base. The students and professor received a commendation at the corporation's annual awards ceremony, generating positive media coverage for the university. The students not only learned how to undertake rigorous audits to test for discrimination and developed a deep understanding of experimental design and data analysis, but they also took special care in writing up their results accurately and with appropriate qualifiers, knowing that the report would be widely read and closely scrutinized.

---

representing multiple perspectives and viewpoints in their interpretations and recommendations. This is all attributable to a number of distinctive features of community-based research: students' desire to make good on their commitment to people they have come to know in the community, the greater autonomy associated with all kinds of learning off-campus, and the recognition that comes with having completed a meaningful project for a purpose other than a good grade. All this makes CBR highly motivating and highly effective in ways that conventional classroom instruction *and* even conventional service-learning simply are not.

Community-Based Research as Critical Pedagogy

Critical pedagogies combine teaching methods and curriculum content with the aim of transforming the larger social order in the interest of promoting social justice, equal opportunity, and participatory democracy. They do this with course content that challenges and critiques conventional assumptions about the social order; by empowering students with skills and predispositions that prepare them to be effective social change activists; and by modeling democratic and egalitarian processes in the

The Impact of CBR on Students

We have learned some things about the impact of CBR on students from comments they share on course evaluations and in informal conversations. Here are some of them:

> "I left your class with a head full of thoughts about some pretty big issues—many things I have never thought about before."

> "Now I know that whatever I do in my career, I want it to make some sort of difference in the world—to make life better for people who don't have the same opportunities that I do."

> "This project took more time than any of my other courses, and I found it frustrating at time. But in the end it was *so* worth it—I learned an amazing amount, about doing research and about myself."

classroom (Giroux, 1992; Shor, 1992). Many academics are drawn to all kinds of community-based learning by virtue of its promise as a critical pedagogy. While some conventional service-learning may accomplish some of the goals of critical pedagogy, the principles of community-based research dovetail especially neatly with it.

Varieties of critical pedagogy, including feminist pedagogy, have made their way into classes at virtually every educational level. They inspire the work of a diverse array of teachers, teaching an even more diverse array of students, who are committed to teaching and learning in ways that fundamentally challenge and transform, rather than reproduce and legitimate, existing social arrangements. To this end, critical pedagogues self-consciously craft both the content and the methods of their teaching to counteract what are considered to be oppressive features of conventional education. Although definitions of critical pedagogy vary considerably, they tend to center on three major goals (adapted from Hartley, 1999):

- A focus on collective and collaborative learning, with a concomitant deemphasis on hierarchy, including authority differences between teacher and student

- A demystification of conventional knowledge, including embracing the notion that objectivity is impossible, that neither the teacher nor education generally is neutral, and that people's lived experiences are valid sources of knowledge

- A focus on teaching for social change

Each of these aims of critical pedagogy is also embodied in the principles and practices of community-based research.

Emphasis on Collaboration and Cooperation

The emphasis on collaboration and cooperation over hierarchy is central to CBR, where collaboration at every stage of the research process undermines the traditional prestige and authority hierarchies that characterize conventional research. Instead, researchers work with community members to design and carry out projects, and community members assume equal or greater authority to identify research problems, design ways to gather and analyze information, and determine how the results will be shared and used. When students are the researchers, they are empowered alongside community members. By participating as full partners in the conduct of meaningful research and the production of useful knowledge, students acquire a sense of efficacy about their own abilities and potential contributions. In this way, CBR can be an effective means to nurture students' commitments to social justice and shape their views of themselves—and perhaps their career aspirations—as activists and action researchers. Although students typically need substantial guidance—more or less depending on their level of training and whether they are undergraduates or graduate students—CBR virtually guarantees that the distance between professor and student is sharply reduced. Roles are blurred as community members, students, and sometimes the professor work together as teachers, students, and researchers.

CBR does more than model nonhierarchical and collaborative research. As students participate as partners in the research process, they invariably confront questions about power and control in the social relations of research, including ways that research is typically shaped by particular interests and points of view that reflect wider social arrangements, including prevailing hierarchies of power and prestige. And finally, collaborative research with a community typically (ideally) casts students, community members, and professors in roles of learners as well as teachers. This means that while students are learning to do research, they are helping others to learn along with them, a surefire way to enhance their own understanding.

Demystification of Conventional Knowledge

The demystification of conventional knowledge helps students to understand better the nature and production of knowledge and challenges the notion that there is any objective or neutral knowledge. This perspective

What Students Bring to CBR

One way that students are empowered by their CBR involvement is by contributing important skills or knowledge that neither the professor nor community members possess. In one case, a psychology student became indispensable to a graduate-level CBR course project because she was the only one who knew Statistical Package for the Social Sciences (SPSS) and was able to coach everyone else about using the computer for data entry and analysis. Another project involved community asset mapping, about which the professor knew very little. Two undergraduate students learned about and ordered geographical information systems software and attended a training session in a nearby city to learn how to use it. They then shared that knowledge with the rest of the research team: professor, students, and community members.

Some students' distinctive contributions are related to their majors: an art major takes charge of designing posters and flyers, an accounting major helps the research team make sense of the county budget. Others bring various life experiences: a returning student with young children may have valuable insights to bring to a research project on problems facing single mothers; a part-time bank teller has useful information for research about discrimination in housing loans; the student who is free to attend the Tuesday night meetings of the Coalition for the Homeless becomes a critical conduit of information for an assessment of countywide services for this population. In many different ways, students' distinctive contributions help to make them truly equal members of the research team.

---

also validates knowledge that is rooted in people's—including students'—own lives and experiences. Put another way, critical pedagogy "demands the examination of how and why . . . knowledge has been legitimated and reproduced" (Knupfer, 1995, p. 220) along with teaching strategies that start with each student's own knowledge base.

This demystification of knowledge suggested by the goals of critical pedagogy also is central to CBR, whose practitioners argue that, contrary to the claims of conventional academic inquiry, scientific research can never be value free, knowledge is a form of power (hence should be collectively produced and controlled), and research participants as well as researchers possess critical knowledge (Small, 1995). These ideas come alive for students in the course of doing CBR. The affirmation of lived experience is most obvious in the stress on local knowledge—the value given to the perspectives and knowledge of community members over the supposed expertise of the researcher in CBR, and a concept that parallels the idea of voice that is essential to feminist thinking about authority, knowledge, and empowerment. In critical pedagogy, this principle is most often applied to the classroom setting, where the students' experience and knowledge, not the teacher's authority, is the starting point for learning. This becomes a way of validating positionality—the distinctive perspectives and worldviews of students with diverse social characteristics that render them marginal in conventional classrooms and within conventional knowledge frameworks. In community-based research with students, the affirmation of lived experience extends to and empowers both community members and students, two groups whose authority does not hold sway in conventional educational or research contexts.

This does not mean that methodological expertise and rigor are discarded for the sake of including diverse experiences. Quite to the contrary, it is the combination of the principle of inclusivity and respect for the lived experience of people who are typically ignored with a methodological principle of acquiring information systematically and reliably that yields knowledge most beneficial to the community. As we discussed in Chapter Four, the community organizations (and their social change agenda) are not well served by flawed research designs, incomplete or biased data, analysis that is unjustified by the data, or conclusions that are unsupported by the analysis.

Social Change

The third and perhaps most important aim of critical pedagogy is social change, a principle central to community-based research as well. Critical pedagogy asserts that education ought to be liberatory rather than oppressive, transformative rather than oriented toward maintaining the status quo. It should contribute to social betterment directly, by challenging existing social relations and structures of privilege—and by empowering students with knowledge, skills, and proclivities that prepare them to be active agents of social betterment in their current and future lives. CBR's emphasis on social change distinguishes it from more conventional charity-oriented service-learning and from conventional academic research. But CBR also serves as a powerful form of critical pedagogy as it helps students develop:

- The capacity to think critically and analytically about existing structures of oppression and injustice
- The skills necessary to operate effectively as change agents in the public sphere
- An abiding commitment to values such as social justice and human welfare

- A belief in their own and others' ability to apply their knowledge and skills to bring about improvement in the lives of people

Community-Based Research as Civic Education

Much of the recent attention to all kinds of community-based learning is connected with growing concern about the apparent failure of colleges and universities to educate students for effective citizenship. Young people are variously described as politically apathetic, cynical, disengaged, self-centered, individualistic, and pessimistic about their ability to have an effect and lacking in understanding of what it means to exercise civic responsibility in a democracy as well as in the knowledge and skills that might prepare them to do so. The challenge to "renew the public sphere, revitalize our associational life, and reinvest in those civic activities that are the nursery of citizenship and civic vitality" (Schneider, 2000, p. 98) has turned attention to the ways that colleges and universities might more

---

The Youth Action Research Group

The Youth Action Research Group (YARG) in Washington, D.C., is studying the displacement effects of economic development in an immigrant neighborhood. The group of high school students who comprise the ongoing core of YARG work with different university students from one semester to the next. One semester, the YARG decides to examine the impact of economic development on housing quality and affordability for the low-income residents of the community. Both high school and college students learn how to do land records ownership research from a community development corporation staff member. They conduct interviews and focus groups with tenants in a building about to be converted from rental units to cooperatives to understand the likely displacement effects of such changes. With faculty and organizational staff facilitators, the high school students—with their deeper understanding of the community—and the college students—with their better understanding of research methods—construct the survey instrument and interview dozens of residents of a large building about to be converted. They follow up with focus groups to determine the residents' preferences and commitments regarding possible next steps. Within weeks, after the college students' semester has ended, the residents have organized themselves into a tenants' association that later buys the building from the corporate property owner.

The combination of skills, efforts, and working together as equal partners led to a more just outcome: rather than being displaced through economic development, the low-income residents were able to become home owners through the cooperative purchase of the building.

---

effectively address their long-time mission to prepare young people for democratic citizenship. The question then becomes, "How might that best be accomplished?"

For many, a large part of the answer lies in community-based learning, which has been widely touted as the current answer to the challenge of preparing young people for civic engagement and political participation. However, although it seems that involvement in service-learning (or any other sort of volunteer work) does enhance students' social conscience, compassion, and civic consciousness (Eyler and Giles, 1999), it does not lead to increased political engagement. Nor does it prepare young people more generally for active citizenship. On the contrary, the dramatic increase in community service among young people has occurred even as their political interest and electoral participation have plummeted (Colby and Ehrlich, 2000).

The problem seems to be some confusion about what we mean by citizenship, as how we conceive of citizenship shapes our notions of how we should go about educating people for the work of citizenship. Kahne and Westheimer (1996) argue that when service-learning experiences are charity oriented, they imply a particular and narrow view of what constitutes preparation for citizenship in a democracy—one that embodies civic duty, compassion, and altruism. They dispute the notion that this is what constitutes citizenship: "Citizenship in a democratic community requires more than kindness and decency; it requires engagement in complex social and institutional endeavors. Acts of civic duty cannot replace government programs or forms of collective social action. Citizenship requires that individuals work to create, evaluate, criticize and change public institutions and programs" (p. 596).

Others (Barber, 1992; Boyte and Kari, 2000; Astin, 1999) make a similar point: democratic citizenship requires more than just moral commitments such as compassion, altruism, and concern for the common good. More important are the capacity to reflect critically about social policies and conditions, as well as the knowledge and skills necessary to take thoughtful and concerted political action to bring about social change. What are the requisite knowledge and skills for citizenship in a democracy? Boyte and Kari cite "the arts of public argument, civic imagination, the ability to evaluate information critically, the curiosity to listen constantly, interest in public affairs, the ability to work with others far different from ourselves on projects that recognize multiple contributions" (p. 51). Astin (1999) would include the ability to develop trust, communication skills, and the capacity to work collaboratively with others. Walshok (1999) singles out the "capacity to evaluate and use information for positive social, civic, and economic purposes," which "requires transforming information into ideas and analysis useful to making judgments" (p. 76).

Community-based research, with its emphasis on critical analysis, collaborative inquiry, and social action, is a powerful way to prepare students for active citizenship. Students become skilled at working collaboratively: allocating and managing myriad tasks, identifying resources, asking for and providing assistance, giving and receiving constructive criticism, listening to conflicting points of view, recognizing differing strengths and weaknesses, resolving disagreements, keeping track of information, speaking up when it matters, and otherwise merging abilities and efforts toward the accomplishment of a common goal. In working collaboratively with the community to answer a question, students acquire knowledge and experience in areas that are essential to active civic participation. Because the goal is social change, students involved in CBR are forced to be analytical as well as creative, thoughtful as well as proactive, idealistic and realistic, leaders as well as collaborators, knowledgeable about what is as well as visionary about what might be—in short, all those things that prepare them to participate in what Barber (1984) calls "strong democracy."

Community-Based Research as Pedagogy: The Drawbacks

Education has long been an important aim of community-based participatory research. Usually, however, that refers to the goal of using the research process as a means of popular education for empowerment of the poor and disenfranchised rather than to how CBR might be an effective

---

Students' Lives Change Through CBR Experiences

"The research project that I undertook in my Social Movements course as a sophomore at Georgetown helped radically change the direction of my college academics, my life on campus and my future career. I chose Social Movements as a last-minute elective because of my interests in social justice and political change. The class explored a variety of social movements. This was my first experience participating in a class that included a service learning component. I was delighted to get off campus and be able to enter the strange and wonderful world of the peace movement. The research that I did with the Women's Peace party so inspired me that I added sociology as one of my majors, started a peace and justice group at Georgetown, and chose a job with a peace movement organization after graduation. Now, I work for an environmental public interest group in Washington State and am attending a graduate program on community and the environment, to pursue a career as an environmental justice advocate."

Amber W. GU '99

---

teaching strategy for undergraduate and graduate education. As we have demonstrated, CBR has much to recommend it as a pedagogy in higher education as well. At the same time, there are drawbacks. One is suggested by the focus of this chapter, which has been the benefits of community-based research not for communities but for students (and, to a lesser extent, for faculty members and institutions). Some recent critics have taken academics to task for failing to consider the impact of service-learning program on communities, even as much lip-service is given to the importance of mutuality and reciprocity between academy and community in the design of service-learning programs and activities. They also suggest that much service-learning neither contributes to solving real community problems nor challenges negative stereotypes of communities as needy and lacking in resources (Ward and Wolf-Wendel, 2000; Benson and Harkavy, 1996). Although CBR is better able to dodge those particular criticisms—as it is, at least in principle, community driven and collaborative—that does not mean that it always brings benefit to the community. Students, especially undergraduates, are simply more likely than academic or other professional researchers to be irresponsible, insufficiently trained, uncommitted, insensitive, incompetent, unavailable, and subject to the constraints of an academic schedule. Instructors with good intentions may end up paying more attention to student learning than to the quality and usefulness of the research for the community, and those with insufficient training, experience, or sensitivity themselves may end up taking on research projects for which neither they nor their students are equipped. This circumstance can bring harm to communities and undermine community-academy relations. In the next chapter, we outline many strategies that instructors might use to enhance CBR's pedagogical value for students as they also ensure its benefit for the community. However, in the end, the community's needs must always take precedence. And that means that some (perhaps many) projects simply are not suitable for some—or any—students.

Another drawback is that CBR requires a great deal of commitment and effort on the part of the professor and the students—far more, as a rule, than conventional kinds of teaching and learning. It also requires a willingness on the part of instructors to tolerate higher levels of uncertainty and "messiness" than most kinds of teaching, even other forms of service-learning. CBR is particularly challenging for instructors who bear heavy teaching loads, whose students are beginning level (for example, community colleges and beginning undergraduates), who are used to highly structured courses and syllabi, and who are uncomfortable venturing outside the domain of their own disciplines and knowledge bases.

Political considerations come into play as well; CBR carries potential career costs for the faculty member and subtle hurdles for graduate students who eschew conventional thesis research projects for community-based ones, which may be considered lacking in rigor or tainted by their goals of social change and social justice.

Despite its distinctive challenges, instructors who are drawn to community-based teaching and learning, teaching approaches that further the goals of social justice and social change, and educating students for lives of meaningful and active citizenship would do well to consider community-based research as a teaching strategy. In the next chapter, we detail many of the nuts and bolts of this kind of teaching.

Summary

Community-based research, when used as a teaching strategy, is an exceptionally effective form of service-learning that is appropriate for a variety of disciplines and curricular levels. With its emphasis on the principles of collaboration, demystification of knowledge, and social change, CBR fits especially well with the aims of critical pedagogies. These same principles make CBR more effective than many forms of more conventional charity-oriented service-learning as a means to prepare students for active citizenship. Despite some distinctive drawbacks and challenges, CBR offers much to academics who are drawn to community-based teaching and learning and are committed to education for the purpose of social justice and social change.

7

TEACHING COMMUNITY-BASED RESEARCH

THE CHALLENGES

WHEN CBR IS DONE AS A FORM of service-learning—that is, with students as researchers—it brings together teaching, research, and service in exciting and promising ways. However, the challenges to professors are substantial. In addition to ensuring that the needs of the community are met, the instructor's major concern must be that the CBR experience provides students valuable learning within and, typically, in accordance with the curricular aims of the course, major, or program. These challenges provide the guiding question for this chapter: How might faculty members go about structuring the CBR experience to ensure its viability, pedagogical integrity, and benefits to the students, as well as to the community?

Finding a Disciplinary Connection

As with other forms of service-learning, CBR is inherently interdisciplinary and enriches learning in a variety of disciplines by means of its contributions to students' overall personal and social development. Because CBR has a particular kind of focus—systematic inquiry, with the aim of solving an identified problem or providing specific, needed information—it also has the potential to enhance academic learning in substantial ways. Often, CBR involves at least some research using secondary sources—that is, finding out what is already known about a topic by studying the relevant scholarly writing, research reports, or databases. Such research may provide important background information, as when students preparing to survey the homeless first read about factors that cause homelessness or use existing data to describe the extent of homelessness in their own county. Occasionally, such secondary data are all that the community partner needs. This was the case when students at Mars Hill College (North Carolina) took on a project with HelpMate, a local agency that assists and advocates for abused women. The research consisted of examining national abuse statements, assessing how the data are collected, and then comparing them with data from the local area. More typically, CBR projects require that students work with community members and their instructors to design and carry out some sort of collection of data in the community. In this respect, CBR serves as a powerful teaching strategy in any course whose pedagogical aims include familiarizing students with the research methods and data collection instruments common to the disciplinary area.

Although courses in virtually any discipline might benefit from incorporating CBR into the syllabus, community-based research seems to be found most often in the social and behavioral sciences and in human service fields (social work, education). This may be because these fields share substantive concerns and methodological approaches that most typically fit with the community's social change agenda. For students who are studying topics such as poverty, public health, early childhood education, urban politics, immigration policies, community development, family violence, illiteracy, or environmental racism, the community offers a rich arena for developing and applying their research skills in a meaningful way. Here, again, CBR can also be a highly effective teaching strategy in courses whose main focus is research methods—social research, experimental psychology, and evaluation methods—as well as courses specifically in participatory action research, community organizing, policy, or social change.

The ways that CBR can contribute to academic learning in other disciplines are sometimes less obvious, but the possibilities are numerous. Research in the sciences—biology, physics, chemistry, and so on—can be brought to bear on a wide range of problems related to environmental quality. Such research might be done for a local agency responsible for protecting environmental quality or on behalf of groups that suffer from the consequences of pollution or natural resource depletion but lack influence on decision making about matters like enforcement of regulations, landfill sites, zoning, and land development. Students have also undertaken science-related CBR projects in educational settings, such as developing and implementing research-based lesson plans for local elementary and high school students.

Courses in the humanities and fine arts can be substantially enhanced by community-based research. Historical research for a community might have as its purpose historic preservation, entitlement claims, or public education, including efforts to challenge prevailing interpretations of historical events. Students who conduct research on the history of a neighborhood, an organization, an industry, or a heretofore neglected group have a chance to develop skills in methods of historical inquiry, such as archival research, oral interviews, photo and personal picture collection research, and site evaluation. Finally, CBR is finding its way into professional graduate programs, including schools of medicine, law, and public health. Here too, CBR gives students the chance to apply specific classroom-based learning in real-world settings that advance teaching and learning goals.

Another reason for the versatility of CBR as a teaching strategy is that projects often employ rather unconventional methods of data collection. As was discussed in Chapters Four and Five, multimethod projects are common as well. This is because CBR is premised on the assumption that "both issues and ways of working should flow from those involved and their context" (Hall, 1992, p. 20), and research methods must recognize the value and legitimacy of experiential knowledge of the research participants—a goal that may be achieved more effectively with less conventional methods. Methodological orthodoxies are far less important here than using methods that are sensitive to the special characteristics of the people and situations being studied. Although some conventional data collection techniques—survey questionnaires, for example—are often used, they are typically joined by any of a number of qualitative and humanistic data collection approaches. These sources of data might include not just unstructured interviews, focus groups, and observation, but also community meetings, video documentaries, legislative records, shared testimonies, public art, and a wide range of others. This variety in methodological approaches is often especially appealing to students and also an effective teaching strategy for professors who want students to acquire experience with a variety of research methods and approaches.

Although they connect well with discipline-based academic content, CBR projects seldom end up being rigidly discipline specific. Rather, students often find they bring and apply many different kinds of knowledge from other courses and disciplines to their work. The students who undertook a needs assessment of the local Latino population, described in the opening of Chapter Six, are a good example of such interdisciplinary learning. They strengthened their Spanish language skills and learned about Central American dialects when they translated the questionnaire; acquired familiarity with immigration law as they did background research and

CBR and Academic Learning

CBR can contribute in myriad ways to the specific academic content or learning objectives of courses in many different disciplines:

- A psychology graduate student worked with a local school to administer diagnostic tests to preschoolers with different kinds of disabilities. She gained substantial understanding of such tests and greater comfort in administering and interpreting them, as well as making referrals based on those interpretations.
- Architecture students joined forces with a local community development corporation to conduct sidewalk surveys, which involved assessing the structural integrity of houses in the neighborhood from the outside by reading indicators, thus ascertaining how difficult and costly it would be to rehabilitate each house.
- At the request of the local human services coalition, students in a seminar class in economics developed a county self-sufficiency standard: a measure of the minimum income needed for demographically varying families to maintain an adequate quality of life in the county. This required extensive research on the cost of living in the county, measures of standard of living, and a host of other social and economic indicators.
- Students in a state and local government class learned about the legislative process by completing a project for a local nonprofit involving research to produce a binder of information about all the pending legislation pertinent to the work of the agency: summaries of each bill, the status of each, and biographical and contact information about the sponsors and cosponsors.
- Students in an interdisciplinary class at Princeton University, "Science, Technology and Public Policy," worked with the New Jersey Environmental Federation to study reductions in pollution and other benefits from shutting down local generator incinerators. They also researched current air emissions and recommended ways to increase composting, recycling, and source reduction as alternatives to incineration. Another group of students assisted the New Jersey Conservation Foundation on a report that summarized the scientific literature on deer population management and became the basis of the foundation's deer management plan.
- Students in a history class at the University of Louisville engaged in archival research with the local historical society, focusing on identifying individuals, building, and geographical sites of importance to the history of African Americans in the Louisville metropolitan area.
- At Emory and Henry College, students in molecular biology worked with local high school teachers to design experiments to teach molecular biology concepts to high school students. Students also work as tutors in those classes, helping students to conduct and understand the experiments.

gained some sensitivity to the fears and insecurities of the Latino community; developed new insights about politics and policy as they presented their findings and recommendations to groups such as the county commissioners; and acquired a deeper understanding about cultural values and worldviews very different from their own.

Faculty members and students who have done community-based research report similar kinds of wide-ranging skills and knowledge outcomes such that much of what students learn falls outside the traditional bounds of the course and discipline. Students who do site analysis with a neighborhood group aiming to build a playground are likely to acquire, in addition to practice applying their environmental science research skills, a better understanding of local politics, urban planning, land use, group dynamics, and child development. Virtually every CBR project helps students develop a new understanding of the relationship between knowledge and power, the relevance of systematic inquiry to social action, and the potential for experts in their own field, as well as ordinary people, to use what they know to make meaningful contributions to their surrounding communities and societies.

Building Community-Based Research into the Curriculum

The faculty member who is looking to incorporate CBR into teaching is faced with many different models for doing so, as it can be integrated into the curriculum in a number of ways. Some academics involve students in their own CBR on a noncredit basis, as graduate research assistants, work-study employees, or interested volunteers. However, for most students, CBR is credit bearing and is done in connection with a course, as an independent study or internship, or to meet the requirement of a thesis at the undergraduate or graduate level. When it is part of a practicum course, often one or more group CBR projects are the centerpiece of the course. For example, a graduate education seminar at the University of Denver, "Community-Based Research in Urban Settings," was organized around a quarter-long project for which students worked with three local extended-service schools to assess young people's views of the adequacy of their before- and after-school programs. CBR can be especially effective in capstone courses. At Hood College, the senior seminar in environmental studies is designed around a community-based project to which students apply a variety of skills and knowledge related to environmental analysis. A recent project involved a site analysis of a large piece of land that had been designated by the local Bureau of Parks and Recreation as a future park.

Sometimes "community based" becomes "community immersed" as students may live for a semester within the community where they are doing research. An example is a course offered by Texas A&M University in which students and their instructor live with families in *colonias* along the Texas-Mexico border as they work with community members to learn about the problems endured by residents of that area and how they deal with and respond to them. In this case, the knowledge gained in the research becomes the content of the course. A course on social movements at Georgetown University requires that each student work with a local advocacy organization in Washington, D.C., on a research project having to do with the work of the organization. In this way, students understand social movements from the inside out rather than simply as they are described and analyzed in texts and class lectures.

Dedicating most or all of an entire course to community-based research is, in some ways, ideal (and having a two-semester course is even better). However, many faculty members do not have that sort of room in their curriculum and courses for CBR. Indeed, a common concern is that introducing community-based research—or any other sort of community-based learning—will require skipping some course material or otherwise compromising existing content and learning goals. Nonetheless, there are many ways to include CBR in existing courses in ways that supplement, rather than take over, the course syllabus. Instructors may include CBR on a smaller scale, as a fourth-credit option or as a required or optional assignment within a course. For example, introductory courses on research methods in the social sciences, which often require a small, independent research project, may offer students the option of making that project a community-based one. This is more viable at this level when the project is a fairly small and simply one—perhaps as a part of a larger project involving more advanced students—and when students work in small groups rather than alone. A drawback is that numerous small CBR projects within a large class may create a particularly heavy workload for the instructor.

Another curricular option is for students to take on CBR projects outside regular courses—as independent studies, in connection with other experiential learning (such as an internship), or as a project to meet requirements for a senior or graduate-level thesis. Many instructors have had students who begin CBR projects as part of a course and then choose to extend their work into subsequent semesters, perhaps on an independent basis or, in rarer cases, as a noncredit-bearing summer project. A graduate student in education at the University of Denver undertook a class-based survey research project with the South West Improvement

Council that explored the relationship between income and housing costs in the lower-income Westwood area of Denver. The following quarter, in a course on ethnography, she built on her housing study by conducting focus groups with residents of that same area, this time to explore in some rich detail their experiences with managing family life under trying economic circumstances.

Often students turn a volunteer or service-learning experience into a CBR project, or college officials make CBR a regular part of what are traditionally direct service programs. Both Middlesex County and the College of New Jersey offer students the opportunity to participate in CBR Corps. At the county college, four teams of students spend three hundred hours during the year engaged in direct service and research activities on behalf of their community partner. At the College of New Jersey, the corps focuses almost entirely on research on behalf of one or two community partners. Both corps are led by professors, and the students receive benefits from the federal AmeriCorps program (a stipend and scholarship) for their participation (Donohue and Paul, 2002). The challenge in all of these cases is to ensure that students do not become so overextended that it affects their performance in their regular classes, and that the community partner does not become too dependent on any one student, team, or corps to take care of all of its research needs.

Finally, graduate students sometimes find an intellectual home in community-based research and undertake a project for a master's or doctoral thesis. This too can be a challenge, especially at institutions where there is little support for community-based learning and in disciplines that are still firmly wedded to conventional academic research. Satisfying the demands of a picky and conservative dissertation committee along with the research needs of a community may prove to be too large a burden for students struggling to finish their advanced degrees.

What seem to be most important with regard to building CBR into courses, curricula, and other campus programs are flexibility and creativity. Incorporating community-based research as a learning option requires enthusiastic instructors who help students find ways to do it within the framework of their institution's curricular and credit arrangements—something that seems to be true of effective service-learning programs in general. This is easier at institutions where there is administrative support for such efforts.

Another issue is whether CBR should be required in a course or program. Many faculty have it as an option, which is also a way to limit the number of students involved in CBR, an important consideration given the extra work they require of instructors and students. Other considerations influence this decision as well. Sometimes CBR is required more readily in fields where the fit of CBR with program goals is clear and more or less assumed—social work or sociology, for instance. In other cases, instructors are comfortable requiring CBR only when it assumes a relatively nonpolitical nature. For example, an education professor did not hesitate to require that students become involved in a project where they tested low-income preschoolers for early diagnosis of learning problems—a rich opportunity to train students to administer the instrument and interpret results. A project such as one where students work with a local minority parents' group to gather and analyze data to uncover differential treatment of children of color in the schools, however, is potentially more controversial and challenging to the status quo—hence, it may be one that is less likely to be required. The fear, it seems, is complaints from students who may dislike having to commit to an action agenda with which they are not politically aligned or even interested. Such a concern is far from universal, however, and is likely to be absent in disciplines (social work is one) that adopt a clear and deliberate social justice agenda.

Ensuring Student Readiness

How do we ensure that students are ready to take on a community-based research project in terms of both their own potential to benefit from the experience *and* their capacity to work well with community members and to produce results that are useful to the community? Three general requirements seem germane to doing CBR:

- Familiarity with and sensitivity to the community
- Understanding of the principles of community-based research
- Relevant research skills and substantive knowledge pertaining to the research problem at hand

The last items, research skills and substantive knowledge, are not as clearly prerequisites to doing CBR and instead might be acquired in the course of carrying out the CBR project. This is, after all, a form of active learning. The first two, however, are prerequisites to undertaking research with the community. Indeed, professors would be ill advised to allow students at any level to begin working with a community group on a CBR project if those students know nothing about the community, are insensitive to its problems and members, and know nothing about the principles that guide community-based research. For that reason, we discuss these first.

Familiarity with and Sensitivity to the Community

A crucial area of student readiness for CBR has to do with knowledge about and sensitivity to the community with which they will be working. One of the challenges of all types of community-based learning—and one of its major strengths—is that students must learn about and work with people and within social worlds that are dramatically different from their own. This is especially true for college students who are affluent, white, and from privileged backgrounds. This experience is important in CBR not only because it contributes to student learning, but also because it is critical to the quality of the project in many ways. To ensure validity, every aspect of the research, from development of the research design to the interpretation of results, requires the researcher's capacity to assume the perspective of community members, which requires familiarity with their language, meanings, and worldviews. This is particularly true for research that is social science related—where community members are the research participants—but it is similarly important for other kinds of projects that require community involvement in the planning, implementation, analysis, and presentation stages of the work. Gaining acceptance in the community is usually crucial to a successful project and requires that students establish a rapport with at least some members of the community. Finally, the goals of CBR can be undermined in many ways if students offend community members out of ignorance or naiveté.

The challenge is to see to it that students have some familiarity with and sensitivity to the community they will work with as they begin the CBR project. A number of strategies help ensure student readiness in this area. One minimally effective one is to require that students have completed certain course work (such as a course on ethnicity) before they do CBR. Better still, but not feasible at many institutions, is a requirement that students have some service-learning or volunteer experience before taking on community-based research. Another way to help ensure familiarity and sensitivity is to build in some community experience at the beginning of the CBR project. This can be informal, where students spend time in the community observing, volunteering, or simply "hanging out" and talking to people. Somewhat more formal methods can work as well. One instructor arranged with a community member (part of a group with which he had an ongoing relationship) to give a sensitivity workshop at the beginning of the project, where students spent a few hours learning about the community—its history, strengths, and problems—and also participated in some exercises that brought them into contact with community members. Students may find it helpful to spend some time at the agency or organization talking to employees and volunteers, perusing written information and facilities, and otherwise learning as much as they can about what the organization does and whom it serves and how.

A somewhat more structured way to acquaint student researchers and community members with each other early on is by means of focus groups. As Lynch (1993) points out, focus groups can serve a number of purposes in the early stage of CBR projects. In one study, students who planned a survey of low-income mothers about their child care needs first met with a small group of women who were enrolled in a program to provide transitional assistance to women leaving welfare rolls. Over pizza and soda in a small room at the Department of Social Services (the agency that initiated the study), the students learned a great deal about the kinds of child care problems the women faced. They also asked for—and heard—ideas about how best to approach women in the study group and how to word questions on the questionnaire in ways that made sense and also began to identify women who might be interested in participating in the study. Just as important, the students (all women) developed a more sympathetic understanding of the difficulties of struggling single mothers and came to realize that they had much in common with the young mothers—enough to allow comfortable interaction despite their different social locations. Finally, the focus group meeting reaffirmed for students the importance of their study as a means of drawing attention to the difficulties facing young mothers under the punitive terms of welfare reform.

Understanding Community-Based Research

Whether or not the central focus of the course is CBR (or participatory action research or some other form of action-oriented research), most instructors assign readings and devote some class time to seeing that students are acquainted with the basic principles—and perhaps also some of the rich history and different forms—of this kind of research. This is important even for students with prior research training. The leap from traditional research to action-oriented, participatory research is an enormous one, and it may take a while for students to grasp, and even to feel comfortable with, the action orientation, flexibility, and participatory nature of CBR as compared to the academic research that they have come to take for granted. This is especially true when their previous research training assumed uncritical acceptance of conventional approaches. (See McNicoll, 1999, for a useful discussion of some of these issues.)

Perhaps the easiest way to introduce students to the principles and process of CBR is by way of well-chosen assigned readings (see Exhibit 7.1).

Exhibit 7.1. Selected Readings for Students on Community-Based Research.

BOOKS AND COLLECTIONS

Bonacich, E., and Stoecker, R. (eds.). *American Sociologist*, 1992, *23*, and 1993, *24*.

De Koning, K., and Martin, M. (eds.). *Participatory Research in Health: Issues and Experiences*. London: Zed Books, 1996.

Fals-Borda, O., and Rahman, M. A. (eds.). *Action and Knowledge: Breaking the Monopoly with Participatory Action Research*. New York: Apex Press, 1991.

Freire, P. *Pedagogy of the Oppressed*. (M. Bergman Ramos, trans.). New York: Continuum, 1970.

Greenwood, D., and Levin, M. *Introduction to Action Research: Social Research for Social Change*. Thousand Oaks, Calif.: Sage, 1998.

Maguire, P. *Doing Participatory Research: A Feminist Approach*. Amherst: University of Massachusetts, 1987.

Murphy, Danny, Scammell, M., and Sclove, R. (eds.). *Doing Community Based Research: A Reader*. Amherst, Mass.: Loka Institute, 1997.

Nyden, P., Figert, A., Shibley, M., and Burrows, D. *Building Community: Social Science in Action*. Thousand Oaks, Calif.: Pine Forge, 1997.

Park, P., Brydon-Miller, M., Hall, B., and Jackson, T. (eds.). *Voices of Change: Participatory Research in the United States and Canada*. Westport, Conn.: Bergin and Garvey.

Stringer, E. *Action Research: A Handbook for Practitioners*. Thousand Oaks, Calif.: Corwin, 1999.

Williams, L. (ed.). *An Annotated Bibliography for Participatory and Collaborative Field Research Methods*. Community Partnership Center, University of Tennessee, 1996.

ARTICLES

Couto, R. "Participatory Research Methodology and Critique." *Clinical Sociological Review*, 1987, *5*, 83–90.

Hall, B. "From Margins to Center? The Development and Purpose of Participatory Research." *American Sociologist*, 1992, *23*, 15–28.

Reardon, K. J., Kreiswirth, B., and Forester, J. "Participatory Action Research from the Inside: Community Development Practice in East St. Louis." *American Sociologist*, 1993, *24*, 69–91.

Reinharz, S. "Feminist Action Research." In S. Reinharz (ed.), *Feminist Methods in Social Research*. New York: Oxford University Press, 1992.

Sarri, R. C., and Sarry, C. M. "Organizational and Community Change Through Participatory Action Research." *Administration in Social Work,* 1992, *16,* 99–122.

Small, S. "Action-Oriented Research: Models and Methods." *Journal of Marriage and the Family,* 1995, *57,* 941–956.

Spalter-Roth, R., and Hartmann, H. "Small Happiness: The Feminist Struggle to Integrate Social Research with Social Activism." In S. Hesse-Biber, C. Gilmartin, and R. Lydenberg (eds.), *Feminist Approaches to Theory and Methodology.* New York: Oxford University Press, 1999.

Stoecker, R. "Making Connections: Community Organizing, Empowerment Planning, and Participatory Research in Participatory Evaluation." *Sociological Practice,* 1999, *1,* 209–232.

Reading about CBR as they begin working on their research projects can be especially valuable, as students are able to start making connections between the principles and the practices of CBR and more specifically think of ways to incorporate the principles of CBR into their projects to best advantage. Some instructors have developed questions that prompt students to make such connections in class discussions or as they write in their own journals—for example:

- In what ways does community-based research or participatory action research draw on long-standing methodological principles and practices in this discipline? In what ways does it diverge from the way research is typically done?

- In what respects is your research study helping you to understand the concept of "friendly outsider"?

- What are some ways that your project might incorporate some principles of feminist participatory action research?

- What do you see as the relationship between the project that you are taking on and the achievement of social justice?

- What are strategies that we might use to involve community members in each stage of this research process—in other words, to democratize the research?

- How do you see this project as contributing to some of the short- or long-range goals of this community group?

- In light of what you have read, what are some particular problems that you might anticipate in connection with your community-based research?

- What are some of your own assumptions, preconceptions, and experiences—about research, about the community, about higher education—that have been challenged by what you have read about CBR? Which of those assumptions and preconceptions present the greatest challenge to you as you take on this work?

Students can learn about CBR in other ways as well. One instructor has more advanced undergraduates who have completed CBR projects talk to her basic research methods class about the work they did. This both acquaints the lower-level students with CBR and gets them excited about doing it. Some instructors have students read reports written by students who have already taken the course. An important source of information and understanding is community partners, who, as Chapters Two and Three suggest, have much to teach students about the community and about doing CBR, and perhaps can share their experiences working with students on other CBR projects.

No matter what the strategy, the aim is to help students appreciate certain important features of CBR—that it relies on collaboration with community members and requires new ways of thinking about knowledge and knowledge creation, and that the purpose of the research is a meaningful one: to contribute to positive social change in the community. Students at every level who are sensitive to and familiar with the community they will be working with, and who know something about the purpose and process of community-based research, are far along toward being ready to undertake a CBR project.

Research Skills and Substantive Knowledge

What kinds of knowledge and skills should students have before undertaking CBR? Some instructors have worked with lower-level students—such as first- and second-year undergraduates or beginning graduate students—who have successfully completed CBR projects. Others argue that CBR is more appropriate for upper-level undergraduate or graduate students far along in their programs, and it does seem to be more common that students do CBR at the culmination of a program in which they have completed a considerable amount of relevant course work, including one or more courses in research methods in the discipline. In either case, what is most important is that instructors consider carefully the fit of the expectations of the community, students' abilities and experiences (as well as their own), and the particular demands of the project.

Community expectations must be considered, and sometimes explicitly addressed, in making decisions about CBR projects and student readiness.

Research *With* Versus Research *On*

Helping students understand and appreciate the similarities and differences between CBR and conventional research approaches can be a real challenge for instructors. At Hood College, a group of five students in an advanced-level social science research practicum had some familiarity with action research. Nonetheless, the first draft of an interview schedule for incarcerated women, aimed at finding out their assessment of substance-related programs in the community, included a series of questions that a more mainstream study—that is, *of* rather than *with* these women—would likely include: What crimes have you committed? How many times have you been here? How often did you use drugs, and what kind? Gentle prodding from the instructor shifted the focus of the questions away from the women themselves to their knowledge and opinions about drug-related services. But the real depth of the difference didn't emerge until the students were standing in a room at the detention center, facing a dozen indifferent—or in some cases, openly hostile—women, to explain the purpose of their study. "We need *your* help," the students implored. "We can't do this study without you. You are the ones best able to tell us what programs and services are out there, which ones are useful and which aren't, what you would like to see in the way of programs and services for women in your situation." There was a palpable change in the atmosphere in that small room when a middle-aged African American woman, whose exasperation had been written all over her face, broke into a half-smile and said, "Gee, no one has ever asked us about that stuff before." Nothing the instructor could ever say, nor the students ever read, would make more clear the distinctive nature of community-based research.

When students have major responsibility for doing the research, which is often the case, the expectations of the community about both the quality and the scope of the project must be a bit lower than when the faculty member is the primary researcher and the students are working as assistants on the project. Similarly, community members must be made aware of other limitations. How much time are students expected to devote to this project? Are the students experienced or novice researchers? How many students will be working on the project? What kinds of other resource limitations will have a bearing on the scope of the project? All of these parameters need to be clarified at the beginning of the project, either as it is being developed and defined or, in some cases, before the agreement is even made to pursue the collaborative arrangement. In fact, the planning stages of a CBR project provide a rich learning opportunity for students, as they must work with community members to develop a plan that is realistic in terms of time, money, and the capabilities of people on both the campus and community sides of the partnership.

One problem that occasionally arises is that community members are willing to work with students but actually assume that it is the faculty members' work and skills for which they are "contracting." Ideally, community members appreciate the students' willingness to work on the project and recognize the skills and enthusiasm they bring, but they also realize that they are students and that the research is a learning process for them. This sets the stage for the best kind of collaboration: where community members and students see themselves as both teachers and learners and the contributions of everyone are acknowledged and appreciated.

This also brings in the wider problem regarding community expectations of research—a problem that may arise in any form of applied research when the clients have an unrealistic sense of what research can produce and what researchers can do. This should normally be less of a problem in CBR, where community members (as opposed to more conventional clients) are more closely involved in the design and implementation of the research itself and thus have or acquire a more realistic sense of what research entails. However, CBR also may exacerbate the problem of inflated expectations because of the very different time frames within which community members and students are working and because community partners may have little or no training or experience in research. A common example has to do with sample size, especially in projects involving survey research of some kind. People who have little experience with social research often mistakenly believe that the size of a sample—the bigger, the better—is the best measure of its quality and, hence, of the validity of research results.

When three students at Hood College collaborated with the local Coalition for the Homeless to survey the homeless population of Frederick, Maryland, the students were able to complete only about fifty interviews over the course of the project, fewer than expected as a result of both time constraints and problems gaining access to shelters. Because the students were careful to make their sample representative of different characteristics of the homeless, had an interview schedule carefully designed to get at issues of importance to the coalition, and were not attempting to make statistical inferences about the homeless population, the sample was in fact adequate for their purposes. Nevertheless, a few community members expressed concern and dismay; they thought that the number of completed interviews was too small to make the study of much value.

If the CBR project ends up being significantly beyond the abilities of the students working on it, the result may be either letting down the community in a major way or forcing the instructor to pick up the slack and complete much of the work on her or his own. In one instance of this, two graduate students at the University of Denver undertook an evaluation of a community health initiative that informed women about breast screening services offered by a local health clinic. Although the project proceeded smoothly in its early stages, when it came time to analyze and write up results, the students proved to be insufficiently adept at analyzing qualitative data and unable to produce a report that was sufficiently coherent and comprehensive. As a result the report was two months late and was written only with considerable work by the professor.

In the end, the report was well received and the relationship between the university and the community partner intact, largely because the relationship was a strong one to begin with and because the instructor kept the community partner informed about the status of the project and the students' progress throughout. The professor learned not to assume that students who are skilled at gathering qualitative data are equally capable of analyzing and reporting it. Others have had experience with students who have an unrealistic sense of their own abilities and end up taking on projects for which they are ill equipped. This would seem to be a more common problem for those who teach undergraduates at large colleges and universities, where professors are less likely to be familiar with the abilities of their individual students.

How much research training should students have before doing CBR? Certainly, working with more advanced students increases options, decreases the instructor's work, and enhances confidence in the usefulness of results for the community. At the undergraduate level, this might mean that CBR, especially substantial projects, is reserved for junior- and senior-level students who have advanced training in the discipline, including its research methodology. When CBR is incorporated in a lower-level course, where some or all students have not had pertinent training in research, it may be an option available only to students who have completed a research methods course or have demonstrated a certain level of mastery of course material. One instructor allows the option of working on a CBR project only to students who have done at least B-level work through the first few weeks of the semester. Another option is to make sure that the kinds of research topics taken on by untrained students do not require much in the way of research and other skills, perhaps by having them work with the instructor or alongside graduate or upper-level undergraduate students. Of course, if the main purpose of the course is for students to acquire those skills, then the CBR project can be an ideal way to motivate students to learn how to do research. However, this sort of learning by doing requires both a fairly simple research project and close supervision by the faculty member to ensure that the final product is of high quality and useful to the community.

Most research projects require that researchers, in addition to having some research skills, also have some relevant substantive knowledge related to the research question. More often than not, acquiring this background information is part of the research itself and requires that students consult community members, outside experts, public records, and scholarly books and journals. Sometimes, however, CBR projects require that researchers bring to the project particular substantive knowledge or expertise. This might be the case where a rather high level of specialized knowledge or expertise is required—for example, projects where fluency in Spanish is essential—or when the time frame for the project is such that students would not have the time to acquire the necessary information.

Finally, CBR also requires that students be exceptionally reliable, resourceful, and mature in their interactions with the community and in their work on the project. Many instructors find it useful to talk candidly with students at the beginning of the project about the distinctive responsibilities it entails—for example:

- The obligation to the community, not just the professor
- The importance of meeting goals and deadlines
- The need for ongoing, open, and honest communication among everyone on the research team
- The fact that CBR will require more time and work than most of their other courses

Also worth mentioning are the many rich rewards they can expect to reap from the experience of doing CBR.

Generally, care must be taken to match project requirements with student abilities and resources. At the same time, students' potential for success should not be underestimated. After all, a major goal is for students to learn, and CBR projects that stretch them are more valuable pedagogically than those that do not require much beyond what they already know and can do. Indeed, many of us have found that students rise to the challenge of CBR and surprise us with their resourcefulness and skills. Stories about average students doing far above-average work on CBR projects and courses abound. This is because the experience of doing CBR, even for the student who starts out with a minimal connection to the project and to learning generally, often becomes deeply engaging as students come to see themselves as valued collaborators with their community partners. As a result of this motivation and engagement, students put extra time and effort into their CBR work. They will delve into the literature about constructing good questionnaires so as to do an exceptionally careful job when they know that community members (and not just the professor) will be looking at the result and that the information the questionnaire produces is of importance to the community. They expend unusual amounts of time and effort writing and revising a research report when they know it will be read not only by their community partners, but ultimately by decision makers at the city and county levels.

Instructors can help cultivate such motivation and engagement on the part of students in a number of ways:

- Making CBR an option rather than a requirement
- Letting students have some choice about the projects they will work on
- Being available as much as possible, by e-mail and telephone when not in person, to provide guidance and support
- Giving the students sufficient autonomy to help them develop a sense of competency, responsibility, and ownership of the project
- Making resources of all kinds—supplies, space, computer access, reading material, and so on—readily available
- Facilitating lots of collaboration, among students (when the project is a group one) and between students and community partners

Structuring the Community-Based Research Experience

Community-based research, like virtually all other active-learning pedagogies, requires that instructors venture outside the comfort zone of more conventional teaching, where they have the luxury of assuming a great deal of control over what is taught, how it is taught, and how learning is assessed. CBR is by nature a messy and emergent learning experience that is far less subject to instructor control and whose learning outcomes are even less predictable than with conventional teaching. In fact, CBR is even less subject to instructor control, in some respects, than other forms of community-based learning, because the progress and outcomes of each project are also subject to the whims and serendipity to which all research is vulnerable. All of this makes structuring the CBR experience, especially when it is a course-based project, a challenge.

As more and more college professors use CBR in their teaching, we have learned some specific strategies for making the experience more rewarding for everyone. Here, we provide some answers to the nuts-and-bolts challenges of doing CBR with students by providing suggestions for scheduling and dealing with time constraints; managing the project;

troubleshooting problem projects; evaluating students; and producing, presenting, and implementing results.

Scheduling and Time Constraints

Scheduling and time problems are common with CBR, as the students' (and instructor's) time constraints are often very different from those of community members and may make it hard to get the research done in a timely way. Students have many other commitments, including family and work responsibilities, and if they are doing CBR as part of a full course load, they are not available for more than a handful of hours each week— something that community members may not fully understanding or appreciate. Similarly, although community partners may have schedules that are slightly more flexible, they also have myriad responsibilities and demands on their time, so that the CBR project may have a lower priority than the students and professor might assume.

The idiosyncrasies of the academic calendar pose particular challenges for student and faculty involvement in CBR. A common difficulty is planning and completing a project within one semester, the typical time frame for a credit-bearing course or independent study. One obvious solution to this problem is to do CBR over two semesters or more. Another is to take care to limit the scope of the project to make it manageable within a short time period. Sometimes this means limiting the other requirements connected with a course in which students are doing CBR—assigned readings and so on—so that students are not overwhelmed by the workload. Another is to have students in a course work for one semester on part of what might be a larger ongoing project; a drawback of this alternative is that students will not have the advantage of seeing a project through from beginning to end. Some of these scheduling problem are more manageable when CBR is done as independent or thesis work.

Midterm breaks and special campus events, such as exam week and parents' weekend, also cut into students' availability to work on their research projects. Community members may not be very sympathetic toward students who are on midterm break and cannot attend an important monthly meeting of the community center board, are never available in the afternoon because of a work schedule, or otherwise do not seem to give the CBR project the same high priority in their lives as it might have for the community members. One way to avoid tension is by clarifying everyone's expectations and schedule constraints early in the project. Also, when students work in groups, some of these time and scheduling difficulties can be avoided because students pick up the slack for one another.

For example, work on a project does not have to come to a complete halt over winter break if one or two students live locally or will be returning early to campus and can attend an important meeting or continue conducting interviews during that time. Students have different class and work schedules, and if a group is working well, the members will be flexible and willing to fill in for one another as schedules demand.

CBR poses other time and scheduling challenges as well. Most instructors agree that regular meetings with students, in groups or individually, are essential. In the case of group projects, and because students' schedules vary widely, having and using a designated weekly or biweekly class meeting seems to work best. These meetings are important even though students are meeting and working, alone and together, outside class as well. The weekly meeting with the instructor may be used to discuss readings, work on the research itself, deal with problems, visit people and places in the community, and keep abreast of how the project is proceeding. Regular meetings with students are important for less obvious reasons too. They provide a measure of social control, which is essential for students who are less self-disciplined and unlikely to work hard if they do not think anyone is aware of what they are doing (or not doing). They also help the instructor stay on top of the research projects and flag problems early on so as to intervene and fix them. And in the case of group projects, they make it easier to assess the relative contributions of individual students to each project, which is necessary for grading. As the project progresses, the class time increasingly may belong to students to use for their work on the project, with the instructor available for help as needed. Some of us have found, though, that regular meetings, even when they are perfunctory, need to be held throughout the project.

CBR the Morning After

In referring to the incompatibility of academic and real-life schedules, one of our CBR colleagues notes with some humor that "there is no spring break in the real world." There also are no senior pub crawls. This event turned out to be the nemesis of one professor who inadvertently scheduled the annual Community Research Luncheon the day after the late-night, long-standing senior tradition at her small liberal arts college. The senior student presenters all made it to the luncheon and managed to contribute to their groups' presentations about their year-long CBR projects. But a couple of the more enthusiastic partyers were in less than top form and apologetically slipped out and back to their dormitory beds as soon as their presentations were finished. "There must be something going around" is how the professor awkwardly explained the students' sudden departure to curious community partners who were in attendance.

Regular meetings with community partners are essential as well. Some maintain that weekly meetings are a must, but others have found that once every few weeks is sufficient as long as more regular contact is maintained by means of telephone calls or e-mail messages. How often the entire research team meets depends on a number of factors: the nature and stage of the project, the availability of community members, how accessible campus and community sites are to each other, and how involved the community wishes to be throughout, and at different stages of, the project. Many of us have found that frequent meetings of the research team are more important early in the project, as the research question and design are being developed, while community members are less frequently involved while the data are being collected and analyzed. When community members are involved in the data collection, regular contact becomes part of the research process. While some professors prefer to be in attendance at every meeting, others attend only when they think their input is particularly important and rely on students to report to them what went on.

Other suggestions about research team meetings and other aspects of communicating with the community partners can make the project run more smoothly:

- Meetings can be held at community or campus sites—ideally some at each.
- Students and community members, and not the professor, ought to share major responsibility for organizing and running the meetings.
- If students make a point of meeting prior to each meeting, they can (perhaps with the guidance of the instructor) develop a clear agenda on such matters as questions to ask and information to share—to allow for the efficient use of time.
- When funds are available, it is nice to provide food of some kind, particularly when the campus hosts the meeting (see Budgeting for CBR box).
- E-mail is increasingly an option and makes the entire communication process easier.

Managing the Project

One of the biggest challenges of teaching CBR is in managing the project on a day-to-day basis: assigning tasks, overseeing work, ensuring that deadlines are met, and so on. Decisions about how to organize the work depend on a variety of factors, including whether the project is course based, how many students are working on a project, the nature of the course, the number and characteristics of students, the scope and form of the projects, and the personal styles and preferences of individual faculty members and community partners.

DELEGATING THE WORK. One fundamental management strategy for a group project is to help students divide the labor. Students are more likely to do the work when they are clear on their assignment, and overall the project is more manageable and likely to be completed when distinct tasks are identified and assigned. At the same time, too rigid a division of tasks means that students will not learn about some important aspects of the research process. All the students, for example, should probably be involved in meetings with community partners, developing the research question or focus, designing the research, collecting the data, and analyzing and reporting results. But delegating distinct tasks within those categories makes sense.

In one four-student survey research project involving the homeless, for example, two students developed the sampling design, while the other two drafted a questionnaire, all of them consulting with the community partner and with the other two members of the group as they went along. Although all four students and two community members (formerly homeless) conducted interviews, they divided the sites—shelters and outdoor sites in the community—between the two groups. Two students assumed primary responsibility for entering, analyzing, and writing up the demographic

---

Budgeting for CBR

Instructors who are fortunate enough to have money for supplies and expenses connected with their CBR work will probably find themselves spending most of it on office supplies (tape recorders and tapes, wipe-off wall calendars, organizers, portable files, and the like), duplicating (all those questionnaires, coding sheets, field notes, and final reports to distribute), transportation expenses (for student travel to and from community sites), and . . . food! CBR means lots of meetings, most of them including some or many people from the community— and a tried and true way to lure busy parents and staff away from family or work responsibilities is to provide free food. Also, serving and sharing food, even if it is only doughnuts and coffee in the morning or pizza and soda for a late afternoon focus group, seems to create a certain kind of ambiance that inspires successful collaboration. Students like to be fed, too, and offering to pay for the pizza during a late night work session is a good way for a professor to gain goodwill and next year's CBR recruits. Finally, food is an essential component of those end-of-project celebrations and presentations.

data, while the other two compiled and wrote up the results from the open-ended questions. Although every group and individual was kept informed about all the work of the project throughout its duration, assigning clear responsibilities made it move more smoothly. Sometimes tasks are taken on more informally, so that a student who is especially well organized ends up being the one to arrange out-of-class meetings, while another—who, say, volunteers or lives in the community—will serve as liaison with the community partner.

Another reason to divide labor, and an argument in favor of group projects, is that some students work harder and are more capable and responsible than others. One instructor, in dividing students into teams to work on CBR projects, tries to make sure that there is at least one very strong student on each research team to help ensure a higher-quality product at the end—admittedly, a more feasible strategy at a small college where instructors are more likely to know all their students well. Stronger and more responsible students may help to "pick up" other students, as well, although this can backfire if lazier students come to depend on the harder-working ones to do the lion's share of the work.

In one case, a three-person team of beginning research students worked with a local safety committee on a small project designed to find out what young people knew and practiced in regard to bicycle safety. They decided on interviews at a mall and quickly learned that only one of them—who happened to be particularly unfocused and irresponsible, but also very personable—was successful at getting young people to stop and talk with her about bicycle safety. As it turned out, she completed most of the interviews, and the other two shared the work of analyzing, writing up, and sharing results. Although the weaker student admittedly learned less than the others about doing research by virtue of her very circumscribed responsibilities, this proved to be an effective way to use her particular abilities to ensure the success of the project.

ASSORTED MANAGEMENT STRATEGIES. Following are some bits of wisdom about managing and structuring community-based research projects with students that are gleaned from the experiences of many different instructors:

• Have an accessible, central place to allow for storing and exchanging materials and information such as copies of questionnaires, articles and books to share, and the like.
• Buy and use a large wipe-off wall calendar for each project.
• Have a journal that serves as the running record of details of each project. Students take turns writing in it at each meeting of the class or

the entire research team (including community members), and record important decisions, assignments, and other information. At each regular meeting about the project, start by having a student read or otherwise review the journal entry of the last meeting with the group. Individual journals can be used instead. The advantage of individual journals is that students may also use them to record their own thoughts, concerns, and personal reflections, and the instructor can use them as a source of information about student learning and about the contributions of individual students to the project for grading purposes. Individual journals work best when students are required or encouraged to write in them weekly and when the guidelines about what to write are fairly clear.

• Use e-mail, when possible, as an ongoing means of communication among members of the research team. This obviously works best if someone from the community group has access to the Internet, but it is very useful even if it is limited to students. Have each student create a group address that includes the instructor, and encourage all of them—even those who are not enthusiastic e-mail users—to check it at least once a day. Another effective means of communication is a course- or project-based Web site, such as provided for by programs like Blackboard.

• Set deadlines, but make them at least somewhat flexible. This increases the chances that the project will be done on time—a key consideration. Once students leave at the end of the semester (especially true for undergraduates), they are unlikely to work further to finish the final report. But even if the students more or less finish the project, if they are rushed at the end, any additional work necessary to bring the final product up to an acceptable level will have to be done by the professor, perhaps with help from community members. Students also appreciate deadlines, as they help them with self-discipline and to schedule their time and work more effectively. One way to accomplish this is by means of a work plan, as The Work Plan example illustrates.

• For group projects, keep the student research team fairly small. The ideal size of a research team for a one- or two-semester project seems to be three to five students, with an equal or smaller number of community representatives. More limited projects can be completed by teams of two or three, and a more elaborate and multifaceted project may require a team of six or more.

Troubleshooting Problem Projects

Community-based research projects are subject to a whole range of glitches, problems, and catastrophes. Usually these are surmountable, but sometimes they are not. Always the aim is to do whatever one can to come up

Using E-mail

E-mail can be a godsend for community-based researchers. It facilitates ongoing communication among hard-to-reach students, instructors, and community members, often at odd hours. Some examples of the kinds of e-mail messages that help move projects along or even get them started:

Dear Ms. B,

I am a doctoral student enrolled in Dr. Cutforth's community-based research class and would like to work with your organization. I am pursuing a Ph.D. in education with a focus in curriculum leadership. Before beginning my doctoral program, I taught for seven years (jr. high, primarily civics) and was involved with developing a service-learning program in my school district. If possible, I would like to meet with you sometime this coming week before Friday to discuss in more detail the research help you would like us to provide.

My home number is (333) 444–5555. During the week I am working with the teacher education program and can be contacted at 333/666–7777. Please give me a call or email me to let me know if we can get together. I'm looking forward to meeting you.

dr. strand,

we are going to the fcaa tonight and faith house tomorrow night to conduct interviews. Mike thompson from beacon house is calling us back today to let us know when we can come in to interview. Other than that things are going well and elena and I are working on the research design even as we speak. See you tomorrow @11 for class. Laura

Hey all,

Sorry I did not get my email out, I was at a funeral today as I explained. I got your message, Laura. Sounds good about Beacon House. I am excited about outreach tomorrow. I am not really sure what we are doing, but we will find out.

You guys can go to the Homeless Coalition meeting on the 20th, right? I wanted to remind you all that I will not be there because I have that conference in DC. We should definitely regroup before then. My schedule is really tight so can we communicate over email about what we would like to say at the meeting. I think that it is important to state all the problems that we have had with organizations. Some Ideas: communication, unreturned phone calls, lack of co-operation for even getting in to do interviews. I think that we should remind them that the Coalition expressed a need to have this project done for them, so we need their cooperation on this, too. Explain that this is community-based research, which means we have to have involvement of the community. I guess we should have a progress report. Also, I will give you the list of people who have returned those site surveys and we need to give another copy to those who never returned it. WE should have them fill these out AT THE MEETING, so we can get them back!

Alright, ladies, please give me feedback on what we should and should not be presenting to the Coalition.

Laura, see you at 12:45!

The Work Plan

Sam Marullo, a sociology professor at Georgetown University, requires that students doing community-based research develop what he calls a work plan, to be completed and submitted by the end of the fourth week of the semester. The work plan, which is designed to be flexible, lays out all the important details of the project: what will be accomplished, the schedule of activities and deadlines, and the assignment of tasks. Although the specifics of the work plan are determined by students and obviously influenced by the nature of the project, Marullo offers some guidelines for one-semester projects. One is that data collection must be completed at the latest by about two-thirds of the way through the semester (although he notes that halfway through is ideal). Normally, he requires that students complete the draft of the research report at least two weeks prior to the end of the semester in order to allow time for community input, revision, and duplicating. And he strongly suggests that students schedule one meeting each week with the community partner.

with something of value to the community and something of value to students in the way of important lessons and learning experiences—keeping in mind that the outcomes of the experience, for both the community and student learning, may diverge wildly from the original plan. Here is where the instructor is called on to be exceptionally flexible and sometimes quite creative.

The sources of problems in CBR vary. Sometimes the problem is students, who may procrastinate, drop out, do a substandard job, or fail to complete the work. If they do this in a conventional credit-bearing independent research project, the result is simply a poor grade. But when students fail to complete a CBR project or produce a product that is of such poor quality as to be of little value to the community, that is tantamount to reneging on an agreement with the community. Consequences go well beyond a bad grade for the students. The college or the faculty member (or both) might well experience loss of trust, face, and a future opportunity to work with this community partner. For that reason, when the problem is the students, it becomes incumbent on the professor to salvage something from the project that is of value to the community. More often than not, that means that the instructor takes over a project in order to see it to completion, perhaps during the winter or summer break.

Sometimes the difficulty comes from the other side: the community partner fails to stay with the project through completion or otherwise does not come through with what is necessary to make the project a success. One example of this occurred when a graduate student researcher arranged to collaborate on a CBR project with a community organization just before its board and staff underwent dramatic turnover. As a consequence, communication paths were lost, and the new leadership was unaware of the research plan developed with the previous leadership. Ultimately, the student had to find a new partner and project when it became clear that the faculty liaison was not positioned well enough to develop new ties and renegotiate the old one. A CBR project can degenerate when just one key community person loses a job, becomes ill, or experiences unforeseen work or family demands. Sometimes the organization overestimates its own capacity or decides in the middle of a project that it no longer is able or willing to commit resources to it.

And, finally, sometimes projects come to a standstill because of circumstances quite beyond the control of the students, the professor, or the community partner. One project involving door-to-door interviews with residents of an African American community fell seriously behind schedule because of a series of severe ice and snow storms during a winter semester. Sometimes research plans just do not work, as is the case with the example described in Chapter Three, when an entire project was aborted midsemester because the Alcohol Prevention and Recovery Agency refused to approve the survey instrument because of concerns about being scrutinized.

One way to avoid threats to the success of a project from the campus side is to work to sustain student engagement with the project. This may require little more than staying on top of what is going on with the project, so that the instructor (sometimes with the help of other students) can pull recalcitrant students back into the fold. Students are inclined to be less motivated during certain stages of a CBR project, such as the research design stage or when background research is required. Often the more or less natural ebb and flow of the research work creates slow times during which student commitment and activity might wane. One way to prevent this sort of time waste is to emphasize to students that they must always be proactive—for example, not simply leave a telephone message but keep calling back, or find a different person who can help—*and* that they should have backup tasks in place at all times. When students are completing the interview phase of a survey or oral history project, for example, they might also be working on writing beginning sections of the final report. That way, when respondents are hard to come by for one reason or another and interviewing slows, a fairly common problem, students can continue to make good use of their time and keep working toward the deadline.

When the problem is students who seem to lack motivation and self-discipline, assigning those students specific tasks with clear deadlines might help, as will teaming those students, in group projects, with other students who are more capable and motivated. The problem of reengaging recalcitrant students is often best handled by frank communication in group meetings or by individual discussions with those students.

Finally, one of the valuable lessons that students learn from CBR is that real research seldom proceeds as neatly as textbooks would lead us to believe and that good researchers are flexible, resourceful, self-motivated, and willing to accept uncertainty and change. All of this is especially true of community-based research, which takes place very much in the real world and requires sharing of control, work, and responsibility. This means there are bound to be more than the usual number and variety of unanticipated hurdles to be dealt with which requires compromise, flexibility, and commitment on the part of the entire research team. Here, the instructor can lead by example. In the end, problems in sustaining student engagement may indicate the need for a system for screening students allowed to do CBR or may indicate other shortcomings in the selection and management of projects.

Evaluating Students

Experiential learning of all kinds, along with group projects, is more difficult to evaluate than conventional, individual classroom-based learning. Unlike some kinds of service-learning, CBR results in a written product, the research report, which can be used as the main basis for the grade, especially when the student worked alone (that is, with no other students). When the CBR is a student group effort, grading becomes a bit more complicated unless the professor has reason to assume that all the students made equal contributions. Typically, they do not. That is when other measures—journals, class participation, and individual contributions to the project—are important. One instructor relies on interviews with individual students during which they provide information about and an assessment of the contribution of each member of their research group (including themselves) to the overall effort. These confidential interviews also alert the instructor to problems with the project or other concerns that might need attention. Another professor requires that students keep detailed records in their individual journals about their own and others' activities and contributions and also to turn in short reflection papers over the course of the semester. Some faculty members ask the community partners to assess the contribution of each student to the research project. This underscores the collaborative nature of the partnership and may provide valuable insights into and information about the quality and quantity of each student's work.

Producing, Sharing, and Implementing Results

The last stages of the CBR project can be at once the most exciting and the most difficult. Research findings may be presented in any number of different forms: oral presentation, poster, video, theater, and so on. However, the most common is the written research report. Following are some strategies for producing a quality report from a CBR project:

- Start writing the report early.

- Plan to revise more than once. For most students, this is the stage of the work where they feel—and often are—least competent. They will need lots of guidance to produce a quality product.

- Involve community members in the writing or, at least (and more commonly), as readers of early drafts.

- Make the report professional and scholarly (bound copies are nice), but also more straightforward and clearly written than typical scholarly research. This may well mean that students whose CBR project is meeting thesis or dissertation requirements will have to write two reports: one for the academy and the other for the community.

- Consider producing a one- to two-page addendum to the main report that lists highlights of the findings. If this is not feasible, emphasize to students the importance of having lots of clear summaries and lists of main points within the report itself. Many people in the community will not read the entire document, so it should be written in such a way that they can know by perusing the report what the researchers did and what they found.

- Ask the partner how many copies of the report they want and try to meet their needs. Give them the original if they want it. Think of the report as belonging first to the community and second to the students.

Often students will be invited to present the research to one or more community groups. Sometimes this presentation is given with community. partners, and especially in small cities or more rural areas, students may find themselves talking about their research more than once and to some influential political bodies in the community: not just the board of the partner agency but perhaps the county commissioners, the county council, relevant local coalitions and advocacy groups, government boards, and even state-level legislative groups. Many professors involved in CBR have been pleasantly surprised at the amount of attention given to this form of student-community research. Because these oral presentations can be critical to the impact of the research—not to mention how they reflect on the college and, less so, the professor—they must be done effectively. This might require some faculty intervention, especially when the community partner is relying solely on the students to do the work (often the case).

Wherever possible, students should be given an opportunity to present their results in a more conventionally academic setting. A good place to start is at a department-based or campuswide forum. One professor takes her CBR students each year to a regional conference devoted to undergraduate social science research (the Mid-Atlantic Undergraduate Social Research Conference). Others, more often graduate students, have been on the programs of state, regional, and national disciplinary associations. In addition to giving students practice in presentation, the value of this sort of participation is that it helps to advance the idea that CBR is indeed real research as it promotes the importance of putting academic training to work in the interest of social justice and community betterment.

CBR is best seen as little more than one small part of a community's larger social change agenda. In addition, and as we have seen, CBR projects frequently do not have clear and immediate social change implications. And even when they do, barriers to change often hold sway so that little happens—at least in an immediate sense—as a result of the research. In other cases, the social change implications of CBR projects are clearer. They may have real implications for how an agency does its work, inform official thinking or action about some pending policy or program at the local level, or provoke a spirited public information campaign to garner support for some sort of policy, group, or idea. When students do CBR, however, they are seldom around to see their results implemented. In fact, students often express some disappointment at the end of their work that they will never know just what, if anything, came of their efforts. Nor do they normally have the chance to work to implement the changes suggested by the research. For all the pedagogical benefits associated with involving students in CBR, this is a clear drawback for both students and the community.

Summary

In this chapter, we have discussed how instructors can meet some of the many challenges that come with doing community-based research with students. CBR can enhance academic learning in many disciplines using any of a number of curricular configurations—graduate and undergraduate courses, theses, independent studies, seminars, internships, and so on. We also suggest a number of strategies for ensuring students' readiness to take on CBR projects, which requires that they be sensitive to and familiar with the community, understand the principles of CBR, have some research skills, and acquire some substantive knowledge related to the project. The most important goal of CBR is to produce usable research for the community, and we recommend a number of strategies for structuring and managing the CBR project to accomplish this goal—from the project's inception to the presentation and implementation of results. Throughout, there is always an eye to helping students acquire the knowledge, skills, and values that will make them effective citizens and agents of social change.

8

ORGANIZING FOR COMMUNITY-BASED RESEARCH

PRINCIPLES AND MODELS OF CAMPUS-BASED ADMINISTRATIVE STRUCTURES

Models for Organizing CBR

Solo Practitioner Model
Professor A teaches chemistry at a small, private liberal arts college in rural Appalachia. She is concerned about mining runoff contamination of the local river and has her class on instrumentation undertake a community-based research project in collaboration with a local environmental justice organization. Each semester, her students work with community residents and environmental activists to test the water levels of harmful metals and write a report documenting their findings. The environmental justice organization uses these reports in its campaign to monitor toxic wastes that are being dumped in the river and to force the mining company to reduce its dumping practices.

Simple CBR Structure Model
Professor B, a sociologist at a medium-sized urban state college, directs the college's honors project and teaches research methods in sociology. With the support of a modest grant from the Bonner Foundation, Professor B has been able to institutionalize the undertaking of CBR projects through the college honors program and in the sociology, social work, women's studies, and criminal justice majors. Each semester, she solicits ideas from community service agencies for research projects. After screening out unwieldy and unrealistic proposals, she and her colleagues present the remaining project ideas to students in the honors program, the senior seminars in women's studies and criminal justice, and her research methods classes. Students undertake the projects and produce research reports that are turned in to the faculty member and to the community agency for which they have undertaken the project.

Complex CBR Center Structure Model
Professor C directs the community outreach center of a major research university. As part of the center's activities, which include operating direct service programs and supporting service-learning courses, the director solicits research proposals from community agencies and posts them on the center's Web site. Center staff try to match community organizations' research proposals with faculty and graduate students from a number of departments who are interested in undertaking such projects in collaboration with community groups.

Each semester, Professor C teaches a course titled "Community-Based Research," assisted by three graduate research assistants, through which thirty undergraduates, with research assistants and faculty support, undertake research projects from among those requested by the community. To support this work, the center awards small grants to help defray the costs of some of these projects, pays for the research assistants who help to organize the research projects, maintains the Web site and posts completed project reports on the site, and organizes an annual conference through which these and other CBR projects are presented to the larger community.

Metropolitan Consortium Model
The Chicago Policy Research Action Group (PRAG) is a network of four universities and fifteen CBOs that has operated in Chicago since 1989. PRAG has a central office consisting of a part-time faculty director, full-time project coordinator and research outreach coordinator, and administrator. The bulk of the research work is done by faculty, student interns, research assistants, apprentices, and CBO staff, with roughly ten to fifteen projects ongoing at any time. They are directed by a core group of twenty-four, split evenly among faculty and community partners, which sets policies and makes decisions about the types of projects and partnerships to support. An executive committee of eight members (four university and four community partners) meets monthly between quarterly core group meetings.

The PRAG collaborative solicits research proposals from a broad net of community partners. It has raised over $4 million from the MacArthur Foundation and other agencies to support collaborative research projects that also function to transfer knowledge-generating capacity to the community rather than foster a dependence of the community on university expertise. Although it casts a broad net to solicit proposals, PRAG has also developed a working group structure that focuses on developing research projects and collaborations in five issue areas: adult education and workforce preparation, residential stability, citizen empowerment, public health mapping strategies, and economic development. A joint university-community review process determines how grant resources will be allocated, from among those solicited through the request for proposal process and those developed by the working groups, primarily in the form of having interns, assistants, and apprentices assigned to the project.

Over the dozen years of its operation, PRAG has supported over 140 collaborative research projects. A collection of case studies and some of the lessons learned from PRAG are contained in *Building Community: Social Science in Action* (Nyden, Figert, Shibley, and Burrows, 1997).

Clearly, no one form of social organization is best suited for undertaking community-based research. Rather, the social organization that is most appropriate for a particular research project depends on things like the scope and complexity of the problem to be examined, the immediacy of the need for results, the ability to mobilize resources of various types, and the research expertise of interested stakeholders.

In this chapter, we examine some principles and models of organizing higher education institutions for the purpose of undertaking CBR. The first question one might raise, however, is why institutions must be organized for undertaking community-based research. Why not just do it? Obviously, individuals with appropriate skills can just do research in the community that will benefit CBOs. This is the case for Professor A in the first example. But as is usually true, benefits and efficiencies may come from creating some sort of organizational structure to carry out community-based research.

Through the analysis in this chapter, we see how CBR structures in higher education represent change both internally and externally—change within the higher education institution itself and change in the community. In the following chapter, we turn to a number of issues that need to be considered in organizing a higher education institution to engage in and sustain CBR work.

Organizing Community-Based Research in Higher Education for Social Change

People working for social change that incorporates the process of community-based research will need to accomplish a number of different tasks or functions connected with that work. And some form of social organization—a number of individuals, organized in a deliberate way—will much more effectively achieve the ends of useful research and social change.

Organizing within higher education institutions to undertake community-based research is done for a number of reasons:

- To mobilize resources
- To build deeper relationships among CBR collaborators
- To maximize efficiency through a division of labor
- To manage information and authority relations among components of the project
- To devise rules and control mechanisms for undertaking research projects

- To manage external relationships
- To create sustainability mechanisms

Institutional organization for effective CBR must do more than carry out these seven functions, however. It must also embody the principles of CBR that we have articulated—true collaboration, the demystification of knowledge and the democratization of the research process, and knowledge dissemination and research directed toward the goal of social change.

In order to achieve social change, committed activists need to mobilize sufficient resources for understanding the problems associated with current institutional arrangements and their operations, exploring alternative possibilities and mapping out the desired changes, and ultimately, carrying out the changes sought in institutional arrangements. CBR can play a role in each of the phases of social change. Yet to undertake even a rather straightforward research project, resources such as people's time and effort need to be mobilized (in other words, become activated and directed) to yield practical results. And just as we need to mobilize the right kind of resources in sufficient amounts to complete CBR research tasks successfully, we also need to go about the process in the right way. We should be mindful of the need to structure collaborative relationships so that they use and build the capacities of each of the partners, respect the knowledge of all participants, and invite meaningful participation of all interested stakeholders. Over time, relationships become more multifaceted, which leads to deeper knowledge of each other's strengths and weaknesses, allowing shared understandings to emerge, and ultimately to forming bonds of trust.

CBR's commitment to egalitarian relationships does not mean that we deny differences in skills, training, knowledge, and experience of the collaborators. Faculty members should not pretend that their research expertise is not of value, and they should not support community residents who take on research initiatives that are unsound or will produce useless information. Instead, what we need to do is value, invite, and structure in community input—the knowledge and experience of community members—in order to increase the likelihood of producing research that will advance social change goals. This requires that we think creatively when we assess the resources that can be mobilized and consider what an effective division of labor would be in order to undertake a successful CBR project. The CBR center not only serves as the vehicle for mobilizing resources but also functions as a repository and sustainer of constructed forms of interaction among higher education and community collaborators.

Collaboration and democratization of the research process suggest that one organizing principle should be the maximum dissemination of information and decision making, as determined by the needs of the project. Information can be empowering, suggesting that there should be substantial effort devoted to sharing information as widely as possible and enabling actors to make use of such information. The rules and control mechanisms flow from the information and decision-making processes that are established. This results in fewer inhibiting hierarchical structures, greater lateral flows of information, and more collaborative decision making.

Social change also refers to changing power and institutional arrangements of the larger community. This requires the ability to interact with and influence myriad external relationships outside the CBR collaboration. Because this work is being done with disadvantaged groups, it typically requires special outreach efforts and accommodations to keep everyone involved. CBR also entails developing the capacity of the disadvantaged so that they are increasingly able to organize, mobilize, and undertake social change and CBR activities themselves. In addition, social change work requires that we influence third parties, engaging allies on behalf of the social change agenda, converting disinterested parties, and neutralizing the efforts of actors interested in resisting change. The CBR center becomes a vehicle for building and maintaining this wide variety of relationships over time, beyond the life of a single project.

We now turn to the seven specific dimensions of effective social organization, applying them to CBR organizations in higher education in order to examine how they can be realized in the light of our principles of best CBR practice.

Mobilizing Resources

The primary incentive for organizing is that a collective of people can accomplish more than an individual due to the benefits of specialization and efficiencies of scale. The research process is a complex task requiring multiple skills and often concurrent tasks. Solo researchers are limited by the number of activities that they can undertake at once and by the particular skill sets that they may or may not possess. The multiple methods to be employed and the challenges of gathering data may be incentive enough for the researcher to seek collaborators from among faculty colleagues, students, and community partners. In addition, there are a number of other tasks that are not specific to collaborative research, such as administering an office, organizing logistics, and coordinating materials; even well-qualified researchers are not likely to be equally well qualified as administrators, organizers, managers, popular educators, animators, and advocates, all roles likely to be involved in the community-based research process.

In a narrow sense, the primary objective for organizing around CBR is to mobilize additional resources in order to help accomplish the research task. For the university-based researcher, this would typically entail mobilizing students, faculty colleagues, and administrative support in order to undertake the project. Other faculty colleagues bring additional research experience, more time that can be devoted to the research project, and policy or context expertise beyond that of the solo researcher. The faculty member may wish to engage students in the research process as a source of labor, in exchange for which the students are taught the principles and practice of research. Faculty members may be able to use university resources, such as administrative support, student office help, and use of equipment, as part of their obligation to undertake scholarship. Furthermore, university development and grants offices may be helpful in identifying and soliciting funding to support the research.

The community partner engaging in CBR also finds advantages in mobilizing additional resources to undertake a research project. Time is one such resource: the community-based researcher is likely to need support to have the time to devote to the project. In addition, there is likely to be a need for technical expertise for undertaking pieces of the project. The needs for administrative and management support, labor for data gathering and processing, and development support are at least as pressing on the community-based researcher as they are on the university-based colleague.

In Figure 8.1, we delineate various types of resources that a CBR center would attempt to mobilize. Although some resources are more likely to be found among either the community or university partners, each type of resource may in fact be found in either location. An initial assessment of these resources should be undertaken by those interested in establishing a CBR center in order to guide its development—for example, to determine where it should be located and who should be involved as the initial stakeholders in its formation. Increasingly, collaboration among university and community partners is not only desirable but may be a prerequisite for attaining funding for community-based research.

Building Multiplex Relationships

Unlike the television commercial for a fast food chicken take-out chain, most of us do not have the luxury of "doing just one thing and doing it right." Community agencies interested in undertaking research are most likely also to be involved in delivering services or organizing their community, managing grants, fundraising, doing community outreach, and advocating for their constituents. Faculty members engaged in CBR may

Figure 8.1. Mobilizing Resources Through a CBR Center.

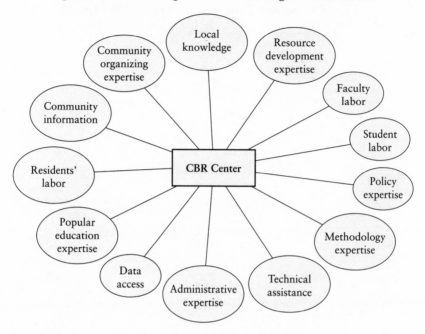

be working on more than one research project, teaching courses, engaging in multiple service projects on campus and in their professional association, and writing grants—so neither can they afford the luxury of "doing only one thing and doing it right." In short, both university- and community-based researchers are involved in many relationships, and each relationship may contain multiple elements (see Figure 8.2).

These multiplex relationships may also consist of role relationships with the same partners who are interacting with each other along different dimensions. For example, in the La Clinica Tepeyac case cited earlier in Chapter Two, the faculty member who is teaching his class and supervising his students' work in the community on behalf of the agency may also be a guest speaker at a community meeting organized by La Clinica, may serve on one of its committees, and may help organize an advocacy campaign with La Clinica. Conversely, the La Clinica staff member who works on the research project may also be helping to teach and supervise the students who work on the project, serving as a guest lecturer or co-teacher for the course, operating as university liaison for La Clinica on the university's CBR center steering committee, and helping to oversee university

Figure 8.2. Multiplex Role Relations Between Faculty and Community Collaborators Engaged in CBR.

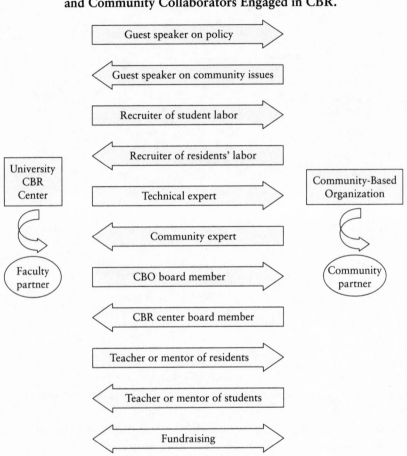

students who volunteer at La Clinica on a direct service project. In sum, there is a multiplexity of relationships that might emerge as a result of the many different roles and role interrelations that two CBR partners might have. Managing these multiplex role relations is likely to be easier when there is an administrative structure that helps to coordinate them and to provide additional staff support to help sustain them.

Maximizing Efficiency Through a Division of Labor

In addition to mobilizing more resources, an organization's division of labor allows for increased efficiency to use better the resources it has mobilized in order to achieve its goals. This refers to the development of specialized knowledge and experience that enable people to become particularly adept in some tasks, to forgo doing others at which they are less adept or less interested, and then to integrate the tasks through cooperation. Developing a center to undertake or support CBR allows for the specialization of research skills and methodologies, substantive expertise, and administrative tasks. It also allows for the development of a greater network of contacts in the community and at the university that may be helpful in advancing both the research and social change agendas.

The multiple stages of and tasks required to complete a community-based research project virtually ensure that there will be some tasks at which a particular researcher is likely to have little competence. For example, a skilled interviewer or field researcher may have limited organizing skills and no experience in keeping track of payrolls and budgets on a large research project. A good public speaker and effective advocate may have limited patience for undertaking data entry and verification and little ability to write grant proposals. A CBR center can bring together people with complementary expertise and create working teams that are more effective and efficient in completing a project than a single person who spends the same amount of time working on various aspects of it.

Managing Information and Authority Relations Among Components of the Process

As research projects grow larger, the complexity of tasks and the division of labor involved require a structure for managing information and establishing ordered interactions among the components. Such a structure is typically depicted in hierarchical terms: authority relations operate so that those at the top exercise authority over those lower in a pyramid-like structure, whereas information flows from lower levels of the pyramid to higher levels. However, both information flows and authority relations can be, and often are, arranged more horizontally. Decision-making authority in modern organizations, and particularly in CBR enterprises, is typically delegated throughout a structure, with participants at various levels throughout the structure being empowered to make particular decisions. Similarly, information flows should proceed in all directions, so that those at the top are sharing knowledge and information throughout the structure with those at all levels, thereby developing the capacity for sound decision making throughout the organization.

Certainly, the development and widespread use of information sharing using e-mail, the Internet, and the World Wide Web make these information flows possible. Students, novice researchers in the community, and faculty researchers can gain access to tremendous amounts of data, sophisticated measurement instruments, and extensive literature relevant to virtually any research topic. Indeed, the more important issue today is having the wisdom to discern which of the available studies, data sources, instruments, and methodologies are most appropriate for a given research project in a particular context. The technical expertise of the professional faculty researcher is not sufficient for making this judgment, since the community-based research partner will have specialized knowledge that is also needed. Developing effective communication among the partners that is ongoing, timely, and relevant is the greater challenge, particularly in the light of the information overload that each of the collaborators may experience.

One of the issues this raises is the credibility and validity of the research across domains that have traditionally been quite separate. From the academic side, the issue is the credibility of "uncredentialed" research collaborators (in other words, those without traditional academic research degrees), such as community residents or CBO staff, who perform data gathering and analysis. From the community side, the issue is the validity of adopting an academic perspective on understanding real-life problems that have a direct impact on disadvantaged people. From each partner's predisposed perspective, the collaborator from the other side is lacking some training or experience that is essential for undertaking needed and valuable work. It takes time to develop an understanding and appreciation of the strengths and weaknesses of each of the partners. Effective communication is necessary to convey the priorities of each perspective and to translate the jargon across the community-academy divide.

It also takes time to develop a level of trust among the partners that the collaborative research goals are being pursued in good faith. From each partner's point of view, there are reasons for preserving discretion and autonomy in determining how data and findings are to be interpreted and used. On this basis alone, we believe that the collaborative practice of CBR offers additional opportunities for scrutinizing, verifying, and reporting data that improve the overall quality of such work. Our claim here is that research designed to meet multiple sets of needs and demands, as CBR does, is both more challenging and more fruitful than traditional scientific discovery because it must be scrutinized and pass muster from multiple sets of interests. Discussing these matters during the process of constructing a memorandum of understanding (MOU) helps to avoid conflicts that may later emerge in the research process. Figure 8.3 illustrates how the traditional university and community's interests and perspectives may differ at each stage of the research process.

Figure 8.3. Traditional University and Community Influences on CBR.

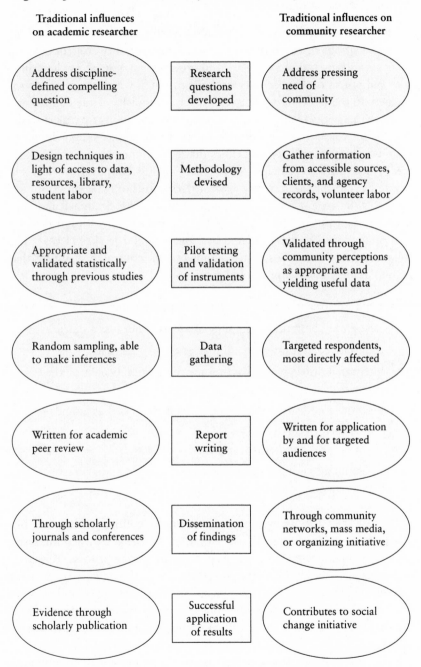

Traditional influences
on academic researcher

Traditional influences on
community researcher

Address discipline-defined compelling question

Research questions developed

Address pressing need of community

Design techniques in light of access to data, resources, library, student labor

Methodology devised

Gather information from accessible sources, clients, and agency records, volunteer labor

Appropriate and validated statistically through previous studies

Pilot testing and validation of instruments

Validated through community perceptions as appropriate and yielding useful data

Random sampling, able to make inferences

Data gathering

Targeted respondents, most directly affected

Written for academic peer review

Report writing

Written for application by and for targeted audiences

Through scholarly journals and conferences

Dissemination of findings

Through community networks, mass media, or organizing initiative

Evidence through scholarly publication

Successful application of results

Contributes to social change initiative

Devising Rules and Control Mechanisms for the Research Process

Under the traditional model of research, the solo researcher makes all the decisions about research design, methodology, quality control of data, analysis, interpretation, write-up, and presentation, guided by the principles and norms of the discipline and institution in which the researcher is located. In the CBR model, the researcher relinquishes some control and replaces this with collaboration, working with community partners to determine the research process. Furthermore, it is no longer simply discipline or university principles or guidelines that govern the practice of CBR; instead, there are also principles of practice of CBR that govern such work. These have been summarized by numerous authors (Greenwood and Levin, 1998; Kretzmann and McKnight, 1993; Sclove, Scammell and Holland, 1998; Stringer, 1999; and Torres and Schaffer, 2000), but here we will present the summary created by Cornwall and Jewkes (1995). The following principles of best practice thus become control mechanisms that help to guide CBR organizational structure:

- Build on strengths and resources within the community.
- Recognize community as a unit of identity, not just a place.
- Facilitate collaboration in all phases of the research.
- Integrate knowledge and action for the mutual benefit of all partners.
- Promote a co-learning and empowering process that attends to social inequalities.
- Use a cyclical and iterative process.
- Disseminate findings and knowledge gained to all parties [Cornwall and Jewkes, 1995, p. 1672].

Because the CBR research process becomes a multiperson partnership among stakeholders with different roles, expertise, and vested interests, organizational mechanisms are needed to govern the process. Research protocols and MOUs are common vehicles for outlining how the process is to unfold. Such agreements are formal in nature, however, and must be put into practice and routinized through everyday practices. Informal and regular communication needs to be established to construct such norms of practice.

Face-to-face interactions, as well as telephone and e-mail communication, informal memos, and regular staff meetings, are some of the mechanisms through which these informal practices are established. Certainly, official MOUs, grant proposals, and even institutional mission statements may be referred to for guidance or to resolve disputes. A designated project director or principal investigator needs to establish trust and be granted the authority to make practical decisions to move the research project forward. The project director can accomplish this by having regular communications with all involved in the project, including all the participants as well as a project steering group (whether it is constituted formally or informally), and sharing information and decision making as much as possible. Figure 8.4 is a schematic illustration of the many authority structures, formal and informal, that guide the research process.

A number of larger questions need to be addressed through the construction of a control mechanism for a collaborative research project, such as:

- Who owns the data?
- What is the internal review process that will be used to review the data and its interpretations?
- What are the major roles, and who will assume responsibility for them?
- How are the work products to be disseminated?

In some cases, not only does the university have an institutional review board (IRB) process that must approve of a proposed research project, so too does the community organization. In Trenton, the Union Industrial Home for Children requires that all research projects, even those jointly developed by its own staff designed to improve the quality of life for its clients, must pass their own internal IRB process to ensure that client interests and confidentiality will not be harmed.

As working relationships are established, shared understandings emerge over time, become routinized, and take on the role of traditional authority governing the relationship. At the most sophisticated level, the Chicago Policy Research Action Group (PRAG) consortium has a steering committee of university and community partners that reviews proposals and exercises oversight over projects through its own set of principles. It publishes work in its own journal, *PRAGmatics,* functioning as a quality control and gatekeeping mechanism for the work done within the consortium.

Managing External Relationships

Because any CBR project is part of a larger social change initiative, the goal is to mobilize resources to become an agent of change and ultimately change the larger society. To mobilize resources, a CBR organization must

Figure 8.4. Formal and Informal Control Mechanisms Governing CBR.

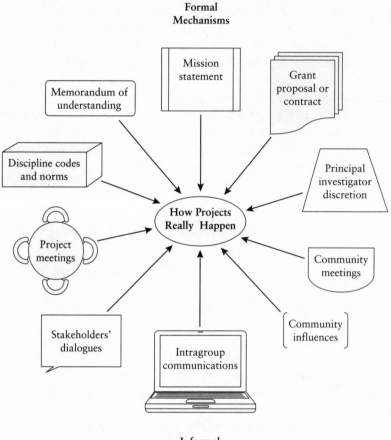

engage in outreach and development activities. To influence the larger society, it may engage in lobbying, organizing, and advocacy work and spread its message to the larger public through the media. Some of this work may turn out to be adversarial in nature, seeking to change the status quo and being met with opposition by forces controlling substantial resources. Figure 8.5 illustrates the types of outreach processes in which a CBR center might engage to reach various outsider publics.

In the most sophisticated CBR structures, each of these relationships might be managed by a professional expert. The publicist, lobbyist, outreach worker, and fundraiser could be dedicated positions within the CBR

Figure 8.5. Outreach Processes and Targets.

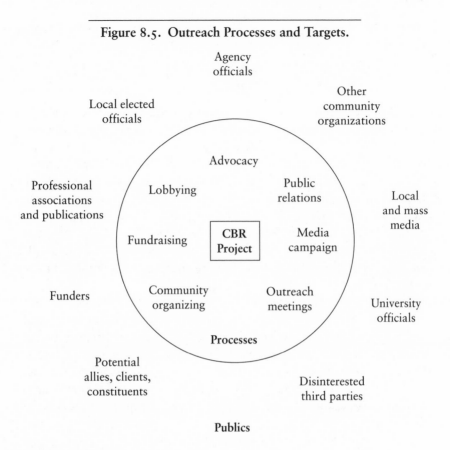

center that are responsible for advancing the center's interests. A publicist would provide news stories and disseminate research findings to mainstream and specialized media outlets in order to make known the work of the CBR center. A lobbyist would be responsible for advocating on behalf of the constituents or clients of the center, applying the research findings to the policy process and promoting legislation and political activism in support of the center's work. A lobbyist would be responsible for advocating on behalf of the constituents and attempt to mobilize additional human resources on behalf of the social change initiative by recruiting and training efforts. The fundraiser would write grant proposals and solicit funding from foundations, corporations, and potential private donors in order to support the center's activities. We are not aware of any CBR center that is large enough and has a division of labor so refined as to have each of these functions filled in a separate position. What is more commonly the case, even among the larger centers, is that it is expected that everyone does some of each of these tasks in the course of undertaking their project.

Creating Sustainability Mechanisms

The ultimate purpose of CBR is to change society to empower those in need, expand opportunities and resources to the disadvantaged, and mitigate structured inequities. Such goals are obviously long term and thus require sustained efforts. The solo researcher is limited not only in terms of the resources that she or he can mobilize at any given time, but also in terms of how these resources can be kept mobilized. From one semester to the next, over calendar breaks, vacations, and sabbaticals, and over the course of a career, the individual faculty member's resources and interest level will vary. An established center is able to mobilize multiple people and resources over time, making it more effective in accomplishing the many different tasks of CBR in a sustained way.

In Chapter Three, we delineate some characteristics of sustainable CBR centers. They are clarity of mission, community demand, organizational leadership, appropriateness of organizational structures, strong human resources, strong financial resources, and ongoing evaluation processes. Clearly, each of these characteristics requires ongoing attention. The successful CBR center needs to build in a self-reflective process so that it periodically considers how well it is achieving these principles. This is done by undertaking strategic planning, process and empowerment assessment, center staff and board reflection, and external reviews.

Four Models of CBR Structures

Community-based research can be undertaken within a wide range of administrative contexts, from the simple form of a solo faculty member working with a single partner to a highly complex consortium of university- and community-based agencies engaging in ongoing collaborative research. Examples of each are presented at the beginning of this chapter. We will examine each of the four models that higher education institutions can use to administer community-based research, moving from simplest to most complex:

- Solo faculty and community partnership
- A small CBR program with regular partners
- A large, complex community-based research center
- A local or regional consortium

These descriptions are offered as models or case studies—and are not intended to be an exhaustive account of the broad range of practices that in fact exists.

The emphasis here is on the models of organization from the perspective of the university partner. These higher education models represent amalgams of CBR centers currently in operation. They also call to our attention the dearth of specialized institutions in the community that engage in community-based research, especially relative to the number of institutions of higher education. The Loka Institute, a national association dedicated to promoting and supporting community-based research, was able to identify only fifty community-based research centers in the United States in the late 1990s (Sclove, Scammell, and Holland, 1998, p. iv). Nevertheless, there are over thirty-six hundred U.S. colleges and universities, suggesting that most collaborations for undertaking CBR will likely occur in the context of a higher education institution-based center.

As CBR structures range from simple to complex, they are increasingly likely to be able to fulfill organizational functions. At the simplest level, the solo practitioner is able to mobilize fewer resources than when there are several faculty collaborators or an entire center operating to support CBR projects. Even small, simple CBR centers are able to afford a division of labor among tasks, create information-sharing systems, and develop control mechanisms that are not possible for a single practitioner. Larger, more complex CBR centers are better able to fulfill all of the previous functions, as well as reach a level of sustainability that is more challenging for a small, basic structure. The large, complex center also may be able to manage external relations well. However, it is likely to be the local or regional center that is best able to influence the external community. It does this by means of policy or socioeconomic change initiatives undertaken on a larger scale than is possible through the other forms of CBR structure. Certainly there are exceptions to these general patterns, such as small structures that have proved to be extremely durable over time, or large centers or consortiums that have not managed to establish good information systems or control mechanisms. However, the increasing size and complexity of CBR structures are likely to correspond to their capacity to achieve the functions described above. Figure 8.6 illustrates this relationship.

Solo Practitioner Model

The simplest model of organizing CBR is a single faculty and community partner collaborating on a research project. In the first case described at

Figure 8.6. Organizational Capacities of CBR Structures.

	Solo Practitioner	Small, Basic Structure	Large, Complex Structure	Regional Consortium
Mobilize resources	X	X	X	X
Build multiple relationships	X	X	X	X
Division of labor		X	X	X
Information management and authority relations		X	X	X
Rules and control mechanisms		X	X	X
Sustainability			X	X
Manage external relationships			X	X

the beginning of this chapter, Professor A has students in her chemistry class work with a community environmental justice organization in Appalachia, which has as its goals the protection of regional waterways and cleaning up mining practices that contaminate the environment. The professor, through her work with the organization, realized the need for ongoing research to test the level of contaminants found in the waterway and to monitor compliance with existing clean water regulations. In her instrumentation course, students had traditionally undertaken lab exercises through which they learned how to operate particular instruments that enabled them to identify unknown chemical substances found in various solutions. Now, as one of her exercises, she has students travel to various sites to·collect samples that they then analyze and record. When she and her students started their evaluation of downstream mining sites, they discovered tremendously high levels of contaminants in the water. Such information could then be used by the environmental justice organization as part of its social change agenda—to advance a lawsuit against the mining operation to force its compliance with clean water laws.

The single faculty member, having her students work collaboratively with a small CBO, undertook a valuable piece of research that produced striking results and led to successful social change. No formal CBR organization structure was needed beyond the informal relationship among the environmental justice organization staff members, the professor, and the students. In this case, the resources mobilized by the CBO staff (such as information about mining operation practices and location) and the professor (her students' labor and lab materials) were adequate to the research task at hand with virtually no other overhead required to complete the project. Furthermore, because the professor and students were acting within the confines of a particular class, academic freedom tenets insulated them from any official university oversight or review processes.

Such projects rarely have such profound consequences in real life, however. In this example, the faculty member and students sized their project to match their limited resource capabilities. Apart from transportation costs, lab expenses, and data analysis costs—the last two covered as part of typical laboratory course costs—there were virtually no real dollar costs to undertaking the project. Also, because of the small scale of the research project, there was no political controversy generated on campus or in the community by undertaking the study, thereby not exposing the professor to any risks of sanction in merit review processes and not requiring any efforts to manage external relations. Potential problems that might have arisen due to the semester system and academic breaks were avoided by keeping the project small and contained so as to be completed within two months, reducing the importance of a more formal organization for sustainability purposes.

Attempting CBR as a solo practitioner has costs as well. The faculty member must invest more time and energy than in traditional classroom-based teaching to ensure the success of the project. She must arrange travel logistics for her students, keep track of costs incurred, and take into account transportation risks and liability issues while coordinating all of this with the community partner. In addition, she must make sure that the students are adequately prepared to undertake the actual research work and appropriately oriented to understand and contribute to the partnership relationship. Professor A also must be concerned about the sustainability of this relationship. Clearly, she is the only point of contact between the university and the community agency. When she takes off a semester or year for a sabbatical, no other colleague is likely to teach the instrumentation course in the same manner, and the monitoring project is likely to miss a year's worth of data. Should Professor A take on a different research interest or be assigned to teach other courses, it might be extremely difficult for her to maintain her relationship with, and organize the monitoring work for, the environmental justice organization.

There is very little of a specialized division of labor in undertaking these projects. Professor A and her community partner are responsible for organizing the project, maintaining the multiplexity of roles required, and mobilizing the internal and external resources necessary to carry it out. They have developed a relationship of trust over time, but Professor A still insists that she and her partners review their work plan each semester to be clear on who is responsible for what pieces of the work. There is good communication between Professor A and her partner, and they have developed norms for sharing information and decision making that works for them. However, all of this would be considered to be informal and is largely dependent on the two key people in this relationship. If Professor A were to leave the university, the environmental justice organization would likely not have a partner for such future collaborations. If the environmental justice organizer was replaced by another person, Professor A would have to start over with the new person, and whether this person would be interested in maintaining this project would be up to his or her discretion, since it is only a small part of the position's formal job description. From both institutional ends of the relationship, such a collaborative project is voluntary, ad hoc, and at risk for long-term sustainability.

Simple CBR Structure Model

In the case of the simple CBR structure, the second example at the beginning of this chapter, we can see that the university program-community partner connection provides support for multiple projects to be ongoing simultaneously and engages multiple faculty and community partners in several different roles. Substantially more university resources, primarily faculty and students' time and expertise, have been mobilized to work with several community organizations. In this case, the CBR director, Professor B, uses a systematic approach to soliciting research project ideas from a limited set of community partners. Such a solicitation process provides a mechanism for the faculty to hear from community partners what their research needs are. The process is more systematic and allows for some level of interaction among potential university and community collaborators, even if the majority of project ideas submitted in response to the solicitation ultimately go undeveloped. The drawbacks of this approach are that the solicitation and research project requests are limited in terms of developing richer understandings of the projects, which is needed to build long-term sustainable relationships, and have the potential to create disappointment among community partners when their projects are not selected for implementation.

In this simple CBR structure, we see a differentiation of roles emerging in that specific administrative responsibilities are defined and play a critical part in maintaining the collaboration. Professor B plays an administrative role that is responsible for processing the solicitation of research requests and matching the requests with university resources that might be able to participate in the project. Professor B solicits possible research projects and then disburses them among potential faculty colleagues who might collaborate in undertaking the project or whose students might undertake the project in the context of one of the several honors, seminar, or research courses at the university. She does this by both routinizing the solicitation process and engaging multiple faculty, students, and administrators in the matchmaking process. At certain times in the year, the database of community-based organizations is updated, and preliminary contacts are made by student assistants on the project. Letters are sent out and forms are created that describe the possible research projects. These are kept on file, and a directory of potential projects has been developed over time.

Once project ideas are submitted, Professor B convenes a committee that is responsible for matching university resources with the community's requests, documenting the process and reporting on its outcomes, and maintaining written records of its activities. This committee engages several university faculty and students, all of whom accept some responsibility for the success of the collaborative research project. These administrative responsibilities are built into Professor B's time—through a course release purchased by a grant—necessitating an altered job description and appropriate review procedures to be developed to hold her accountable for fulfilling these responsibilities. Administrative staff and student support roles are also established to carry out various parts of the solicitation, matching, and documentation processes. Professor B is responsible for overseeing these operations as part of her grant management responsibilities. Corollary to such a division of time accountabilities of staff comes budget accountabilities as well; in other words, it is now possible to document the amount of money that is being spent to administer various components of the collaboration process.

The larger scale of this operation and the involvement of multiple faculty members raise the visibility and accountability of such an initiative in the eyes of faculty colleagues and the institution as a whole. Because these CBR initiatives are not the equivalent of an academic program or department, they do not receive comparable levels of institutional support, scrutiny, and review. However, faculty colleagues are aware of these collaborative activities because they are being solicited to participate in them (more or less selectively) and being asked to evaluate the work of colleagues who are so engaged. Because such work often cuts across disciplinary boundaries, wider-scale institutional review procedures are questioned as rewards and incentives from several departments are brought to bear. To the extent that particular courses, or sets of courses, emerge or are revised to accommodate CBR activities, department- and college-level curriculum committees are asked to review such developments. Such encounters with ongoing university structures—departments, curriculum committees, merit review processes, workload expectations—set the stage for institutional reform to accommodate (or deter) this work.

Because new faculty members are being approached to participate in CBR projects, those already engaged should pay attention to the faculty development process in order to ensure the growth and sustainability of the enterprise. Few faculty receive training for undertaking this type of work in graduate school, so it is necessary to teach the principles, perspectives, and applications of CBR. A number of models of faculty development can be applied to introduce faculty to CBR, and selective incentives may be used to encourage their involvement. Single workshops on the CBR process or presentations of research done through CBR may be effective for encouraging the involvement of faculty predisposed to undertaking this type of work. A one- to two-week intensive institute on CBR may provide substantial training and support for faculty who are novices to this endeavor and may link them with potential partners in the community. An ongoing seminar or learning circle may serve the dual purpose of introducing faculty to CBR as well as providing ongoing support for sustaining this type of work. The Partners in Urban Research and Service-Learning (PURS) project, described in Chapter Two, is an example of an ongoing academic seminar that serves as a partners' development workshop and an incubator for developing collaborative research projects.

In the case of the PURS project, collaborative research projects are developed more organically, through the seminar format, which has enabled community and university partners to work together over a sustained period to define the projects and arrange funding support for them. The PURS process trades breadth and systematic outreach for selective and in-depth partnership development, which leads to more sustainable long-term relationships. However, this comes with a greater cost of initial investment of faculty and community partners needed to sustain the ongoing seminar, which serves as the incubator for such projects. At Georgetown, the PURS cofacilitators assume responsibility for managing the seminar and maintaining the PURS infrastructure, while project teams emerge to undertake grant-writing responsibilities and carry out the research projects. In this case, as well as for the small structure described in the second example in this chapter, such differentiation of roles leads to the need for communication among the multiple actors, documenting and recording actions and decisions, mechanisms for disseminating information, and procedures for handling problems that emerge. Another type of administrative specialization of functions emerged in PURS as some of the members demonstrated a talent for and commitment to grant writing, some were more adept at budget management, some were more committed to advocacy work (either within the university or with respect to local politics), and others were better skilled at outreach and partnership building. This administrative specialization requires even further development of communication skills to enable all the collaborative members to keep up with developments in areas relevant to their work, but in which they are not directly involved.

Complex CBR Center Structure Model

Similar to the third case at the beginning of this chapter, several higher education institutions have developed CBR centers that also contain other community outreach activities, such as direct service programs or community-based learning initiatives. Locating CBR activities within such complex, multipurpose centers is done in order to promote the integration of community service into the university's activities through service-learning, student and faculty participation in community service, and community-based research.

At the University of Michigan, for example, the Edward Ginsberg Center for Community Service and Learning describes itself in its brochure as building on a long tradition of service and learning. The center joins academic programs with community service so students and faculty can forge a link between theory and practice, knowledge and action, and campus and community. Faculty members participate by integrating service into teaching and conducting research that is responsive to community needs. At Georgetown University, the Center for Social Justice Research, Teaching and Service supports faculty and students' service-learning work and administers the Service-Learning Credit program, oversees (and funds) students' direct service organizations (through its volunteer and public service office), and supports faculty and students' engagement in CBR. This model of integrating CBR with service-learning curriculum development and support for direct service organizations is the approach taken with most of our peer Learn and Serve grant-supported universities, including the University of Denver's Center for Service Learning and Civic Engagement, Middlesex County College's Community Research Center, the Brisbane Institute at Morehouse College, and the Appalachian Center for Community Service at Emory and Henry College.

There are three keys to the success of these centers: (1) the mobilization of sufficient resources, (2) creating ongoing partnerships with community-based organizations, and (3) institutionalizing the work as part of higher education's research and teaching activities. In terms of resources, we refer to both financial and human resources, which may be mobilized internally (using permanent university resources) as well as externally through grant support. The benefit of establishing ongoing partnerships allows for the development of trust among the partners, shared understandings of problems and programs, sustained commitments that reside in positions rather than particular individuals, and efficiencies of scale derived from reduced start-up costs and in-place communications and administrative systems. Our stress on institutionalizing the CBR work as part of the university's teaching and scholarship mission is to ensure the long-term development of projects that are needed to accomplish structural change and sustain the participants in this work. We explore each of these three characteristics of successful center development below by examining the case of the Center for Community Partnerships at the University of Pennsylvania.

As Benson and Harkavy describe the success of the WEPIC program, they place a heavy emphasis on their success in securing external funds from sources as diverse as the DeWitt Wallace and the Hewlett foundations; city and state grants for job training, educational program development, and health care delivery; federal funds for establishing a community outreach partnership center through the Department of Housing and Urban Development; and quite limited university funds for pilot projects. Benson and Harkavy are modest about the University of Pennsylvania's success in securing grants, attributing some of it to being at the right place at the right time, acquiring some good publicity from early successful demonstration projects, and having some good connections. Of course, none of these would matter if WEPIC had not been effective in producing quality outcomes and being able to document them to disinterested or skeptical parties. Benson and Harkavy note that the process has been slow in evolving (painfully at times, given the false starts and

Center for Community Partnerships

The Center for Community Partnerships is the home base of the University of Pennsylvania's practice of strategic academically based community service, which refers to the university's mobilization of its intellectual resources to address the manifestations of globalization and mass society at the local level by transforming the education system (Benson and Harkavy, 1997). Operationally, it includes the practices of community-based research and service-learning that are tied to the institution's strategic plan for collaborative community development through the creation of community schools that support mass democracy. This concept evolved from ten years of practice and reflection, carried out by the West Philadelphia Improvement Corporation (WEPIC), linking West Philadelphia's public schools with the university's undergraduate and graduate education program in activities designed to produce civic cosmopolitan community schools, which would serve as the cornerstone of creating cosmopolitan neighborly communities. The university, through institutional commitment and strategic partnership with its surrounding community, has dedicated substantial human, intellectual, and financial resources to undertake collaborative research, teaching, and direct service for the purpose of addressing community problems. Motivated by its concerns to stave off the increasing deterioration of its surrounding community of West Philadelphia and its desires to improve its instrumental research, teaching, and learning, the University of Pennsylvania committed support for the WEPIC program both to secure its own long-term survival and further its own pursuit of excellence (Benson and Harkavy, 1997).

The Center for Community Partnerships is housed in the office of the university president and reports to the academic provost as well as the president. The tremendous success of the center, according to its director (and university vice president) Ira Harkavy, results from (1) the dedicated and talented faculty, students, teachers, and community partners undertaking the work at the community level; (2) the emergence of a strategic vision (through practice, theory, trial and error, reflection, and contingencies) that focuses work on the creation of cosmopolitan community schools; (3) the integration of this work into the routine teaching and research activities of faculty, students, and administrators; (4) support from the top administrators within the university—both previous university president Sheldon Hackney and current president Judith Rodin have been active participants in and supporters of WEPIC projects; and (5) the intentional as well as incidental success in mobilizing resources for collaborative initiatives. From its first experimental project of providing job training to a handful of youths through a school beautification project in 1985, WEPIC has grown to include twelve West Philadelphia schools involving forty-five hundred children, parents, and community members in a wide range of programs. As of 2002, WEPIC projects and the center had raised over $3 million in grants from private foundations, state and local government, corporate gifts, and university endowment. As Benson and Harkavy (1997) paraphrase the real estate industry's mantra about the key to success, as applied to WEPIC, the three rules of successful academic innovation that Penn has followed are: "(1) Get money. (2) Get money. (3) Get money" (p. 57).

paths not taken that they cite), but that successful efforts have now been rewarded with increased funding and institutional commitment.

The lesson for centers in start-up phases is that not only does the enterprise need to undertake successful projects, but it also needs to document them and publicize them in order to attract further funding and that it needs to pursue multiple sources of funding for its projects, assuming that any given funding request is likely to be unsuccessful, and even if successful, limited in duration. The timing, publicity, connections, and other contingencies to which Benson and Harkavy refer may in fact help increase the odds that a particular project will receive funding, but it is the number as well as quality of requests that one must keep in mind when seeking to establish a center. They also point out that as an institution-building strategy, it is helpful to point out to university officials that such an enterprise may bring in funding to which the university would otherwise not have access. Such a financial incentive may convince fiscally cautious university officials that investment in the development of community outreach centers may in fact be a sound fiscal investment as new resources, along with their overhead, are brought to the institution.

Establishing a center at the college or university will likely entail deepening of particular community partnerships. Obviously, with social change being the ultimate goal of CBR projects, it is unlikely that any single project will be a success in transforming a community from being poor, underdeveloped, or failing to educate its children to becoming an economic, social, and educational model. Thus, even the successful completion of a particular project is likely to result in only incremental change at the community level. Community organizers and advocates are well aware of the long time frame needed to achieve structural change and the implications of this for sustained, multifaceted approaches to social change. Such a time frame is not particularly conducive to the academic calendar, with its semester and summer breaks, to students with a fourteen-week semester or ten-week quarter, or a faculty member's semester-long courses and annual review processes. It is the establishment of a center that enables faculty, students, and courses to coordinate their efforts and work with one or a small number of community agents over time, on a number of different projects, that will afford the collaborative social change enterprise the opportunity to succeed.

Each particular disadvantaged community has unique circumstances and conditions that help to explain the challenges it faces. Understanding these problems and acquiring a body of knowledge that appreciates the particularities of the community, beyond a more academic understanding of general theories, requires an investment in time and study. In some senses, such preliminary investigations are sunk costs that all investigators must absorb in order to address a particular research problem. In the case of CBR, researchers confront not only the traditional academic research needs to understand the theory and literature related to their projects, but they must also invest in learning about the uniqueness of the community in which the research is to take place. To capture and build on the knowledge of the community is one function of the research center that helps to reduce some of the initial start-up costs of undertaking community-based research.

Local or Regional Consortium Model

The regional consortium serves a larger area and combines the resources of several universities and CBOs. The Just Connections network serves the entire Appalachian region, covering six states and linking five higher education institutions with a half-dozen or so community organizations. The Trenton Center defines the entire city of Trenton, New Jersey, as its target community and has begun networking among community organizations and four local institutions of higher education. One of the main reasons for constructing this more complex level of organization is to undertake projects that address larger problems or to effect change across greater areas. The Trenton Center offers a second objective of supporting a larger number of projects, relying on greater efficiencies of scale and enhanced fundraising capacity through the center. The geographical dispersion among multiple sites creates additional challenges, but the participants believe that the greater the resources are that are brought to bear and the potential for structural or policy changes are worth the additional effort to overcome such challenges.

The Chicago Policy Research Action Group is a premiere example of such a regional consortium and a model for other such developing consortium efforts. The administrative structure of PRAG is kept small intentionally for two reasons: one pragmatic (limited resources) and one principled (the desire to remain responsive to community needs). All important decisions are made jointly by university and community representatives: policy decisions are made by the core group, and operational decisions are made by the steering committee; research funding allocations are made by a jointly staffed grant review committee; and new projects are developed by joint issue area working groups.

The purpose of PRAG's work is to improve the quality of life for the less advantaged members of the Chicago community. The work is done intentionally to contribute to a social action and social change agenda, specifically to empower groups that would otherwise be passed over by economic development or, worse, be victimized by it. To this end, PRAG sponsors policy forums, undertakes briefings for elected officials, meets with local government agency staffs, and holds policy breakfasts organized jointly with the mayor's office. Such a local policy impact is made possible by the size of the collaboration.

Summary

In this chapter, we have applied the principles of community-based research to organizational requirements in order to examine the institutional forms that CBR centers can develop. We demonstrated how the three principles of collaboration, demystification of knowledge and its construction, and social change advocacy shape the institutional requisites of mobilizing resources, building multiplex relationships, maximizing efficiency through a division of labor, managing information and authority relations, devising rules and control mechanisms, managing external relationships, and creating sustainability.

We then turned to four models of organizing CBR in higher education: solo practice, small programmatic structures, large complex structures, and regional consortium structures. In theory, the larger, complex structures and regional consortia are better able to achieve the organizational requirements for successful institutional operation and social change. However, the wide range of contexts, resources, histories of collaborations, and organizational development variations suggests that successful implementation of CBR is not based on adherence to a specific model of evolutionary path. Each collaborative team must determine for itself, based on these considerations, what path is likely to be most fruitful for achieving its goals.

In the next chapter, we turn to more specific nuts-and-bolts matters about developing and operating CBR centers, in order to support practitioners in making sound judgments regarding their center's development.

9

MANAGING COMMUNITY-BASED RESEARCH

PRACTICAL MATTERS

IN THIS CHAPTER, we examine some exemplary practices of organizing community-based research at colleges and universities around the United States. Our focus here is on concrete and practical issues, in order to provide guidance and resources to those who wish to advance their practice of CBR by creating a center to support their work. Even small, rural, liberal arts colleges such as Mars Hill College can find creative and effective ways to collaborate with the surrounding community in order to undertake productive, valuable, and transformative research projects. This chapter is about how to implement, administer, and develop CBR in higher education institutions.

In the previous chapter, we underscored the importance of locating the CBR organizing structure in an academic unit that reports to a dean or provost rather than in a community relations office, within student affairs, or in campus ministry (as is the case for some service-learning programs). We also stressed the importance of establishing a CBR center as a self-governing entity—in order to ensure its survival and its success. As a self-governing unit, requiring a real line item in an institution's budget, the CBR unit can determine its own actions and create positions and programs to achieve its mission.

Higher education institutions can best sustain and advance the practice of CBR by creating CBR centers. Relying on individual faculty to undertake CBR projects without such institutional support virtually ensures that when the faculty member leaves, changes interests, or goes on sabbatical leave, the CBR partnerships will be disrupted or dissolved. The multiple

Organizing for CBR at Mars Hill College

The Center for Assessment and Research Alliances (CARA) at Mars Hill College in western North Carolina is rooted in a long tradition of CBR. Mars Hill College, a liberal arts college with Christian roots that still influence its sense of service, was named the first "College of Promise" in North Carolina in conjunction with Colin Powell's America's Promise program. Directed by Thomas Plaut, CARA is one of the means that the college uses to express its culture of engagement, in addition to the Lifeworks Center, which coordinates service-learning activities.

Research alliances between community groups and agencies began at Mars Hill with its Community Development Institute in the 1970s. The agencies needed research, and the college had the expertise and equipment to help them meet those needs. The college faculty needed to educate students and fund computer hardware and software for teaching and research. CARA grew through the collaborative ventures that this complementarity produced and now has an innovative and sophisticated data analysis center geared toward both community and student development. Through the 1990s, they provided assessment and evaluation services for an emergency telephone installation project and other health initiatives, schools, the Red Cross, a sustainable farming project, and the Bonner Foundation.

Students are recruited from research classes as *apprentices* to CARA for basic data gathering, entry, and cleaning work. A few become intrigued and are trained as CARA staff *sojourners,* who help design projects and carry them through to completion. Each year, two or three students are named CARA *fellows,* who are responsible for running the center, helping organize projects and training, and supervising apprentices and sojourners. Apprentices are paid six dollars an hour, sojourners eight dollars, and fellows ten dollars. Faculty are recruited project by project; often they already are involved with an agency or community group. If the project is big enough, CARA can buy faculty time to reduce their course load.

dimensions of and activities associated with CBR require a support staff to make the workload manageable for faculty members. Furthermore, the center serves as a repository of intangible assets—of relationships, community knowledge, previous and ongoing work—that are essential to the successful completion of CBR projects. Even small institutions can mobilize sufficient resources to establish a center for sponsoring and supporting community-based research.

There is much overlap in the characteristics that support the successful practice of service-learning as well as CBR: clarity of mission, effective leadership, efficiency of operations, and effective mobilization of human and financial resources. Although sustained service-learning partnerships are important, the success of a CBR center in some ways requires greater organizational capacity than that needed for successful service-learning centers. Managing and sustaining CBR partnerships assumes great importance because the research process requires a better understanding of the community organization's change goals, its location within the community, and its strategy for social change. Typically, the collaborative research process requires more of the CBO leadership's time, which is facilitated by having longer-term relationships and better-developed levels of trust. More technical skills, as well as knowledge of the community, are required of the faculty, students, and community researchers. When results are produced through the research, more follow-up action is required of both the community organization and the faculty and students in order to advance the social change agenda. All of these additional needs can be supported better through the establishment and effective operations of a CBR center.

In the areas we describe in this chapter, a wide range of practices has evolved that reflects differences in institutional and community contexts, idiosyncrasies of historical relationships, and personnel considerations. In delineating some practices, we note the specific benefits and costs of the options being considered. There is no one perfect model for managing CBR activities. Each group of practitioners needs to consider its own assets and limitations, distinctive institutional context, potential resources, and priorities when deciding how to proceed.

Getting Started

The first task for an individual faculty member undertaking community-based research is identifying a community partner who shares common interests. These interests may be topic related or community related. In Chapter Two, we noted that partners often must seek additional support to complete CBR projects. The obvious place for the faculty member to seek additional support is from his or her own campus, and the important next step is to find some like-minded colleagues and to initiate conversations about common interests. We have found that although there may not be many (or any) other faculty colleagues engaging in CBR, there are likely to be at least a few other faculty members, as well as staff and students, who are familiar and comfortable with working in the community. This small group of faculty, which may also include supportive staff, administrators, students, and community partners, becomes the nucleus for a CBR structure.

Strategic Planning

Once the core group is identified, the next task is to find or create occasions to come together to discuss each other's community work, partnerships, and visions for social transformation. Such conversations may well turn to challenges of and supports for engaging in such community-based work and strategies for transforming the institution to provide greater support for it. These discussions are themselves the preliminary work for undertaking a more serious strategic assessment of the institution's potential support for establishing a CBR center and strategic planning for institutional change.

Eventually the nucleus group will have to undertake a more systematic strategic planning process by considering the following questions:

- How does their proposed work fit within the institution's mission?
- What is the institutional culture—for example, faculty beliefs about scholarship and publication, institutional rewards systems, student beliefs about the community—within which the program will have to operate?
- What is the nature of ongoing and past relationships of the institution with the community?
- What are the community's priorities and its capacities?
- What ways are students involved in the community, and what is their capacity to engage in collaborative research under faculty tutelage?
- What are some of the internal resources—people, material, networks, and financial—that can be mobilized to undertake and support CBR?
- What are some of the potential external sources of support for the institution and the community to undertake collaborative research?

Finally, the core CBR group should create an action strategy for mobilizing the resources needed to support CBR and reducing barriers that hinder its development. Such strategies are primarily bottom-up, as is the case for all of the programs we discuss in this book, but most have also benefited from some top-down resources for supporting CBR within the institution. By bottom-up strategies, we are referring to the faculty-, student-, and staff-led initiatives that create and develop CBR projects and begin to operate as if they were in fact a center, which ultimately leads to mobilizing additional resources that enable them to become a CBR center.

The College of New Jersey Learning Circle

Since 1999, The College of New Jersey (TCNJ), a residential state liberal arts college with a few graduate programs, has chosen a new president, provost, two vice provosts, and several new deans and has written a new mission statement. The mission statement calls for TCNJ to be "a national exemplar in the education of those who seek to sustain and advance the communities in which they live." Congruent with this new mission, top administrators have actively supported a faculty groundswell of community-based research at TCNJ.

Prior to the spring of 2000, the college's School of Education and School of Nursing had applied practica and collaborative projects with community partners. Many undergraduate departments had preprofessional internship and independent study opportunities. The college also had a well-developed, nationally recognized service-learning program that required all first-year students to complete ten hours of service for a wide range of local nonprofit organizations.

In the spring of 2000, sociology professor Matt Lawson encouraged students in his research methods class to undertake applied projects for a local shelter for runaway and homeless youth. Patrick Donohue, interim director of the nascent Trenton Center for Campus-Community Partnerships, learned of the shelter collaboration through local nonprofit networks and contacted Lawson about the Trenton Center. They discovered their mutual interests in mobilizing TCNJ faculty to engage in collaborative research projects with Trenton CBOs and strategized a process for engaging additional faculty members' involvement.

As they strategized, Lawson went to the provost to discuss this initiative and learned of his interest in supporting it. That spring, Lawson posted an electronic message to all faculty suggesting applications of community-based research in many disciplines and invited his colleagues to a breakfast meeting to discuss their interests and meet Trenton Center director Donohue. Eight faculty members, as well as the provost and the director of service-learning, attended the meeting. This group met biweekly in a learning circle throughout the summer, educating themselves, formulating an institutional strategy, drafting a mission statement, and designing an organizational structure that would foster CBR on campus.

Over the course of the 2000–2001 school year, members of this learning circle and a few additional faculty colleagues completed twelve projects with community partners—compared to one the previous year. Thirty-four faculty members and five administrators continued an electronic discussion list for mutual support and sharing ideas. In 2001–2002, the administration provided resources to establish a center and hire staff to coordinate faculty and student collaborations with community partners. This center has become the focal point for coordinating TCNJ's community engagement with Trenton and the surrounding communities through community-based research and service-learning.

A number of activities are critical for supporting and expanding CBR, so the core group will have to decide where to expend its limited resources for institutional development. Some of the successful CBR programs described in this book have succeeded by giving priority to the following activities:

- Attaining external funding to build administrative support and buy faculty time to undertake CBR projects
- Undertaking faculty development programming—to socialize faculty to the value of undertaking CBR, broaden uninvolved faculty colleagues' perceptions of legitimate research, and alter peer evaluation processes related to merit and tenure reviews
- Building from ongoing community partnerships, developed through direct service or service-learning program activities, thereby deepening the relationships and strengthening social change impacts

This core group also should define some practical and attainable short-term goals, an important step toward achieving institutional change. This is an old organizer's maxim: win early victories, even if small ones, in order to sustain early supporters and win new support from sympathetic bystanders. The core group needs to be sensitive to undertaking such winnable initiatives and then publicizing their achievements in order to broaden their net of mobilized resources. Such publicity can take the form of publishing a project report, getting media coverage of a successful collaborative project, or having students present their research at an academic conference.

The Role of Community Partners

An issue that needs to be considered early in the process and revisited as the CBR structure emerges is the role of community partners. This is a sensitive issue, and our experiences vary considerably in terms of community partners' inclusion throughout the development process, their advisory or decision-making responsibilities, and their control over resources.

In an idealistic first consideration of this issue, enthusiastic CBR advocates within the higher education institution may feel that community partners should be consulted, included, and have shared control over all CBR structure decisions. However, there are not only legal and liability considerations that preclude such sharing of authority within the university or college setting, but also strategic, practical, and political considerations that necessitate a thoughtful consideration of how roles, responsibilities, and authority can be shared. For example, on a strictly practical level, CBO staff and community residents typically have little interest in, knowledge of, and time for internal institutional politics and decision-making processes that are vital to the successful development of a CBR center at the institution. At the same time, this should not be used as an excuse for excluding community partners from participating in decision making that affects them or their capability for collaborating with the institution.

The Trenton Center deliberately and intentionally created itself to stand independently within the community, with community partners constituting a majority of the decision-making board. The center's board retains control over the center's resources, including approval of campus plans to use joint grant money. However, this is more the exception. In most cases, community partners are consulted on important issues, or a small number of the center's advisory board are community partners, or community partners share decision-making authority with faculty members in particular realms.

Organizational Structure and Internal Operations

In the previous chapter, we discussed the various forms that CBR initiatives can take, ranging from a single faculty practitioner collaborating with a community partner to a complex center through which multiple collaborative research teams undertake numerous projects. In examining the possible organizational structures of CBR centers, particularly with respect to staffing arrangements, budget and funding issues, and technology, we refer to different models for CBR centers located within higher education institutions, including simple, freestanding centers such as Mars Hill College, CBR units embedded in a complex center such as Georgetown University (see Figure 9.1), and multicampus CBR superstructures based on the work of several campus structures such as Chicago's Policy Research Action Group.

A more recent approach is to organize a CBR center as an independent, freestanding nonprofit organization in the community. Two community-based models that have emerged recently, the Trenton Center for Campus-Community Partnerships in Trenton, New Jersey, and Just Connections, in the Appalachian region, are independent, nonprofit organizations that assist in developing and coordinating campus-community partnerships. Established by faculty and community leaders, these organizations work to:

- Nurture, support, and at times manage community-based research partnerships.
- Organize training sessions on CBR and other topics, including strategic planning, introduction to geographical information systems, and participatory neighborhood planning.

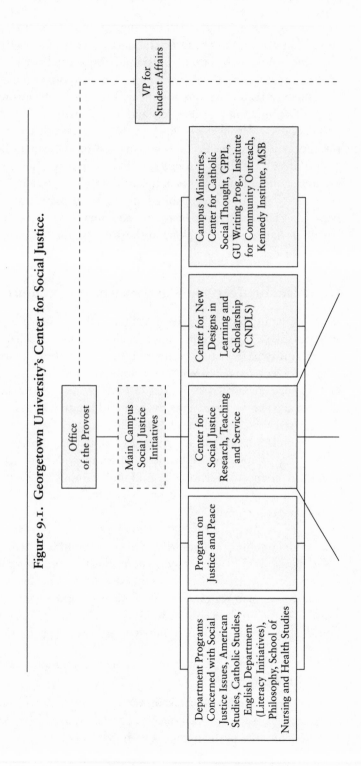

Figure 9.1. Georgetown University's Center for Social Justice.

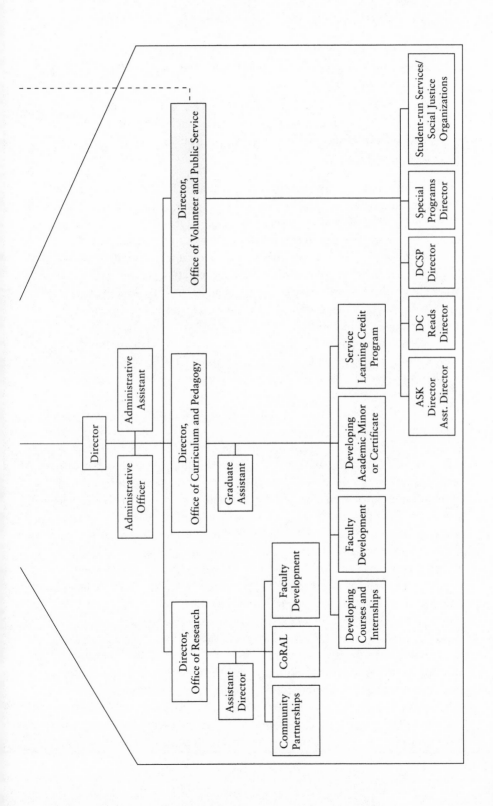

- Assist member campuses in developing their campus-based CBR centers, including helping to raise funds, bring in outside consultants, and train staff.

- Organize study circles, regional conferences, and other vehicles for dialogue about common issues of concern among a broad cross-section of nonprofit, academic, student, foundation, and government leaders.

These intermediary organizations play a central role in cultivating the common ground between the missions of the local higher education institutions and the needs and interests of community groups. A key aspect of this model is the emphasis on coordination and community control. In both organizations, their board of trustees consists of at least half community members along with representatives from participating campuses. Among other things, these boards have controlled significant grant funding that in part has been subgranted to the colleges based on a review of proposals submitted by colleges. In addition, both organizations have played a significant role in developing and coordinating campus-community partnerships. For example, the Trenton Center has a Campus-Coordination Committee that is co-led by a Trenton Center staff person and the director of one of the campus centers that gathers the community research questions and then works with their peers to match these requests with faculty and student teams.

At each of the academic institutions, the director of the CBR center is a faculty member who reports to an academic administrator, such as the dean or provost. There are other possibilities: the director can be defined as an administrator rather than a faculty member and report to another administrative office rather than to an academic office. There are institutional variations that influence the leadership and reporting lines for the CBR center, and the institution's historic location of community outreach activities may play some role in this determination. It might even be tempting to establish the center through the president's office or through the office of a vice president for external relations and community affairs, for administrative start-up ease and budgetary matters. We would argue, however, that it is imperative for the unit to be placed in an academic reporting line to a dean or provost in order to ensure the academic integrity of the CBR work of the center. Similarly, we believe that it is important to have a tenured faculty member to serve as the director in order to enhance credibility of center's work with other faculty colleagues.

Although the faculty member–director may also work on particular CBR projects, his or her distinctive role as center director is to ensure the overall effective operations and sustainability of the center. The administrative support staff helps to carry out the work of the center as well as the work on particular CBR projects. As CBR center operations become even larger, there may be multiple administrators whose roles are further differentiated; for example, different people may take on budget and financial responsibilities, operational and logistics management, fundraising, and public relations. Researchers may begin to differentiate their roles as well, so that within the center, one could find experts on specific research methodologies (for example, a survey researcher or ethnographic field researcher), specific substantive areas of expertise (such as an economic development expert or a family violence specialist), or with specialized knowledge of particular communities.

CBR Staffing

As the CBR center becomes institutionalized, the leaders need to define positions, write formal job descriptions, and recruit individuals to fill roles through job searches targeting appropriate professionals. In the early stages of the center's development, many of these roles may be filled by faculty or staff who are not paid for their time to do this work. With increasing awareness of and financial support for the center's activities, pieces of faculty time may be bought out by the center for this work, particularly through release time from other teaching, research, or service commitments. Also, community members may volunteer their time or CBO staff may be loaned to, or bought by, the center to assist with particular start-up tasks.

As positions become better defined and funding is secured to hire people, it is important to select people with the right skills and experience to fill these positions. For jobs requiring community-specific expertise, the center should advertise for applicants from among community organizations and local media. For administrative positions, the center should advertise through local media, university channels, and community organization newsletters, as well as appropriate professional networks. For CBR research expertise, the center might solicit applications from university and community partners and from national networks such as the listservs of the CRN network, PARnet, and COMM-ORG. During the search process, community partners should be brought into the selection and interviewing process. This may be achieved by having community partners serve on the search committee or interview final candidates during their campus visits.

On campus, students typically provide some staffing support. They can serve in administrative assistant positions or help with office management, financial support, and logistical operations. Undergraduate students in CBR classes serve in research roles as part of their course learning—for example, helping to gather or codify data or undertaking library or Internet research—which may require a substantial amount of training and supervision by the faculty member. These research positions also may be paid (in whole or in part by federal work-study funds), linked to independent study credit, or voluntary, such as through a research internship program. For more experienced undergraduates and graduate students, paid research assistantships and internships can be created to assist with research projects, affording students more responsibility in supporting the CBR work. Nevertheless, such students still require preparatory training and regular oversight while in the field.

Community members may assume formal roles within the CBR center beyond their role as community partner on a given project. For example, grant funding can be used to hire community members as paid research staff on a particular project. On some projects, youths may be paid or provided internship opportunities to engage in research projects alongside community adults, faculty, and university students. Community partners should be invited and supported to participate in center initiatives, such as strategic planning processes and hiring searches. The center director may wish to create more formal consultant roles that enable community members to have ongoing relations with the center, facilitating projects, undertaking fundraising, or developing technical assistance resources. Some of the CBR centers, such as the Policy Research Action Group (PRAG) in Chicago and the Philadelphia Higher Education Network for Neighborhood Development, have established more permanent, formal positions on their steering committee assigned to community partners (with stipends and expense support) to ensure community voice in the center's decision making.

A diversity of skills and perspectives strengthens CBR projects. However, it also presents challenges, such as how to facilitate open communication among all the members of a research team and the center and how to deal with conflicts due to differences of perspective, methodologies, ideologies, and personal values. And just as center leaders must be sensitive to factions and differences in perspectives among potential faculty collaborators, they must also be cautious in assembling community partners who are willing to work together on a project or on the board. Community members are no less likely than faculty members to engage in heated battles over scarce resources, personal matters, and interactions that took place long ago.

Budget Issues

For the solo CBR practitioner or teacher, CBR may be a low-cost venture. The cost of the faculty member's time is covered by the teaching and research obligations associated with the professional role. Additional office and administrative expenses, as well as course-related travel and supplies costs related to CBR projects, may also be covered by an academic department. Other out-of-pocket expenses may be covered by department or university discretionary funds or would be tax deductible as research-related business expenses for the faculty member.

As CBR projects get larger, costs increase. Money is needed to pay for additional help in gathering and processing data, managing the program's operations and budget, staff training and development, space rental, equipment purchase, and public relations. At some point, externally generated resources will be required to pay for the costs of the research beyond the time of the researchers engaged in the project as part of their jobs. Such funding may come from grants or contracts from external agencies or university resources allocated for such purposes—for example, through endowments earmarked to support such work. Salaries for research positions can come from soft funds (those raised from grants or contracts targeted for a specific purpose and limited in amount and time) or hard funds (permanent positions that are institutionalized as part of the university's staff). Soft funds enable researchers to identify needs and respond flexibly to priorities identified in the community and by specific funders. The drawback of relying on soft funding is that the researcher or the center has to dedicate some substantial amount of resources to grant seeking. Permanent funding of research positions through the university or external endowment frees the researcher from having to seek funding on a continuous basis. However, such permanent funding requires that the CBR unit pay special attention to ensure that it remains responsive to the community's needs over time rather than being driven by internal university interests.

Once a university's CBR initiative reaches some scale of operation, it is likely to hire administrators to manage the center's operations. This includes the support activities of paying staff, managing logistics of meetings and allocating resources, arranging transportation, and other support activities that may be only tangentially related to the undertaking of a particular CBR project. Furthermore, there needs to be a mechanism to recruit faculty and students' involvement in CBR projects, solicit projects from the community, and match resources to projects. The community research clearinghouse concept has been developed at several institutions to solicit project ideas and potential faculty and CBO partners, using Web-based databases and search capacities to link those with common interests. This too incurs real budget costs because data have to be solicited and input in an ongoing manner, and partnerships have to be initiated, supported, and sustained—all of which is done by permanent center staff. Also, securing the long-term success of the enterprise requires some staff development activities that train and recruit the next generation of researchers and socialize potential community partners into the CBR process.

Overhead is both a fuzzy, catch-all term and a specific, federally regulated activity. In its nebulous form, *overhead* refers to all the costs of running and administering a center that is not typically specified in a line item of a grant or contract. It may refer to an implicit rent for the use of space and other equipment such as computers, telephones, and photocopiers; it includes the cost of university personnel in offices such as human resources, payroll, accounting, public relations, and grants management that help to support the work of the center but do not receive earmarked fees for the services they provide for such work; and it includes funds for the general upkeep and maintenance of the university's capital resources. In the technical sense, government grants allow for charging overhead as a fixed percentage of costs to allow for the grant to pay for some of the university's infrastructure used by the grant. As of 2002, the Department of Housing and Urban Development's Community Outreach Partnership Center grants include a 25 percent overhead charge.

Community Research and Learning Network Clearinghouse

The Community Research and Learning (CoRAL) Network in Washington, D.C. calls itself "a partnership among higher education institutions and community based organizations (CBOs), the purpose of which is to mobilize the universities' educational and scholarly resources for the purpose of supporting CBO's social change missions in pursuit of social justice." One of its early initiatives was to create a Web-based clearinghouse (www.coralnetwork.org) to solicit CBR project interests from CBOs and solicit higher education–based resources to undertake such projects. This Web site operates as a tool for CoRAL staff and participants to help make matches between potential university and community partners. New users are invited to suggest projects or solicit partnerships based on the information on the Web site. The clearinghouse also serves to disseminate information about ongoing and completed projects, announce upcoming events, and serves as a repository of resources and technical assistance.

As a large center, PRAG has a well-established center that operates from its base at Loyola University with a steering committee of twenty-four members, evenly split between university and community partners. Its annual operating budget is over $1 million, with funding from university resources, foundation grants, and contract work. The PRAG center has benefited from the support of the Chicago-based MacArthur Foundation, which has provided over $4 million in support over the past decade. The consortium of universities in Chicago has contributed several million dollars of in-kind support by creating campus centers at each university to recruit, sustain, and develop faculty and student interest to undertake this work. External grants and contract work have provided over $10 million in support of community-based research during the past decade. Overall, funding has been split among these three types of funding—foundation, university, and grants and contracts—demonstrating a sound principle of having a diverse funding base for the center to ensure its long-term stability.

Princeton University's Community-Based Learning Initiative (CBLI) adds an innovative wrinkle to the funding mix of CBR centers: alumni donations. Princeton University alumni from the class of 1955 created an endowment campaign at the time of its thirtieth reunion, spearheaded by a challenge from classmate Ralph Nader. Funds from this endowment now go to support a number of community-oriented activities, including community service programs, service-learning, and community-based research. The activities are housed at the independently incorporated CBLI to ensure that the alumni organization maintains control over the funds. CBLI funds are not intermingled with the university's operating budget, although CBLI does collaborate with numerous service programs and service-learning activities organized through other university offices, such as the college dean's office and the Princeton Community House, which sponsors students' direct service activities.

Whether a CBR center should undertake contract work for clients who are able to pay is an ethical dilemma that the center must consider. Presumably, CBR centers are engaging in research with and on behalf of disadvantaged groups that have limited ability to pay for the costs of undertaking such research. Thus, the ability to pay for the research, even to cover the costs of the materials needed for the research itself, may be severely limited. If a community organization has received a grant to do this work, this is less an issue, although the CBR center and the CBO still have to negotiate what expenses should be charged against the grant. Increasingly, service agencies are required to undertake evaluation research to demonstrate the effectiveness of their operations, providing the opportunity for collaborating on evaluation research. Funding built into the agencies' grants or contracts for evaluation work can be paid to the CBR center for undertaking this work. Even when the CBO has some ability to pay for research done by university faculty and students, there is an inherent and perceived power differential that must be considered when negotiating contractual arrangements between the university CBR center and the community partner.

A CBR center may decide to undertake research with some partners that can pay to subsidize projects for clients or partners who cannot. Or the center may decide not to pursue such opportunities, restricting its activities to developing partnerships with and seeking funding for clients who are disadvantaged. Even this approach, however, is not free from ethical challenges in that the university may seek funding from local foundations and agencies, and thereby find itself competing with the same CBOs with which they are attempting to partner (see Figure 8.3). The CBR center and its partnering CBOs will need to think strategically about which grants are more appropriately submitted by the higher education institution-based center and which are appropriately submitted through the community organization.

The best way to ensure long-term sustainability of CBR within the university is to have hard-line positions within the university's budget—in other words, positions that are permanently funded. In larger centers, specific faculty lines and administrative positions will be paid for with funds allocated to the center by the university, parallel to funding for academic departments and programs. Endowment funding for such positions, and possibly for the center as a whole, ensures their existence into perpetuity.

Technology and Transportation

New technologies have improved the practice and capabilities of community-based research with respect to communication, sharing information, and management. At the lower end of the technology spectrum, access to transportation (or lack thereof) may play a role in limiting the opportunities for collaborative work; long distances, limited public transportation access, costly private transportation, and safety are transportation issues that can deter CBR partnerships. These practical matters must be addressed in order to undertake successful CBR projects.

Communication among university and community partners is greatly improved with widespread access to low-cost telephones and fax machines. Even most small CBO offices can afford fax machines, copiers, an-

swering machines, or voice mail, which are readily accessible at colleges
and universities. The increased popularity and lower costs of wireless
phones are making communication continuous and inexpensive. In fact,
the new challenge seems to be communication overload: too many messages requiring too much time to filter through and respond selectively.

Widespread access to e-mail has also dramatically improved communication capabilities. Although some smaller CBOs still lack access to
powerful enough computers to maintain Internet and e-mail access, their
numbers are declining rapidly. On the college and university side, virtually
all faculty now have access to computers—if not on their own desktops,
then in convenient labs—that are powerful enough to provide full electronic
communication and access using the Internet. Electronic address lists for
e-mail allow for targeted communication with multiple others working on
a project. The growth of regional and national listservs of CBR participants
allows for the exchange of ideas, best practices, and troubleshooting among
those who are not directly involved on a particular CBR project but may
have helpful experiences to share. Numerous CBR center Web sites contain
large amounts of helpful information and links to useful data sources. Here
too the challenge is moving quickly from lack of access to information overload due to the declining costs of technology and the mushrooming growth
of information available at relatively little cost.

The tremendous growth of information available on the World Wide
Web is another source of potential overload for CBR practitioners. Of
course, the value of the information obtained from the Web has to be evaluated in the light of one's own experience and context, requiring time and
expertise to assess such information. Raw data that might appear useful
for some research purposes have to be evaluated in terms of their appropriateness and reliability for others. Smaller organizations may in fact turn
to university partners to provide such expertise for determining the value
of data as well as to providing analysis to respond to specific queries.

The increasing sophistication and user friendliness of computer software have made undertaking data management and statistical analysis
procedures dramatically easier. Widespread access to database management software (such as Quattro Pro and Dbase) and spreadsheets (such
as Excel and Lotus 1–2–3) has made it much easier for community organizations to build data sets needed for community-based research from
their own records. The new versions of statistical analysis software, such
as Statistical Package for the Social Sciences (SPSS), Minitab, and Stat-
View, make it possible to undertake even quite sophisticated data analysis with little statistical training. Geographical information systems that
enable researchers to map problems and assets at the neighborhood level

and link them to census data or other government agency data are becoming increasingly accessible and easier to use.

Universities are likely to have resource management software that CBR centers can use for their own purposes. Clearly, the spreadsheets that come bundled with most new personal computers are powerful enough to maintain budget and financial information even for quite sophisticated projects. Human resource management software can keep track of the activities, hours, and pay information for personnel. For centers employing large numbers of volunteers as well as paid staff, software such as VICTA is quite helpful in keeping track of their activities.

Transportation can become a serious challenge to CBR projects when the university and community partners are not located near each other. In urban areas where the university and community partners are geographical neighbors, walking and short public transportation rides can fulfill the need to have the partners meet face-to-face, regardless of the time of day, day of week, and irregularity of such meetings. At the other end of the spectrum, in rural areas, virtually all CBO and campus partners will be located at some distance from each other, and there is unlikely to be any public transportation that can suit the timing and travel needs of faculty and student researchers to get to community sites. In other urban and suburban settings where the university and community are not geographically colocated, public transportation may not be accessible or convenient in terms of its fixed schedules. In such cases, it may be necessary to travel by private vehicles, taxicabs, or university-owned vehicles. The costs of such private transportation may be substantial, as are the costs of travel time. Safety and liability matters need to be considered as well. The CBR center may be able to assume responsibility for supporting these transportation needs.

Faculty Considerations

Recruiting, supporting, and developing faculty involvement in community-based research is challenging for several reasons:

- Most doctoral-prepared faculty were not formally trained in CBR in graduate school and have had little exposure to it.
- The perspective or orientation of faculty research is toward a scholarship of discovery rather than a scholarship of application or engagement (Boyer, 1990).
- Professional norms of research and discipline-based questions tend not to be place specific.

- Institutional reward and incentive systems, particularly at doctoral research institutions, emphasize publications that conform to norms of traditional theory and hypothesis testing, have a focus on abstract or theoretical issues, and examine national or regional policy matters (Boyer, 1990; Edwards and Marullo, 1999; Hesser, 1999; Nyden, 1997; Porpora, 1999).

- Heavy teaching loads at some higher education teaching institutions impinge on the time available for faculty there to undertake CBR.

- Lack of familiarity with CBR by faculty peers and administrators leads them to treat such work as "service" work rather than innovative pedagogy and engaged scholarship, which devalues the work and faculty incentives to participate in it. Beyond these training and normative impediments to engaging in CBR, additional practical challenges must be overcome before a faculty member can become involved in collaborative community-based research.

- The interested faculty member must become familiar with the community, local CBOs, and the issues of greatest concern to underprivileged community members.

- The faculty member must establish a working relationship with community collaborators, which includes developing shared understandings of problems and language to describe them, common perspectives on possible responses to the problem, and a level of trust.

- The faculty member must mobilize sufficient resources to undertake the project. (As indicated in Chapter Eight, these resources may include other academic colleagues, graduate or undergraduate students, money, other volunteers, and appropriate materials, equipment, and services.)

For the solo researcher, ignoring disincentives and overcoming these obstacles is mainly a matter of individual effort. A CBR center can provide support for overcoming the practical challenges of becoming familiar with the community, establishing working relationships, and mobilizing resources. The center may also play a role in helping to (re)develop the faculty expertise needed to undertake CBR and in altering institutional rewards systems. We now turn to some of the strategies and programs that have been used to develop, support, and sustain faculty who are engaged in CBR.

Finding and Recruiting Faculty

Some faculty members are predisposed to engaging in CBR. Such a predisposition may be based on values commitment (which may be discipline based, faith based, or humanistic in its origins), previous experience, or atypical training. Others might be enticed to undertake a CBR project by the offer of financial support—for example, through offering small grants through the CBR center to develop such projects. Once these faculty are identified, the next step is to engage them in conversations about and orientations to CBR in a particular locale. Personal follow-up and individualized support prove to be most helpful in moving interested and potential CBR collaborators into active partners. Invitations by students to faculty have also been effective as a means of recruiting faculty, particularly through their teaching. Another recruiting tool is to organize forums that feature engaging speakers, offer lively conversation, and provide some food and drink. A talk given by a high-ranking university official that encourages such faculty activity may also provide encouragement for those predisposed to community engagement. Another device that we have used is to offer "reality" tours of the communities that we work with in order to have interested faculty meet potential or actual CBO partners working in their own milieu. Periodic mailings to the entire faculty about such speakers or other forums organized by the CBR center help to maintain a level of visibility and legitimacy for CBR work and serve as an open invitation (albeit a passive one) for those with an interest to become involved.

Once potential CBR faculty members have been identified, they may desire more information about what is entailed in doing collaborative research and specific opportunities available in the community. Information about just what can be done to get involved and how it can be conveyed on a one-to-one level or through more formally organized workshops, institutes, seminars, fellows programs, or mentoring programs. One form of CBR workshop would be a relatively short training activity (ranging from a half-day to two days) that introduces CBR to interested faculty members and suggests opportunities for future engagement. A more comprehensive institute would be a longer block of time (one to two weeks) through which potential CBR participants are introduced to research opportunities and take initial steps to become engaged in whatever format may be appropriate for their interests. A seminar would be an ongoing, longer-term forum through which interested potential partners work through the process of transforming potential projects into actual research initiatives. Bringle and associates at the Indiana Campus Compact has used a service-learning fellows program to provide training, ongoing support, and institutional change initiatives to engage faculty in CBR as well as developing service-learning courses and curriculum (Bringle, Games, Ludlum, Osgood, and Osborne, 2000). We have also used a more informal mentoring program, which entails matching a seasoned CBR veteran with a newcomer in order to provide support and advice for the neophyte in launching a successful collaborative research endeavor.

Another strategy for developing faculty CBR projects is to provide support, in terms of time or money (or both), for the researcher to begin a project. This may take the form of release time from other commitments, such as a course release or freeing a faculty member from other administrative responsibilities. An institution may also offer mini-grants (for example, for summer research projects) to undertake pilot CBR projects. University-sponsored faculty fellows programs or other faculty research support mechanisms may be adapted to accommodate CBR projects. The state of Maryland offers faculty sabbatical research support for service-learning and CBR projects through its "sabbaticorps" program.

Support and Reward Structures

One of the major challenges facing researchers engaged in CBR is an institution- and discipline-based reward structure that does not readily accommodate community-based research. At doctoral research institutions, applied research is devalued in most disciplines and relegated to journals that are perceived to be second tier during faculty review processes. CBR, done collaboratively and directed toward the needs of a particular community or agency, is likely to be viewed even more skeptically by department, university, and discipline colleagues in merit review processes (Porpora, 1999). Although there are efforts under way to educate faculty and administrators about the value and legitimacy of such engaged scholarship, such peer appreciation for this type of work is limited. This places an additional burden on the CBR practitioner and a campus CBR center to educate colleagues and academic administrators on the value and legitimacy of this work, the benefits produced for the community, and the secondary benefits that accrue to the university as a result of goodwill generated in response to professional contributions to the community.

This raises the issue as to how this work is to be counted in the academy—as teaching, research, or service. Obviously, if such work is counted in the faculty evaluation process as service, it is relegated to tertiary status, which carries little weight in promotion, tenure, and merit evaluations, particularly at research universities. In our view, this work is not community or professional service—at least, not in the narrow sense in which this term is used for faculty evaluation purposes. In institutions where teaching is highly valued and rewarded, undertaking CBR projects in conjunction with one's courses allows the professor to set learning objectives for students and document the enhanced learning and powerful impact such courses have on students' development. Standardized teaching evaluations may provide some evidence of students' enriched learning in CBR courses as reflected in their higher overall evaluation of the course. However, it may be worthwhile to develop additional course and teaching assessments that capture other elements of students' learning. As Chapter Six indicates, CBR enriches students' learning in a variety of ways. Citing published accounts of such learning outcomes and conducting research that documents them in one's own teaching may be useful in the faculty evaluation process, especially at institutions that reward teaching excellence and value the scholarship of teaching and learning.

At institutions where scholarship is the key determinant of faculty rewards—particularly as measured by the quantity of journal articles published and the journals' prestige—the challenge of having CBR count is substantially greater. The reporting form required by community groups to use the collaborative research results differs substantially from that required by discipline-based research journals. In our experience, community partners are less interested in detailed reporting of methodology and have very little interest in how the current research fits within the appropriate theoretical and research traditions of the discipline. Instead, they are much more interested in descriptive findings, the caveats and nuances of the research results, and their implications for social change and policy action. At the very least, this means that faculty partners seeking to attain scholarly credit for such work need to rewrite their collaborative research in a format that conforms to the expectations of the discipline's research journals. Furthermore, such work runs the risk of being assessed as too narrow or too applied by peer reviewers who evaluate the work according to their (implicit) standards of discovery scholarship. Even if the journal accepts and acknowledges the value of engaged scholarship, there may be an assumption that the entire social change agenda needs to be played out successfully (and documented in the academic research report) to make the article worth publishing. Such an assumption leads to a biasing of published reports of CBR—toward social change projects that achieve success—that is partially determined by a political outcome that itself is determined by myriad social forces, many of them unrelated to the quality of the research process and its findings.

Another development in this area is the emergence of specialty journals to create a forum for publishing the results of engaged scholarship. In this category, we include the *Michigan Journal of Community Service Learning*, which carries research and pedagogy articles; the University of Pennsylvania's *Universities and Communities Schools*; the *Journal of Higher Education Outreach and Engagement*; and journal of the Association for Research on Nonprofit and Voluntary Associations, *Voluntas*. In addition, some long-standing journals with a broader mission have had made editorial decisions to feature articles on these topics and even to devote entire issues to this work. For example, the *American Behavioral Scientist* devoted two issues to the related subjects of university-community collaboration and cutting-edge developments in service-learning and CBR (volumes 42:5, 1999, and 43:5, 2000); the American Sociological Association devoted a section to service-learning pedagogy and CBR in its journal *Teaching Sociology* (26:4, 1998); the *American Sociologist* (23, 1992) and *Sociological Imagination* (33:2, 1996) each devoted issues to participatory action research; and the Department of Housing and Urban Development's journal, *Cityscape*, devoted an entire issue (5:1, 2000) to the experience of community outreach partnership centers, funded by the department to undertake community-based research. To further the legitimacy of such work, the American Association for Higher Education has sponsored a series of eighteen discipline-based monographs to document the best practices in service-learning, which include some examples of CBR.

In addition to institutional rewards that support a faculty member's engagement in CBR, there are other forms of support: interpersonal (from individuals in the community, profession, and the university), financial (apart from university salary and grant support), symbolic, and intrinsic. One innovative form of interpersonal support that has emerged is the ongoing learning circle, a forum in which colleagues engaged in similar work meet to share their work and their struggles, and otherwise interact with each other to create a support network. National associations such as Educators for Community Engagement (formerly the Invisible College), the National Society for Experiential Education, and the Community Research Network serve as alternative professional associations for CBR practitioners, providing forums for sharing work, convening for annual meetings, and organizing regional meetings of practitioners. Financial support may come from additional stipends or consulting fees paid to researchers for their CBR work or travel or training fees provided beyond wages. Support in the form of human labor may be provided through a department or CBR center providing research assistants or interns to a researcher working on a project. Symbolic rewards may take the form of special awards to acknowledge outstanding work, recognition ceremonies to acknowledge and thank contributors publicly, or special honors or meals for CBR contributors.

We believe that the most important factor that sustains the work of CBR practitioners is the intrinsic satisfaction and reward of knowing that one's work is making a difference in the lives of people, of maintaining the belief that one is doing the right thing, and the expressions of appreciation and gratitude from partners, students, and beneficiaries that reaffirm the value of this work.

Faculty Sustainability

In order for CBR practice to be sustainable over the long run, the supports and institutional rewards must be institutionalized. Each of the supports may require some institutional change within the university to bring them about, so faculty advocates should be prepared to devote some energy to this domain of social change as well. A CBR center, with hard money positions and endowment for research and program initiatives, provides the greatest security for the institutionalization of CBR and the base for pressing for such institutional change. For CBR that is undertaken within courses, creating a home for such courses in departments' permanent course offerings, or even among their requirements, ensures the sustainability of such activities. Finding a place for such courses within the university's core curriculum provides a tremendous level of sustainability. We have been able to identify CBR courses being offered in fulfillment of universities' requirements for service-learning, diversity, and discipline-based scientific inquiry.

Mobilizing students to create academic interest and legitimacy is an additional resource that can be used to build faculty support. A student research conference not only provides students with a forum to showcase their work and their enthusiasm for CBR, but demonstrates to other faculty the value of this work and the impact that it can have on students. In some instances, earmarked student resources—such as activities fees, speakers' bureaus resources, and scholarship funds—can be directed to supporting CBR activities undertaken by students with positive visibility for faculty. The Bonner Foundation's Bonner Scholars program, which provided $6 million in funding for roughly fifteen hundred student scholarships in 2000–2001, allows less affluent college students to engage in CBR as one means of fulfilling the scholarship's service requirement.

Efforts to educate faculty colleagues and academic administrators also require a long-term strategy. Creating a task force or CBR center committee charged to address such institutional change requirements through a strategic planning process, although tedious and time-consuming, may prove to be fruitful in the long run due to the extensive conversations, education, and vetting process entailed. The cultural capital of an institution is also an important resource. A university's mission statement will undoubtedly employ one or more frames establishing the institution's commitment to the community and to society. The following mission frames can be employed for establishing the legitimacy of and mobilizing resources for CBR:

- Moral (especially for faith-based institutions)—the responsibility of the institution to support those in need and educate its students to adopt such personal values
- Civic—the obligation to prepare students to be contributing citizens to the common good
- Social responsibility—the responsibility of the institution to be a model corporate citizen and contribute to the community's well-being
- Reciprocity—for land grant and public institutions, the obligation to contribute to the public good in exchange for favorable treatment and public financial support

Center-Campus Relations

A CBR center identified as or located within an academic unit is better able to evaluate, monitor, and assess its own professional work (within the broader university academic context); faculty members can build courses and professional research work around their community-based research; and external considerations such as students' service interests or town-gown relations are not the primary forces driving the CBR process. Status as an academic program also ensures that there are positions, both administrative and faculty lines, that are assigned to and responsible for undertaking this work and that they have a budget from the university with which to do the work.

Matching Institutional Research Assets to Community Research Projects

When CBR has academic program status, faculty members can undertake their CBR work in the context of the curriculum as part of their teaching commitment or as faculty research in fulfillment of their scholarship commitment. If CBR is built into a faculty member's course offerings, the professor must decide how it will fit into the course and how the students will be trained and used appropriately in undertaking research. Students may also be involved as teaching assistants for the course or as research assistants on projects that are operated through the center. As research assistants, students may be paid appropriate wages for their role in the process, or such positions may have a modest stipend attached or be totally voluntary internships, with the student receiving training in exchange for her or his labor. Another vehicle for structuring student involvement is through independent study: the student undertakes a piece of a larger project and is supervised by the faculty researcher and receives academic credit for the research project undertaken. Graduate students may also undertake doctoral or master's thesis research in conjunction with larger CBR projects, and undergraduates may undertake senior theses or honors projects on CBR projects. Organizing such projects will always have an ad hoc nature to some degree, as individual faculty and students with shared interests come together to work on projects with CBOs as they find each other. To make this process more organized and systematic, CBR centers can develop a clearinghouse and matchmaking function for themselves in several ways:

- Soliciting research projects and maintaining lists of potential and ongoing community research projects
- Soliciting interest and resources from faculty and students interested in participating in such work
- Taking steps to match the resources with research needs, such as setting up meetings, making introductions, and providing tangible financial and human support

The third element is critical and requires proactive staffing, as the lists by themselves do not automatically translate into matches. In practical terms, this means that partnership building and management becomes a part of some CBR center staff member's job description.

Review, Approval, Informed Consent, and Liability

Considerable variability exists in the amount and nature of universities' oversight of community-based research projects in areas such as the kinds of research that require formal IRB approval, the nature of informed consent required for participation in research projects, and whether course-based research projects fall under the same review criteria. We have found that universities' risk management policies vary considerably regarding the level of support, or opposition, they offer community-based research projects. Although we point out some potential problems and pitfalls, each potential CBR practitioner will need to discuss these issues with college or university officials who oversee the institutional review process for human subjects research and deal with risk management issues.

As we pointed out in Chapter Five, university policies regarding the review process for research on human subjects vary widely. Some institutions do not require that any CBR projects go through a review and approval process, some require review under certain circumstances, some require reviews for virtually all projects, and those with established CBR centers have created their own internal review mechanisms. When proposals do require review, the concern is with the human subjects who are participating in the study: whether they are being exposed to risks as a result of their participating in the study; whether the informed consent process provides the participant with adequate information to grant such consent, privacy, and confidentiality concerns; and the documentation of such information and consent forms. Such a review process seems to be inspired in reaction to a medical research process that puts subjects in a study at risk due to exposure to untested medications or, conversely, from failing to treat life-threatening conditions. As applied to the social, political, economic, interactional, and policy research commonly undertaken in CBR, exposure to such physical health risks is generally nonexistent. Instead, concerns are raised about the potential social costs of participating in such a study, for example, through the risks of stigma, loss of privacy, or loss of program benefits or privileges. Even merely associating with an outsider—a university partner on the research team—may expose a participant to some level of risk.

Two practical matters emerge in the review process: the appropriateness of applying conventional IRB processes to CBR and the timeliness of such review processes. In most instances, IRB committees asked to review CBR proposals will likely be unfamiliar with such requests and will attempt to translate standard research protocols to the process under review. Conversely, the CBR practitioners and, especially, the community partners may be asked to translate their procedures into a scientific model (of discovery) that does not particularly fit research objectives. Such cross-cultural communication is fraught with the challenges of misunderstandings, questioning of assumptions and motives, and mistrust that might emerge from starting with different assumptions about the nature of scientific inquiry. Our experience has been that the best way to deal with such challenges is to keep open the lines of communications, address such questions forthrightly, clarify assumptions, and treat such interactions as an opportunity to educate colleagues unfamiliar with CBR.

Such cross-cultural communication challenges might require additional work and lead to delays before an IRB process approves a particular study. In addition, the urgency of community problems and short deadlines for grant applications and program review often place the community partners on a faster time line than the faculty partner. Furthermore, the academic calendar, with its slow times during the summer, semester, and midsemester breaks, and its overall more deliberate pace, may also lead to delays detrimental to the collaborative effort. The university partners should do all that is possible to avoid such delays, and the community partners must become sensitive to such constraints. It may be possible for the CBR center to negotiate an expedited review process that establishes guidelines for human subjects research that does not pose risks to the community collaborators, thereby enabling some CBR projects to be reviewed more quickly under these guidelines. Again, managing expectations through open communication is the best approach to avoid such delays and potentially detrimental misunderstandings.

From the university side, another dimension of review and control that needs to be considered is that of risk management and liability. When faculty members and students are off campus, perhaps riding in university-owned vehicles or transporting community members while undertaking official university business, they are exposing themselves to different types of risks from what university risk managers may be accustomed to. Students especially need to be told about the different types of risks to which they will be exposed while in community settings, especially if the research project is part of a required program of study. University risk managers should be informed of the nature of such research projects and should be given an opportunity to raise their concerns and pass along their expertise. As CBR is conducted as part of the teaching and research activities that are defined as part of the faculty member's job obligations, and students are participating in their role as students or student employees of the university, the risk management staff needs to understand the university's responsibility for accepting liability for possible mishaps.

CBR project directors should devote some of the students' training to matters of risk and liability. Presentations about risk and safety should not invoke unnecessary fears, but neither should they ignore or minimize the types of risk posed. Some institutions require students to sign waiver forms indicating that they have been informed of the risks involved in undertaking community-based work, are undertaking the work willingly, and do not hold the university liable for accidents or damages. Such waivers nevertheless do not release universities from their responsibilities to provide appropriate support, care, and caution on behalf of its students. They do, however, ensure that the faculty members and students talk seriously about risk-related issues. Students might instead sign a consent form, indicating their voluntary participation and perhaps providing emergency contact information.

In terms of the faculty CBR project director's personal liability, the college's or university's insurance (and legal counsel) should serve to cover against lawsuits and liability in the case of accidents or damages. However, it is wise for the CBR practitioner to clarify this with risk management officials. We would also recommend that the faculty practitioner consider purchasing a personal umbrella liability policy as another form of protection against calamitous mishap, weighing the amount of exposure one faces, the numbers of students involved, the nature of the community in which one's students are working, and one's assets (house, retirement accounts, savings, and so on) that are exposed.

Center-Community Relations

In this section, we examine the university-community partnership from the point of view of the higher education–based center. This is the reverse perspective from Chapter Two, in which we examined some of the same issues from the perspective of the community partner. For the partnership to work, these issues must be addressed in a way that is suitable for all partners in the collaboration.

Partnerships

Precisely who are the partners engaged in a community-based research project and how the relationship is established and maintained through the center are the issues we examine here. Partnerships can be created as a result of ad hoc relationships—chance meetings of individuals with common interests—or established deliberately, resulting from a systematic approach to partnership creation. In the first situation, research partnerships may grow out of shared interests or experiences, a common colleague, attendance at an event, or any number of other chance meetings. At the more deliberate end of the spectrum, the partnership formation may result from a strategic planning process or a rational match-making process, or it may develop out of an existing relationship, for example, one based on a direct service program partnership. For some urban institutions, especially those located in poor neighborhoods, their potential partners may be found immediately outside their gate. The Neighborhood Center at Trinity College in Hartford Connecticut; Howard University's Center for

Urban Progress in Washington, D.C.; and the University of Pennsylvania's WEPIC project in Philadelphia describe this as their experience. At Chicago's PRAG and at Hood College, a formal solicitation of research proposal requests from the community leads to a matching process with institutional research resources to determine projects. At Georgetown, the PURS project actively sought partners from among two targeted communities that already had long-standing university direct service programs operating there. The University of Denver's Center for Service Learning and Civic Engagement targeted solicitations for collaborative research from two communities in which it had established direct service and service-learning programs.

Such partnerships are formed initially out of a common research interest. If a project is launched, it is the work itself that structures the initial form of the relationship. At the completion of the project, the relationship may simply end as the collaborators move on to other priorities. However, the relationship may continue over time and develop in response to changing research needs and challenges and as new opportunities emerge for additional collaboration, such as future funding opportunities. The relationship is maintained as long as the needs of all the collaborators are being met. However, these needs may change from rather narrowly defined research interests on a specific topic to broader obligations; in the long run, traditions of partnership may emerge. The center plays three key roles here:

- Center staff are familiar with the CBO's larger change agenda and help to foster relationships between the CBO and different faculty over time.

- Working relationships are already understood and agreements are in place, reducing the challenges of placing and supervising students, negotiating contractual relations, clarifying liability issues, transacting financial matters, and other logistical matters.

- Interpersonal relationships are already established and experiences are shared, so that certain norms of operating are understood.

Advisory Boards

The university may establish an advisory board for the CBR center that has some community members or partners as board members. Such boards may perform a number of functions, including these:

- Establishing priorities for collaborative research projects
- Recommending how resources are to be allocated

- Raising funds to support the work of the center
- Developing common understandings of problems and operations among both actual and potential partners
- Creating and monitoring operational guidelines for the conduct of collaborative projects
- Evaluating the center's effectiveness in achieving its goals

Some institutions have decided explicitly against having community members serve on their advisory board, for several reasons: the amount of time and cost incurred by board members is not justifiable to impose on resource-strapped community partners, and university politics and bureaucracy limit what the board can do, setting up a mismatch between community expectations and what the board can deliver. However, some other center directors who have community partners on their boards have expressed to us that community members have come to learn about and understand better the university's constraints as a result of serving on such boards. In the long run, this experience helps to create realistic expectations about the assets and limits that the university brings to the collaborative enterprise.

Public Relations

Managing public relations is a task that is not often done very well. Indeed, some of the participants in CBR eschew the need for, and intentionally avoid participating in, public relations. The reasons for such avoidance vary: humility about the work, the distraction and redirection of scarce resources that participants believe would be better used on the work, and a mistrust of media and fear that the work will be misrepresented and cause harm to the enterprise. On the positive side, projects and centers can benefit from letting the public know about the work that is going on:

- Recruiting potential allies and future participants and funders
- Effecting social change through publicizing the results of their work
- Creating a general public more receptive to the process and results of such work

We do not know of any CBR centers that have public relations specialists on their staff, and only some of the larger centers include media relations as a (minor) job responsibility for any of their staff. Yet all institutions of higher education have public relations offices and staff who work for the institution and could play a role in promoting the work of the center. Often, it takes some initiative and effort to contact and educate university public relations staff about the mission, projects, and value of the CBR work being done. However, given the public service and social responsibility mission of all universities, colleges, and community colleges, the benefits of CBR can be framed in such a way as to inspire the institution's media specialists to generate positive stories about the work being done. Most institutions have their own internal media, such as campus newspapers and student-run papers, in which positive stories can be printed. Many also have more externally directed productions, such as alumni magazines or fundraising newsletters, which enable them to spread news about positive university developments to a wider audience. Often, there may be smaller community papers that would be interested in publishing community-university collaboration stories. In addition to professional staff working in the institution's public relations office, there may be journalism classes or students who would be willing to write stories about CBR work that can be published in campus or community papers. There are a number of good resource books with suggestions and practical information, explaining how even small groups with few resources can generate positive publicity for their work (Ryan, 1991; Salzman, 1998).

Summary

This chapter has offered practical suggestions about how to operate a CBR center at an institution of higher education. We started by suggesting a number of initial issues to raise on a campus in order to help a group of interested faculty and administrators launch a center. We then examined a range of alternative structures that the centers can take, focusing on issues such as staffing, budgeting and funding, and uses of technology. Our examination considered faculty matters, such as recruitment, development, and sustainability through the institution's rewards structure. We focused on the center's relationship to the rest of the campus, examining how its location may affect its operations in terms of mobilizing institutional resources, risk management, and human subjects research. Our discussion turned finally to community-campus partnership matters, focusing on the factors that affect university faculty and staff decision making regarding their participation in CBR, the role of advisory boards, and managing public relations.

10

A LOOK TO THE FUTURE

IMAGINE A FUTURE in which community-based research has become business as usual in higher education. Here is what voices from campuses and communities might sound like then:

FROM A STUDENT

College is turning out to be an incredible experience for me. It seems I spend a lot of my time out in the local community, working with different people on projects that we hope will bring about some real changes. Just last week I helped interview two dozen or so residents of the public housing project about all the things that need fixing in their building, and I'll be joining their association president in presenting our findings to the Housing Commission at their next meeting. In the meantime, I'll be reading about lead-based paint for my environmental biology class and talking with my political science professor about strategies for getting the city officials to pay more attention to local housing issues. I can't believe how much I am learning in and outside the classroom and from so many different people. I get to be a "teacher" too. In fact, there is something about working on a research project together—me and other students, our professor, members of the community—that makes us all teachers and learners and researchers. I love that feeling of being depended on and of having something important to contribute, even though I am "just a student."

When I graduate, I'm not sure just what I'll do. I am already thinking that I might want to continue working on housing-related issues, but then there was that exciting oral history project when we interviewed peace activists from the 1960s that really grabbed my interest. I'm even thinking about staying in the community, because I have made so many friends here. No matter what I end up doing, I know I want to apply all that I have learned as a student at this college to make the world better in some way. And I feel confident now that I can really do that.

FROM A FACULTY MEMBER

I was just awarded tenure at my university, thanks to a whole range of things, including a strong letter of support from a member of the board of the local community action agency and a pretty solid c.v. that includes a number of research reports that were never published in academic journals. That's because most of my research is community based— "real" research that is a bit different from the more traditional academic research that many of my colleagues do. I teach at a university that values that kind of work, and that is very important to me. The administration here appreciates the excellent course evaluations that I get from students who are involved with me in CBR projects and they recognize that it is also really good for university-community relations.

The city council just passed an ordinance banning smoking in many local public places based in part on research that one of my students and I conducted with the local health clinic. A few people are displeased with that outcome, of course—smokers, mainly—but my university received much positive publicity for supporting our participation in this collaborative research project. As for me, I continue to get enormous satisfaction from being able to combine a strong commitment to teaching, a passion for meaningful research, and a belief in the importance of service in my work as an educator and researcher at this institution. It doesn't get any better than this!

FROM A COMMUNITY SERVICE PROVIDER

I love that word *partnership,* and it certainly describes the relationship that my agency has with the local college. We've always had students come in to tutor our youngsters, but now their involvement with us is much deeper and wider. It seems that hardly a day goes by when there aren't students—and usually one or two professors too—hanging around our building: conducting interviews with young people from the community, meeting with client-staff research teams, accompanying staff members to hearings, and so on. Of course, we spend time on the campus too. Right now, I am helping to teach a course on youth programming with an education professor whose class last semester helped us identify some shortcomings in our after-school program. They also taught us how to gather information in a way that will let us conduct a similar study of our school-based tutoring program next year.

It's wonderful knowing that we can call our college partners anytime we need advice about a grant proposal or could use their help gathering information about new federal regulations or ways to strengthen our programs. And their students have become indispensable to us—especially those whose commitment to our agency and our community extends through their college years and even after their graduation. In fact, our current executive director started off as a student on one of our research teams.

FROM A COMMUNITY MEMBER

I used to think that colleges and universities were places where rich kids and overeducated professors talked about irrelevant things and conducted meaningless research. Now I have a different view. That's because some professors and students from one of our city's universities have been spending time in our neighborhood, helping us figure out what sorts of changes we want to make in our community and how we might go about doing it. We finally have our own grocery store as a result of the information they helped us collect and that we then presented to the local chamber of commerce. And the best thing is that they aren't *telling* us what to do; they are *asking* us what we think should be done. They aren't talking *at* us but rather *with* us. And they aren't doing this for their *own* benefit but for *ours*. They really seem to care about this community. They have become our friends and colleagues.

We have become members of their campus community as well. We are invited to seminars and concerts there, and last week my elderly neighbor gave a talk in a history class about how our neighborhood has changed over the past fifty years. She told us later how great it was to feel as if she had something important to share with people at the university! Her view of colleges and universities, along with those of everyone in this neighborhood, has really changed. We all feel good about that.

FROM A FUNDER

My job as a foundation executive has certainly gotten easier. One reason is that some colleges and universities have finally gotten serious about working with their local communities to address community problems. As a matter of fact, we just renewed funding for our local CBR center for the fifth straight year because, once again, they were able to show that they've made a substantial and positive contribution to the community through their work. In one case, they brought together professors and students from three different disciplines and staff from the local health clinic to create a wildly successful, countywide immunization program. This model program, whose development we helped to fund, was featured in a national news magazine as well as many health-related publications. How can we not want to continue to support that sort of work?

The CBR center exists because the university took seriously this idea of engaging the community and made some major changes in the way they operate, providing resources for staff and a space right in the community for this work. I expect we will continue to give them money for a long time to come, as we continue to see all kinds of benefits that come from combining community programming and university research in such important and effective ways.

FROM A COLLEGE OR UNIVERSITY ADMINISTRATOR

I'm going to erect a statue in our quad in honor of the faculty members who introduced community-based research to our campus some years ago. We all know about the seemingly formidable challenges that have faced higher education over the past few decades: increasing student diversity, legislative mandates, faculty dissension, and the nagging sense that we should be devoting some of our substantial resources to helping the communities that struggle outside our campus walls. My institution has addressed them all, with rousing success. The answer? Well, a big part of it is community-based research.

We support and reward faculty involvement in CBR, and as a result, a substantial number of our faculty are involved in it in some way. Because of that, we have a diverse and growing student body whose needs we are meeting. Students get the best of active, experiential learning and leave here with skills, knowledge, and a commitment to active participation in democratic society—just like our mission statement promises. We are truly engaged with our community, and we don't have town-gown problems.

Faculty morale couldn't be higher. We attract top-notch scholars and teachers from around the country who want to be at a place where they can combine teaching, research, and service in innovative, meaningful ways. Our commitment to community collaboration infuses all that we do on campus as well, making ours a model of academic democracy. All this also means that we attract lots of grant money, along with the stamp of approval from state and local legislators. When they ask me to make a presentation telling them all that we have contributed to the community lately, there is just too much to say, so I bring along folks from the community to help me. CBR has indeed proved to be transformational, and I am proud to have been a part of these important changes in higher education.

The Vision: A CBR Future

The vision of the future expressed by these voices is dramatically, though not unrealistically, different from the world of higher education as we know it now. And it is a vision of the future that we hope this book, and the work it may inspire, will help bring about.

These voices express a very different vision of the classroom. The classroom of the CBR future will be one without walls, where students move freely into the community and community members move freely onto and across the campus. In this world, the community is part of the educational process, and the classroom extends and melds into the community on community members' terms. It is also a classroom without rigid roles and hierarchies. The teacher can be a student, the student can be a teacher, and the community member can be both. Learning becomes a mutual process, with community stories holding common footing with academic information and questions of the community having greater importance than answers found in textbooks. The classroom of the CBR future is a place where hands-on active learning takes precedence over passive book learning and where the activities of the course fit with the work of the community, and matter to it. Learning, in this model, is a bottom-up process such that theories and models emerge in the context of the real world and their value depends on their relevance to it. Participants in this educational world leave the process with deeper moral conviction and clarity, enhanced practical skills, and broader intellectual perspective.

Beyond the classroom, the CBR future also implies different higher education institutions. The college and university of the future will be much more interdisciplinary than it is today. Students will no longer be confined to discipline-bound majors, and faculty will no longer be held to rigid and narrow disciplinary standards. Indeed, institutions may be organized around interdisciplinary programs, and not around discipline-defined departments at all.

The tearing down of walls between institution and community will also require much more democratic institutions of higher education, where decisions about resource distribution, programmatic emphases, and future expansion will be informed as much by the powers of faculty-community partnerships as by boards of trustees. The civic engagement philosophy promoted by higher education will require new institutional decision-making structures that reflect the democratic practices CBR attempts to create and sustain. The artificial division between teaching, research, and service will no longer exist as research becomes part of the pedagogy and useful in service to communities. The split between basic and applied research will also dissolve as research begins to address community problems and advance knowledge generally. Rewards for both faculty and students will reflect a new value placed on knowledge that is produced collaboratively, creatively, and in service to the ideals of a better society.

Dedicated CBR spaces—on campuses, in the community, or in jointly claimed areas—are central to the vision of the CBR future. These will be open, safe homes where faculty, community members, and students can come together freely. Community-based ways of expressing knowledge will be respected equally with academic ways of expressing knowledge. All who enter these homes will be valued for their individual experiences and unique skills and will be welcomed to integrate these experiences and skills with others to build more comprehensive and complex forms of knowledge. Ultimately, these homes will provide access to all seeking knowledge, as well as to all who wish to contribute to its creation and discovery.

The communities of the CBR future will be supported in myriad ways as they develop their organizations and their members toward more effective, informed practices. Community organizations will no longer have to choose between gathering the information necessary to do successful programming and doing the actual work; they will be able to do both. They will no longer feel compelled to meet externally imposed standards of the sort that often separate them from their community constituencies. Instead, they will be able to incorporate the values of CBR into their own missions, building programs from the wisdom of community members and thus transforming them from recipients to participants. Put another way, social service and social change will no longer be mutually exclusive goals. Higher education institutions without barriers to community participation can help community organizations make these changes. The result will be a reduction in the anti-intellectualism of American culture, because research and knowledge will be useful and practical, as well as thoughtful and intellectual.

Those who give financial support to CBR and its values will also experience new horizons. Funders, recognizing the synergy created from research informed by action and action informed by research, will be able to see communities as producers of knowledge and higher education institutions as partners in social programming. Responding to the ground-up process of CBR, they will define their funding priorities as much by the advances of CBR as by the desires of foundation staff and board members. Governments will no longer think of communities as uninformed recipients of expert-defined programs, but instead will recognize their central role as participants in policy development. The result will be more democracy and a return to the ideal of government by the people, of the people, and for the people.

Idealistic as this future may seem, it is achievable. Indeed, we have shared in the previous chapters many small pieces of this vision that have already been realized on campuses and in communities across the country. However, creating the sort of large-scale transformation that we propose here will require a number of changes in the way that we organize and operate our colleges and universities, community-based organizations, and government and other funding organizations. These changes—what we think of as action steps—have three central aims:

- To enhance the infrastructure or capacity to undertake community-based research
- To assess the practice of CBR in order to demonstrate and ensure its continuing value to our institutions and the community
- To promote and advocate for the expanded practice of CBR

Infrastructure Development

The following action steps provide the support and sustainability needed for the effective practice of CBR. We start with steps that need to be taken at the local level—on campuses and in community-based organizations—and then move to steps at the regional and national levels that are needed to advance CBR:

1. *Establish centers or offices, with staff and budgets, to support CBR.* The practice of CBR flourishes with appropriate support and skilled practice. We need to create spaces to mobilize these resources and nourish the practice of CBR so that it may develop its potential for social change. Each local community and its local CBR practitioners need to determine the institutional framework that might be best suited to support their work. We have noted several different forms around which this work can be organized and urge higher education and community leaders to develop and support the framework that seems most appropriate to support their practice.

2. *Change faculty reward structures so that community-based research is recognized and valued as legitimate scholarship, service, and—as applicable—an important contribution to innovative teaching.* Faculty

reward systems were designed to promote and ensure the quality practice of teaching, research, and service. These vary among institutions, depending on their mission, size, and location, as well as other factors. The indicators for how teaching, research, and service are evaluated typically do not accommodate the integrative practice of CBR. Some institutions, such as Portland State University, Indiana University/Purdue University at Indianapolis, and San Francisco State University, have developed innovative procedures that enable CBR practices to be considered for evaluation through the rank and tenure system. To advance this practice, we will have to document stories of how CBR has affected the community, professional practice, and students' learning. We will need to broaden the types of publications and scholarly products that can be evaluated during such reviews. We should create a space for community members to help document the impacts of CBR projects in the community.

3. *Deepen existing partnerships and develop principles for collaboration for each institution.* Most institutions already have in place some forms of partnerships with community organizations through direct service programs, student volunteer organizations, or service-learning partnerships. We suggest that undertaking collaborative research projects with such partners is an effective means for deepening these partnerships and expanding their effectiveness. Both the community organizations and the university should consider establishing principles for engaging in such collaborations to ensure that their long-term goals are being met through such partnerships.

4. *Develop institutional program components to support CBR practice.* These might include the following:

- Continuing-education programs. These programs can be made available to community partners, enabling them to take courses at the college or university for free in recognition of their contribution to students' learning.

- Cocurricular programs. These programs can provide training and supervision for students who volunteer to work in communities and undertake CBR in ongoing collaborative projects.

- Leadership development program. Whether curricular or extracurricular, student leadership programs can provide training support for undertaking CBR.

- Student scholarship programs. Student financial aid funding can be tied to training and incorporation of students to participate in CBR projects. Creative uses of federal work-study funds, Ameri-

Corps funding, research assistantships, and traditional scholarship funds can support students who wish to engage in CBR.

5. *Incorporate CBR into graduate or other formal training.* One way to do this is to create certificate programs or areas of concentration within graduate programs for students engaging in CBR. Another is to support, in every way possible, students who wish to undertake CBR for their doctoral or master's thesis research.

6. *Work with admissions staff to promote CBR in admissions materials and programs aimed at recruiting students.* Some students will find opportunities to engage in CBR so appealing that they will base their college matriculation decisions on the opportunity to work in the community. We will have to educate admissions office staff about the appeal of this work and assist them in developing promotional materials to disseminate to prospective students. This will increase the pipeline of students interested in CBR. It is also likely to improve retention, as the increasing number of students attracted to community-based learning will experience greater satisfaction in their undergraduate program.

7. *Develop Web sites for matching community research needs with campus resources.* As a support mechanism to help the campus and community share information about projects and resources, CBR centers can host a Web site that describes projects desired by community partners and research assets and interests offered by the university. We recommend that this be part of a larger enterprise that through interpersonal outreach seeks to solicit matches among potential CBR partners. A Web site can serve additional purposes, such as providing research reports and instruments, partnership agreements, and other support documents to support the partnerships that develop.

8. *Start CBR-oriented learning circles that include campus and community participants.* It is challenging for community and university partners to learn how to work together and understand the institutional constraints faced in each other's work. Learning circles enable participants to come together as equals, share their experiences, and explore with each other possible solutions to problems they encounter. The time that the participants invest in such a process is time taken from other pressing demands—hence, stipends or other compensation should be offered to the participants.

9. *Develop the community's (as well as the faculty's) capacity to work on CBR projects.* We already mentioned the need for faculty development workshops, so here we focus on the parallel need to enhance the community's ability to work on CBR projects. In a material sense, the community partner's time spent working on a CBR project may come at the expense

of his or her work on other day-to-day program or organizing activities. This trade-off needs to be recognized, and the CBO should be compensated in financial terms or other in-kind support. Furthermore, the expectation is that the community partner is accepting some responsibility for educating and supervising students who are working on the project. This may require additional training and support to be provided to the CBO.

10. *Establish ongoing networks and associations with other people and institutions engaged in CBR work.* To coordinate efforts and learn from each other's experiences, we need to establish networks to promote and advance the development of CBR practices. These may take the form of a national association of CBR practitioners or institutions, regional networks or associations, or local networks. At the national level, the association would serve to establish best practices, do outreach and advocacy work, and provide forums for new developments. At the regional and local levels, CBR practitioners can coordinate their activities and share project information and funding support. We need to integrate this work across sectors as well, infusing CBR work into substantive and project developments in areas such as housing reform efforts, participatory community development, school reform, and environmental justice initiatives.

11. *Work with kindred national associations to advance the practice and institutionalization of CBR.* National organizations such as the Campus Compact, the American Association for Higher Education, the American Association for Community Colleges, and Educators for Community Engagement have played a role in supporting the development and spread of CBR. We should continue to work with them to use their networks and resources to advance these developments in the areas of promoting best practices, reconsidering faculty roles and rewards, and integrating CBR into the curriculum.

Assessing and Enhancing the Value of CBR

We also need to take action steps to ensure that quality CBR work is being done and to demonstrate its effectiveness to educators, the community, professional and practitioner associations, and the larger public. As we demonstrate effective practices, we can begin to establish best practices and examine the conditions under which these practices vary:

12. *Develop and share a working list of best practices in community-based research.* Much as practitioners have established principles for best practice in service-learning, we need to establish such principles for CBR. To do so will require that we solicit and share these widely in order to develop some consensual principles. These should be shared among univer-

sity and community practitioners and reviewed continuously in the light of what we learn from ongoing CBR work.

13. *Design, conduct, and support research that looks at the impact of CBR—on students, communities, institutions, and faculty members.* In this era of accountability, we need more than anecdotal and impressionistic evidence of the impact of all kinds of community-based teaching and learning—not only on students but also for the communities we hope to help transform. We will need thoughtful outcome goals and measures that can be applied across sites and projects. As our evidence accumulates, we will want to undertake meta-analyses in order to demonstrate patterns and conditions for successful CBR work. Some of the outcomes that we will want to assess are:

- Students' learning outcomes—indicators of the extent to which participation in CBR improves students' learning in the areas of critical thinking skills, civic responsibility and engagement, substantive content of courses and disciplines, creating knowledge and understanding of the research process and career development

- CBOs and community outcomes—indicators of the extent to which participation in CBR has a positive effect on the community and the organization in the areas of skills development of CBO staff and community members, internal operations of CBOs, program effectiveness and implementation of new initiatives, increasing community power and participation in decision making, access to resources and raising funds, and coalition building and working with other CBOs

- Faculty outcomes—indicators of the extent to which participation in CBR has an impact on faculty work in the areas of job satisfaction and morale, tenure and promotion and the rewards process, and teaching effectiveness

- Institutional outcomes—indicators of the extent to which institutional participation in CBR has an impact on the institution in the areas of town-gown relations, adaptation and fulfillment of institutional mission tenure and promotion, faculty rewards procedures, and curriculum content

Outreach, Promotion, and Advocacy

To further the practice of CBR requires that we enthusiastically promote it among our community and higher education colleagues. The best place to begin such advocacy is among predisposed colleagues and practitioners.

We will also want to educate potential funders and the larger public about the effects of CBR practice:

14. *Promote CBR in the undergraduate curriculum through related educational reform initiatives.* A number of current innovations in undergraduate education are particularly compatible with CBR. These include promoting undergraduate research (including collaborative research with faculty members), student leadership development, education for civic engagement, and problem-based learning. CBR advances each of these, and they, in turn, provide rich opportunities and justifications for building CBR into undergraduate courses and curricula.

15. *Offer workshops on and off campus—for faculty members, administrators, community members and organizations, students, and funding agencies—about community-based research.* We must expand our outreach to potential new practitioners of CBR by offering workshops to introduce the practice of CBR and recruit potential collaborators. To support this practice, we must develop educational materials, modules, workbooks, training guides, and document collections and make them readily available for dissemination. Web-based resources and information technology expertise can be applied to make this information readily accessible. We need an experienced training corps that can provide training for trainers in the practice of CBR.

16. *Develop relationships with local media and take advantage of them to promote and publicize CBR work.* We need to promote our successes and provide documentation for local media to help disseminate information about effective CBR practice. This means writing in accessible language and nurturing relationships with the media. We should think broadly about media venues, including community newspapers, university newspapers, and nonprofit organization newsletters. We must work with community media advocates to learn how to communicate CBR project successes effectively.

17. *Promote CBR in disciplinary and other associations connected with higher education.* We need to work with professional associations to create space for CBR within conventional academic venues, such as conferences and journals. Beyond the obvious social science disciplines, we need to expand the visibility of CBR in the arts, humanities, and natural sciences. We need to work with practitioners' associations to provide support and legitimacy for CBR. When making presentations at these conferences, we should try to include community partners as presenters. We also need to promote CBR among student associations. The 2002 annual conference of the Faculty Roles and Rewards initiative of the American

Association for Higher Education was dedicated to "The Engaged Campus." A major theme of the conference was community-based research, and the result was a roster of informative workshops and presentations that drew significant numbers of participants. We need to create continuing forums similar to this to promote the development of CBR.

18. *Write and submit to mainstream disciplinary and interdisciplinary journals manuscripts that report the results of community-based research.* We need to demonstrate to journal editors the value of this work and write quality articles for submission. We need to place ourselves on editorial boards to give such manuscripts favorable reviews. We should create a specialty journal that will publish quality CBR articles.

19. *Promote the inclusion of community-based research in textbooks, especially those that deal with research methods.* We must advocate with textbook writers and publishers to include a chapter on community-based research in methods texts. We will want to publish texts that present the results of CBR studies and the methods used in community-based research.

20. *Talk with funding agencies about CBR.* Funders have been promoting collaboration as a means of stretching shrinking funding to effect community change. Funders also want agencies to demonstrate the effectiveness of the funding they have been awarded. Community-based research is consistent with funders' process objectives and their outcome goals. We need to educate funders about the potential of CBR and demonstrate to them successful collaborations.

A Vision of the Future

This, then, is our vision: a future in which campus-community research partnerships are prolific, deep, sustained, reciprocal, and actively committed—in myriad ways, in every corner of the United States—to transforming communities and realizing a more just society. It is a future in which colleges and universities have finally become places where teaching and learning are vigorous and vital, scholarship is valued for its relevance as well as for its rigor, and the ends of knowledge truly are the benefit and use of life. We hope you will join us in working to achieve it.

REFERENCES

Adams, F. *Unearthing Seeds of Fire: The Idea of Highlander.* Winston-Salem, N.C.: John F. Blair, 1975.

Ansley, F., and Gaventa, J. "Researching for Democracy and Democratizing Research." *Change,* 1997, *29,* 46–53.

Astin, A. "Promoting Leadership, Service, and Democracy: What Higher Education Can Do." In R. Bringle, R. Games, and E. Malloy (eds.), *Colleges and Universities as Citizens.* Needham Heights, Mass.: Allyn & Bacon. 1999.

Barber, B. *Strong Democracy: Participatory Politics for a New Age.* Berkeley: University of California Press, 1984.

Barber, B. *An Aristocracy for Everyone: The Politics of Education and the Future of America.* New York: Oxford University Press, 1992.

Beckwith, D. "Ten Ways to Work Together: An Organizer's View." *Sociological Imagination,* 1996, *33,* 164–172.

Benson, L., and Harkavy, I. "Communal Participatory Action Research as a Strategy for Improving Universities and the Social Sciences: Penn's Work with the West Philadelphia Improvement Corps as a Case Study." *Educational Policy,* 1996, *10,* 202–223.

Benson, L., and Harkavy, I. "School and Community in the Global Society: A Neo-Deweyan Theory of Problem-Solving Schools and Cosmopolitan Neighborly Communities." *Universities and Community Schools,* 1997, *5*(1–2), 16–71.

Benson, L., Harkavy, I., and Puckett, J. "An Implementation Revolution as a Strategy for Fulfilling the Democratic Promise of University-Community Partnership: Penn–West Philadelphia as an Experiment in Progress." *Nonprofit and Voluntary Sector Quarterly,* 2000, *29*(1), 24–45.

Bledsoe, T. *Or We'll All Hang Separately: The Highlander Idea.* Boston: Beacon Press, 1969.

Bledstein, B. *The Culture of Professionalism: The Middle Class and the Development of Higher Education in America.* New York: Norton, 1976.

Boyer, E. L. *Scholarship Reconsidered: Priorities of the Professorate.* Princeton, N.J.: Carnegie Foundation for the Advancement of Teaching, 1990.

Boyte, H. C., and Kari, K. N. *Building America: The Democratic Promise of Public Work.* Philadelphia: Temple University Press, 1996.

Boyte, H. C., and Kari, N. N. "Renewing the Democratic Spirit in American Colleges and Universities: Higher Education as Public Work." In T. Ehrlich (ed.), *Civic Responsibility and Higher Education.* Phoenix, Ariz.: American Council on Education and Oryx Press, 2000.

Bringle, R., Games, R., Ludlum, C., Osgood, R., and Osborne, R. "Faculty Fellow Program: Enhancing Integrated Professional Development Through Community Service." *American Behavioral Scientist,* 2000, *43,* 882–894.

Bringle, R., Games, R., and Malloy, E. *Colleges and Universities as Citizens.* Needham Heights, Mass.: Allyn & Bacon, 1999.

Brown, L. D., and Tandon, R. "Ideology and Political Economy in Inquiry: Action Research and Participatory Research." *Journal of Applied Behavioral Science,* 1983, *19,* 277–294.

Brydon-Miller, M. "Accessibility Self-Advocacy at an Independent Living Center: A Participatory Research Approach." In P. Park, M. Brydon-Miller, B. Hall, and T. Jackson (eds.), *Voices of Change: Participatory Research in the United States and Canada.* Westport, Conn.: Bergin and Garvey, 1993.

Campbell, J. R. *Reclaiming a Lost Heritage: Land Grant and Other Higher Education Initiatives for the Twenty-First Century.* Ames: Iowa State University Press, 1995.

Cancian, F. M. "Conflicts Between Activist Research and Academic Success: Participation Research and Alternative Strategies." *American Sociologist,* 1993, *24,* 92–106.

Colby, A., and Ehrlich, T. "Higher Education and the Development of Civic Responsibility." In T. Ehrlich (ed.), *Civic Responsibility and Higher Education.* Phoenix, Ariz.: American Council on Education and Onyx Press, 2000.

Cornwall, A., and Jewkes, R. "What Is Participatory Research?" *Social Science in Medicine,* 1995, *41,* 1667–1676.

Couto, R. "The Promise of a Scholarship of Engagement." *Academic Workplace,* Spring 2001, pp. 4–8.

Couto, R. A., Stutts, N. B., and others. *Mending Broken Promises: Justice for Children at Risk.* Dubuque, Iowa: Kendall/Hunt, 2000.

Deegan, M. J. *Jane Addams and the Men of the Chicago School, 1892–1918.* New Brunswick, N.J.: Transaction Books, 1988.

Dewey, J. *Democracy and Education.* Old Tappan, N.J.: Macmillan, 1916.

Dewey, J. *Experience and Education.* Old Tappan, N.J.: Macmillan, 1938.

Donohue, P., and Paul, B. "Transcending the Walls of the Classroom: An Alternative Pedagogical Model for Community-Based Research." Unpublished manuscript, 2002.

Edwards, B., and Marullo, S. "Editors' Introduction: Universities in Troubled Times—Institutional Responses." *American Behavioral Scientist,* 1999, *42,* 754–765.

Ehrlich, T. *Civic Responsibility and Higher Education.* Phoenix, Ariz.: Oryx Press, 2000.

Eyler, J., and Giles, D. E. *Where's the Learning in Service-Learning?* San Francisco: Jossey-Bass, 1999.

Eyler, J., Giles, D. E., and Braxton, J. "The Impact of Service-Learning on College Students." *Michigan Journal of Community Service Learning,* 1997, *4,* 5–15.

Farrington, B. *Francis Bacon: Philosopher of Industrial Science.* Old Tappan, N.J.: Macmillan, 1973.

Fetterman, D. M. *Foundations of Empowerment Evaluation.* Thousand Oaks, Calif.: Sage, 2000.

Freire P. *Pedagogy of the Oppressed.* New York: Continuum, 1970.

"Getting Started/Key Questions." In Resource Guide for Faculty and Students (brochure). Edward Ginsberg Center for Community Service and Learning, University of Michigan. Retrieved January 22, 2003, from http://www.umich.edu/~mserve/ucomm/brochures8b.html.

Giroux, H. *Border Crossings: Cultural Workers and the Politics of Education.* New York: Routledge, 1992.

Glen, J. M. *Highlander: No Ordinary School.* Lexington: University Press of Kentucky, 1988.

Greenwood, D., and Levin, M. *Introduction to Action Research.* Thousand Oaks, Calif.: Sage, 1998.

Hall, B. L. "From Margins to Center? The Development Land Purpose of Participatory Research." *American Sociologist,* 1992, *23*(4), 15–28.

Harkavy, I., and Puckett, J. L. "Lessons from Hull House for the Contemporary Urban University." *Social Services Review,* 1994, *68,* 299–321.

Hartley, H. "What's My Orientation? Using the Teacher-as-Text Strategy as Feminist Pedagogical Practice." *Teaching Sociology,* 1999, *27,* 398–406.

Hesser, G. "Examining Communities and Urban Change: Service-Learning as Collaborative Research." In J. Ostrow, G. Hesser, and S. Enos (eds.), *Cultivating the Sociological Imagination: Concepts and Models for Service-Learning in Sociology.* Washington, D.C.: American Association of Higher Education, 1999.

Highlander Research and Education Center. 2003. http://www.hrec.org/.

Horton, A. I. *The Highlander Folk School: A History of its Major Programs, 1932–1961.* Brooklyn, N.Y.: Carlson Publishing, 1989.

Horton, B. D. "The Appalachian Land Ownership Study: Research and Citizen Action in Appalachia." In P. Park, M. Brydon-Miller, B. Hall, and T. Jackson (eds.), *Voices of Change: Participatory Research in the United States and Canada.* Westport, Conn.: Bergin and Garvey, 1993.

Jackson, T. "A Way of Working: Participatory Research and the Aboriginal Movement in Canada." In P. Park, M. Brydon-Miller, B. Hall, and T. Jackson (eds.), *Voices of Change: Participatory Research in the United States and Canada*. Westport, Conn.: Bergin and Garvey, 1993.

Kahne, J., and Westheimer, J. "In the Service of What?" *Phi Delta Kappan*, 1996, 77, 592–600.

Kellogg Commission. *Returning to Our Roots: The Engaged Institution*. Washington, D.C.: National Association of State Universities and Land-Grant Colleges, 1999.

Kennedy, M., and Stone, M. "Bringing the Community into the University." In P. Nyden, A. Figert, M. Shibley, and D. Burrows (eds.), *Building Community: Social Science in Action*. Thousand Oaks, Calif.: Pine Forge, 1997.

Kolb, D. *Experiential Learning: Experience as a Source of Learning and Development*. Upper Saddle River, N.J.: Prentice Hall, 1984.

Knupfer, A. M. "Conflict Resolution or 'Convict Revolution': The Problematics of Critical Pedagogy in the Classroom." *Urban Education*, 1995, 30, 219–235.

Kretzmann, J. P., and McKnight, J. L. *Building Communities from the Inside Out*. Evanston, Ill.: Center for Urban Affairs and Policy Research Neighborhood Innovations Network, Northwestern University, 1993.

Lewin, K. "Frontiers in Group Dynamics: Concept, Method, and Reality in Social Science, Social Equilibria, and Social Change." *Human Relations*, 1947, 1, 5–41.

Lewin, K. *Resolving Social Conflicts*. New York: HarperCollins, 1948.

Lynch, J. "Community Participation in Community Needs Assessment." *Journal of Applied Sociology*, 1993, 10, 125–136.

Lynd, M. "Creating Knowledge Through Theatre: A Case Study with Developmentally Disabled Adults." *American Sociologist*, 1992, 23, 100–115.

Maguire, P. *Doing Participatory Research: A Feminist Approach*. Amherst, Mass.: Center for International Education, 1987.

Martin, L. L., and Kettner, P. M. *Measuring the Performance of Human Service Programs*. Thousand Oaks, Calif.: Sage, 1996.

Marullo, S. "The Service-Learning Movement in Higher Education: An Academic Response to Troubled Times." *Sociological Imagination*, 1996, 33, 117–137.

Marullo, S., and Edwards, B. "From Charity to Justice: The Potential of University-Community Collaboration for Social Change." *American Behavioral Scientist*, 2000, 43, 895–912.

Mathias, C. n.d. SWOT Analysis. www.panasia.org/sg/iirr/ikmanual/swot.htm.

Maurrasse, D. J. *Beyond the Campus: How Colleges and Universities Form Partnerships with Their Communities*. New York: Routledge, 2001.

McKnight, J. *The Careless Society: Community and Its Counterfeits.* New York: Basic Books, 1995.

McNicoll, P. "Issues in Teaching Participatory Action Research." *Journal of Social Work Education,* 1999, *35,* 51–63.

Miller, J., and Brydon-Miller, M. "Changing Lenses: Family Therapy and Participatory Action Research." Poster session. American Psychological Association Annual Convention, Washington, D.C., 2000.

Mooney, L. A., and Edwards, B. "Experiential Learning in Sociology: Service-Learning and Other Community-Based Learning." *Teaching Sociology,* 2001, *29,* 182–194.

Murphy, D., Scammell, M., and Sclove, R. *Doing Community Based Research: A Reader.* Amherst, Mass.: Loka Institute, 1997.

Neuman, W. L. *Social Research Methods: Qualitative and Quantitative Approaches* (5th ed.). Needham Heights, Mass.: Allyn & Bacon, 2003.

Nyden, P., Figert, A., Shibley, M., and Burrows, D. (eds.). *Building Community: Social Science in Action.* Thousand Oaks, Calif.: Pine Forge, 1997.

Nyden P., and Wiewel, W. "Collaborative Research: Harnessing the Tensions Between Researcher and Practitioner." *American Sociologist,* 1992, *23*(4), 43–55.

Park, P. "The Discovery of Participatory Research as a New Scientific Paradigm: Personal and Intellectual Accounts." *American Sociologist,* 1992, *23*(4), 29–43.

Park, P., Brydon-Miller, M., Hall, B. L., and Jackson, T. (eds.). *Voices of Change: Participatory Research in the United States and Canada.* Westport, Conn.: Bergin and Garvey, 1993.

Patton, M. Q. *Qualitative Research and Evaluation Methods.* Thousand Oaks, Calif.: Sage, 2002.

Polikoff, B. G. *With One Bold Act: The Story of Jane Addams.* Chicago: Boswell Books, 1999.

Porpora, D. "Action Research: The Highest Stage of Service-Learning?" In J. Ostrow, G. Hesser, and S. Enos (eds.), *Cultivating the Sociological Imagination: Concepts and Models for Service-Learning.* Washington, D.C.: American Association for Higher Education, 1999.

Reardon, K. M. "An Experiential Approach to Creating an Effective Community-University Partnership: The East St. Louis Action Research Project." *Cityscape: A Journal of Policy Development and Research,* 2000, *5*(1), 59–74.

Ryan, C. *Prime Time Activism: Media Strategies for Grassroots Organizing.* Boston: South End Press, 1991.

Salzman, J. *Making the News: A Guide for Nonprofits and Activists.* Boulder, Colo.: Westview Press, 1998.

Schensul, J. J., and Schensul, S. L. "Collaborative Research: Methods of Inquiry for Social Change." In M. D. LeCompte, W. L. Millroy, and J. Preissle (eds.), *The Handbook of Qualitative Research in Education.* Orlando, Fla.: Academic Press, 1992.

Schneider, C. G. "Educational Missions and Civic Responsibility." In T. Ehrlich (ed.), *Civic Responsibility and Higher Education.* Phoenix, Ariz.: American Council on Education and Oryx Press, 2000.

Sclove, R. E., Scammell, M. L., and Holland, B. *Community Based Research in the United States: An Introductory Reconnaissance, Including Twelve Organizational Case Studies and Comparison with the Dutch Science Shops and the Mainstream American Research System.* Amherst, Mass.: The Loka Institute, 1998.

Shor, I. *Empowering Education: Critical Teaching for Social Change.* Chicago: University of Chicago Press, 1992.

Small, S. "Action-Oriented Research: Models and Methods." *Journal of Marriage and the Family,* 1995, *57,* 941–956.

Stoecker, R. "Are Academics Irrelevant? Roles for Scholars in Participatory Research." *American Behavioral Scientist,* 1999a, *42,* 840–854.

Stoecker, R. "Making Connections: Community Organizing, Empowerment Planning, and Participatory Research in Participatory Evaluation." *Sociological Practice,* 1999b, *1,* 209–232.

Strand, K. "Community-Based Research as Pedagogy." *Michigan Journal of Community Service Learning,* 2000, *7,* 85–96.

Stringer, E. *Action Research: A Handbook for Practitioners.* Thousand Oaks, Calif.: Sage, 1999.

Tax, S. "Values in Action: The Fox Project." *Human Organization,* 1958, *17,* 17–20.

Torres, J., and J. Schaffer. *Benchmarks for Campus/Community Partnerships.* Providence, R.I.: Campus Compact, 2000.

Torres, J., Sinton, R., and White, A. *Establishing and Sustaining an Office of Community Service.* Providence, R.I.: Campus Compact, 2000.

Walshok, M. "Strategies for Building the Infrastructure That Supports the Engaged Campus." In R. Bringle, R. Games, and E. Malloy (eds.), *Colleges and Universities as Citizens.* Needham Heights, Mass.: Allyn & Bacon, 1999.

Ward, K., and Wolf-Wendel, L. "Community-Centered Service Learning: Moving from Doing For to Doing With." *American Behavioral Scientist,* 2000, *43,* 767–780.

Whyte, W. F. (ed.). *Participatory Action Research.* Thousand Oaks, Calif.: Sage, 1991.

Williams, L. *Grassroots Participatory Research.* Knoxville: Community Partnership Center, University of Tennessee, 1997.

Witkin, B. R., and Altschuld, J. W. *Planning and Conducting Needs Assessments: A Practical Guide.* Thousand Oaks, Calif.: Sage, 1995.

Yin, R. K. *Case Study Research: Design and Methods.* Thousand Oaks, Calif.: Sage, 1994.

Zlotkowski, E. "Pedagogy and Engagement." In R. Bringle, R. Games, and E. Malloy (eds.), *Colleges and Universities as Citizens.* Needham Heights, Mass.: Allyn & Bacon, 1999.

Zlotkowski, E. "Civic Engagement and the Academic Disciplines." In T. Ehrlich (ed.), *Civic Responsibility and Higher Education.* Phoenix, Ariz.: American Council on Education and Onyx Press, 2000.

INDEX

A

Academic disciplines: academic learning and CBR, 127; disciplinary connections in CBR, 138–142; discipline-specific learning, 125–126; flexible boundaries in CBR projects, 78–80; student preparation for CBR, 147–150

Academic research: challenges of CBR for, 79–80; conventional vs. community-based, 8, 9; credibility and validity of CBR, 178; reporting CBR results, 115–118; researching *with* vs. *on*, 151; studying impact of CBR, 239; tailoring topics to academic schedule, 103; traditional influences on researchers, 179

Accessing community-based resources, 20–22

Action research, 6

Action vs. research, 81–84

Adams, F., 5, 114

Addams, Jane, 4–5

Advisory boards, 226–227

Alienating rhetoric, 35

Altschuld, J. W., 86

AmeriCorps program, 144

Analyzing data, 113–114

Ansley, F., 27

Appalachian Center for Community Service, 192

Asset mapping, defined, 87–88

Associations: establishing ongoing CBR, 238; promoting CBR through existing, 240–241

Astin, A., 134

B

Bacon, Francis, 1

Barber, B., 25, 134, 135

Barber, Benjamin, 28

Beckwith, David, 23, 26

Belle, Jan Marie, 19

Benefits of community-based research, 16–42; accessing and using resources, 20–22; credibility in eyes of decision makers, 26; engaging policymakers in research results, 25–26; enhancing capacity through collaboration, 22–25, 39–40; identifying community, 16–18; improved civic efficacy and competence, 26–27; social change as, 18–20. *See also* Partnerships

Benson, L., 2, 136, 192–194

Bibliography of student readings, 148–149

Bledsoe, T., 5, 114

Bledstein, B., 2

Boyer, E. L., 2, 66, 121, 214, 215

Boyte, H. C., 3, 134

Braxton, J., 122

Bringle, R., 217

Brisbane Institute, 192

Brown, L. D., 6

Brydon-Miller, M., 7, 8, 34, 81, 82

Budgets: for CBR projects, 159, 209–212; community members stipends in CBR projects, 53–54. *See also* Financial support

Building Community (Nyden and others), 170